DATE DU

Surviving Twice

Surviving Twice

Amerasian Children
of the Vietnam War

Trin Yarborough

Potomac Books, Inc.
Washington, D.C.

Library of Congress Cataloging-in-Publication Data

Yarborough, Trin.
    Surviving twice : Amerasian children of the Vietnam War /
Trin Yarborough. — 1st ed.
        p.   cm.
    Includes bibliographical references and index.
    ISBN 1-57488-864-1 (hardcover : alk. paper)
    1. Amerasians—Vietnam.   2. Children of military personnel—Vietnam.
3. Abandoned children—Vietnam.   4. Amerasians—United States.
5. Vietnamese Americans.   I. Title.
DS556.45.A43Y37   2005
959.704'4'086945—dc22   2004029597

Potomac Books, Inc.
22841 Quicksilver Drive
Dulles, Virginia 20166

First Edition

10 9 8 7 6 5 4 3 2 1

*This book is dedicated with love to the memory of
my mother, Louise Replogle Edwards;*

*And to my children and children-in-law: Inez and Michael,
Francey and Don, Dakotah and Connie, and Sophie and Dan;
to my grandchildren, Amber, Madeleine, Gracie, Rosie,
and Donovan;*

For all their help, patience, and support.

Contents

Preface

IN 1996 I was a freelance journalist researching and writing an article about the thriving Vietnamese American pop music scene in the large Vietnamese immigrant community of Little Saigon, the so-called "Vietnamese Motown" in Orange County, California, some thirty miles from Los Angeles. There I met separately, among other performers, two Amerasian singers, who had been born during the Vietnam War to Vietnamese mothers and U.S. soldiers. I learned that these two—"Randy" Tuan Tran and Louis "Luu Quoc Viet" Nguyen—were among approximately 30,000 Vietnamese Amerasians who had begun immigrating to the United States under a special law called the Amerasian Homecoming Act (AHA) in late 1988, thirteen years after the war's end on April 30, 1975. Their story was complex and fascinating, and I decided to write about this special group.

I had another reason, one I have found very hard to explain to others. I have trouble putting it into words because is it not based on words, but on a collection of mental images—my own emotional memory-pictures going back to childhood. The situation of the Amerasians stirred in me these images and their attached feelings. As a white American who grew up and lived under segregation, and witnessed every day the cruelty and injustice of racism, I recognized from childhood that I was a member of the group that caused and perpetuated that cruelty and injustice. Then, as an American, I again was inescapably part of the group that created the policies that affected the mixed children born of the Vietnam War, and particularly their suffering after they arrived in the United States, where, under different policies, they could have been treated so much better. This is the deeper reason I needed to write this story.

Although the literature on the Vietnam War and its aftermath has been voluminous, very little research and writing has been done about this group of Amerasians, and most of it has centered around their ar-

rival in America and their first years here. Very few of the thousands of
books about the war even mention the Amerasians, although at one
point the media and officials estimated more than 100,000 had been
born. The group that came under the AHA lived very different lives
from those few thousand (at most) Vietnamese Amerasians who came
to the United States as infants or young children before the war's end
through Operation Babylift and the few early adoption channels, and
grew up speaking English in American families and attending U.S.
schools. By contrast, the average age of the Amerasian AHA immigrant
arriving in America was seventeen—about one year younger than the
average age of U.S. servicemen in Vietnam during the war. On the
April day Saigon fell to victorious North Vietnamese Communist
troops, thus ending the war, an American journalist who was pushing
through panicked crowds of South Vietnamese attempting to flee the
city noticed dozens of abandoned children, some as young as two years
old, with half-Vietnamese, half-American faces. Some stood all alone
sobbing; others were wandering, bewildered. Long since left behind by
soldier fathers who had returned to the United States, they had been
pushed frantically into the streets or left at orphanages by terrified Vietnamese mothers or other family members convinced the Communists
would murder anyone ever connected to the American enemy.

This book is not about the political or military histories of the Vietnam War, but they do provide a context and show the effects of certain
historical moments and political policies on the Amerasian children. In
general, the children left behind on April 30 were not harmed by the
new officials. But these Amerasians were usually among "the poorest of
the poor," growing up under a repressive political system during years
when poverty, famine, and diseases affected everyone in Vietnam. They
were the victims of racism, of classism (many were children of prostitutes, all were children of foreigners) and—because of their American
fathers—of political discrimination. Those half-black were especially
mistreated, and Amerasians who faced taunts and beatings when attending school often dropped out. This was the Amerasians' first struggle for survival, and many did not survive.

When the Amerasian Homecoming Act eventually was pushed
through Congress in 1987 by the American public, the despised Amerasians suddenly became a hot property. Vietnamese hoping to escape
the poverty and political climate in Vietnam realized that if they could
convince an Amerasian to claim them as relatives, and could pay the
costly bribes and fees few Amerasians could afford, then they could go

with them to the United States. Suddenly the Amerasians were courted, lavished with gifts and affection, or purchased outright. Fraud swamped the program, until all significant U.S. support for it was shut off in 1993. But about 30,000 Amerasians eventually were accompanied to America by about 80,000 Vietnamese "family members," many or most of them fake relatives.

Now that members of the AHA group have been in the United States since 1988 or later, I have written this book to attempt to explore what has become of them. I will also touch on the question of what has become of the estimated 3,000 to 15,000 Amerasians still living in Vietnam. Because so few records exist, either in the United States or in Vietnam, especially of the Amerasians' later years, much of their stories must be informed guesswork and anecdotal.

Little Saigon, peopled by South Vietnamese (and their relatives) who fought or worked for the United States during the war, is the home of the largest Vietnamese expatriot community in the world. With its huge, affluent Vietnamese malls and its countless Vietnamese restaurants and stores, it is a magnet for Vietnamese Amerasians and other Vietnamese who first settled in other parts of the country. The Amerasian resettlement program at St. Anselm's Cross-Cultural Community Center on the edge of Little Saigon was the largest of approximately fifty sites established by the United States under the Homecoming Act. The government ended funding of St. Anselm's program in 1994, but the center was still in close contact with many Amerasians and helped me contact several. I was also able to read hundreds of files on Amerasians and those who had immigrated with them.

I planned to follow the standard device of selecting several key interviewees who were representative of subgroups within the Amerasian population, and, by gathering their life stories, learn about the Amerasians in general. I was only partially successful, because over six years, the interviewees I was able to stay in touch with were among the more stable of the group, and thus not representative of some of the more disadvantaged Amerasians. Even Tiger Hoa, the gangster, who perhaps would have drifted away as other Amerasians did, was stable in a sense, because he was arrested and imprisoned days after my first meeting with him, making it possible for me to talk with him over the following years.

Unfortunately, the U.S. resettlement program was hopelessly inadequate. Benefits were meager, and lasted about eight months at most. The Amerasians often arrived with physical and emotional problems, illiterate in any language, speaking little or no English, and with few skills sought in an industrial nation. The fake relatives who accompanied the Amerasians very often abandoned them within weeks—even hours—after they had reached the United States, and only 2 percent of the Amerasians found their American fathers, many of whom rejected them. In America, the Amerasians began their second struggle for survival, with little or no family to help them.

This Project and Problems

To learn their stories, I conducted extensive interviews with the Amerasians whose lives I have profiled in this book (Louis, Son, Nan, Sara, and Tiger) and with the Buddhist nun Miss Dao (Chi Lien). I also interviewed social workers, resettlement workers, and police gang officers, many of whom were of Vietnamese origin. I traveled to Vietnam with an interpreter for several weeks to talk with relatives and friends of Amerasians living in America and interviewed a few Amerasians still in Vietnam. I checked countless news clippings and the few books and theses I could find about this group of Amerasians. I read reports from the Office of Refugee Resettlement, the Government Accounting Office, and other government documents, including police records. Few contained material about years after 1995.

Some of the difficulties I faced are obvious ones, such as crossing cultural barriers I was often unaware of and gaining trust and closeness with an interviewee through an interpreter. But there were other barriers I did not understand until long after I began. For example, an American journalist's style of interviewing—double-checking names, places, dates, and so forth—is very similar to police questioning. Moreover, some Vietnamese immigrants assume that any "journalist" is probably representing some publication with a strong political view. Most Amerasians had little conception of the American journalists' stated goal of attempting to gather unbiased and accurate information.

In addition, often the Amerasians themselves do not know basic information about themselves and, having no understanding of any need or purpose for accuracy, simply make up answers to satisfy questioners. Writes one Vietnamese author: "In responding to a question, [Vietnamese are] motivated by the desire to satisfy or please the person who inquires, and thus reply in the affirmative, whether, in actuality, [they mean] 'yes,' 'no,' or 'perhaps.'" Therefore, I made extra efforts to double-check my interviewees' stories with more than one source. I have changed the names and some identifying facts in the stories of Tiger and his family, and of a few others, particularly those in the chapter on "Other Amerasians." I also changed the name of Nan because I was unable to locate her as I concluded this writing.

A Universal Situation and a Vanguard Population

Throughout history, wars and military occupations everywhere in the world have created mixed children. The United States left 250,000 mixed children—at least half illegitimate—in Europe after World War II, and hundreds of thousands of mixed children in Korea, Japan, and the Philippines. Armies of other nations have left similar populations. Race and ethnicity differences always have affected their treatment.

The suffering of children born into these situations demands that we find solutions. As with slavery or the universal oppression of women, two situations once thought unchangeable, we may eventually find at least partial answers. Meanwhile, in the twenty-first century, multicultural societies are becoming increasingly common. People of mixed heritage, although seldom fully accepted by both groups of their ancestors, do have partial membership in two groups, and for that reason alone have a special value. Often able to move between both groups, and thus to provide a valuable link and "translator" function, they can help us develop a perspective and policies for a world in which there must be more acceptance of diversity, and more bonds formed not on the basis of race or "blood" but on shared values and experiences.

The Amerasians I came to know had unique courage and generosity. This is a story of the Amerasians, some of whom survived twice, some of whom did not survive at all.

Acknowledgments

THIS project has passed through many phases, and thus the help and support of so many friends and family members have been especially precious. Owed special thanks are the many Amerasians who talked with me about their lives—particularly Sara, Nan, Tiger, Son, and Louis; the Vietnamese Buddhist nun, Chi Lien (Miss Dao); and Joseph Love, the father-finder, all generous sources of important help and information.

In the beginning I received special assistance from St. Anselm's Cross-Cultural Community Center in Garden Grove, California, from its director, Marianne Blank, and the former head of its Amerasian Resettlement Program, Peter Daniels. The program was already closed when I first approached St. Anselm's in 1997, but I was able to see files, clippings, documents, and photographs and to locate most of the Amerasians in this book. The Southeast Asian Archives at the University of California, Irvine, created and maintained by Anne Frank, had unique resources. I also thank Patton State Hospital.

Throughout my work on this book, three friends helped me constantly, with advice and emotional and practical support—Marie Tyler-McGraw and Howard Wachtel of Washington, D.C., and Taylor Stoehr of Cambridge, Massachusetts. Marie and Howard read every draft and gave invaluable suggestions and encouragement. Taylor, a marvelous writer and editor, volunteered to help reorganize and edit my early manuscript, spending countless hours until it emerged 100 times better. I cannot thank these three friends enough.

Other constant support came from June Pulcini, center of a worldwide network of friends and acquaintances, and who is always generous with contacts and ideas; her husband Marvin May; Donald Freed, leader of my writers' group, who helped me develop several early drafts; his wife Patty Rae Freed; and the very supportive members of the writers' group itself. Several special Vietnamese American friends whom I knew through earlier projects were especially helpful, including Alex Hoa, Thanh Nguyen, Nam Hau Doan Thi, Andrew Le, Anthony Huynh, Tuan Le, and Le Ly Hayslip. Alex, Le Ly, Nam-Hau, and Thanh read drafts, explained Vietnamese culture, and gave many insights I would otherwise have missed.

Author A. J. (Jack) Langguth, always generous with his help and advice; Judy Dugan, my friend and outstanding editor when I free-lanced for the *Los Angeles Times*; and Don White were among others who helped greatly at several stages of this work. I also thank the Rockefeller Foundation (I spent several months as a Rockefeller Fellow at the William Joiner Center for the Study of War and Social Consequences based at the University of Massachusetts, Boston). Special Cambridge friends, in addition to Taylor Stoehr, included Joan Albert, Jim Lapierre, Merry "Corky" White, Ruth Perry, and Elinor "Bunny" McPeck.

During the months in Cambridge, I was helped by Kevin Bowen, director of the Joiner Center; by its staff; and by another Rockefeller Fellow, Caroline Kieu Linh Valverde, an Amerasian scholar. An article she had written years earlier was one of the first things that sparked my interest in this subject. Other helpful friends include Gary Wintz, Drew and Diane Carolan, Mark Hertsgaard, Saul Landau, Gloria and Irving Jaguden, Gerald Nicosia, Tom Grunfeld, Gil Dorland, Carla Kaplan, David Murphy, Tony Russo, Richard Cohen, Margie Bernard, Marc Raskin, Betty DeVise, Jon Lewis, Aris Davoudian, Melissa "Mojo" Davidsonstad. Tom Edwards gave indispensable help with the many photographs (some more than thirty years old).

I'm very grateful also to my children and children-in-law, to whom I have dedicated this book. My daughter Sophie Yarborough, a journalist and a former editor at the *Miami Herald*, helped me research and shape early versions; my son Dakotah Yarborough helped solve endless complicated computer and photograph problems; my daughters Inez VanderBurg and Francey Yarborough, and daughter-in-law Connie Yarborough, read drafts and gave important suggestions.

As I write this list of acknowledgments — probably incomplete — I see that although I often felt alone in this work, I was actually incredibly lucky to have had so much wonderful assistance and support. Thanks to everyone who helped in even the smallest way.

I

Meeting the Amerasians

My American dad really cared for me. And he was crazy in love with my mom.

—Amerasian Son Chau

Alan "Tiger" Hoa

"I have spent eleven years in America—ten of them behind bars," the Vietnamese Amerasian Alan "Tiger" Hoa jokes during a collect phone call from a California prison. "And in all of North America, I have seen the inside of all the jails and prisons—not just in the United States but even also in Canada and Mexico." Tiger's convictions have been mostly for minor crimes—car theft, burglary, and one more serious case when he was drunk and tried to shoot into a neighbor's apartment.

But he also has been involved in certain graver crimes for which he was never caught or charged. He mentions home burglaries and extortions of businesses—typical gang crimes—and running prostitutes, dealing cocaine, Ecstasy, and other drugs, even once hinting at a failed involvement in a gun-running scheme between Vietnam and the United States. Although usually he will not admit it, he has abused drugs and alcohol since childhood. Many of the violent things he has done and seen throughout his life came back to haunt him during a serious emotional breakdown years later in America.

Many women have been drawn to Tiger. "When you are a big gang leader, getting girls is easy," he boasts. Like many Amerasians he has had liaisons with both men and women. Small but powerfully built and muscular, Tiger has curly dark hair, dark skin, and dark long-lashed eyes. Sometimes his face looks almost angelic. Yet when certain muscles shift beneath the surface, the velvet-smooth sheen of his skin changes to a rougher fabric, and Tiger appears like a different person, hard and frightening.

Tiger's body bears the scars of more than thirty knife cuts and fifty cigarette burns. Except for a few scars from gang fights, these are wounds he made himself. One arm bears a broad, ugly slash mark from a suicide attempt after a breakup with a girlfriend. Such self-mutilations are not uncommon in certain Vietnamese subcultures, yet Tiger's scars are far more numerous than most. His scars intermingle with tattoos in Vietnamese and English, some beautifully scripted in Gothic letters, some crude and misspelled.

On Tiger's right knuckles is tattooed "TLSVD," (Where is Life Going?). Other tattoos read: "Kho Vi Con" (The Mother Suffers Willingly for the Child); "On Cha Chua Tra" (The Debt to the Father Has Not Been Repaid); "Nghia Me Chua Quen" (The Love of the Mother Has Not Been Forgotten). On the back of his neck, "My Crazy Life," and on his neck "Tiger Canada." On his chest is a tattoo of a gun. Still another tattoo reads in Vietnamese: "I Bow to My Mother Before Leaving," indicating the reverence shown to an older person on departing, or to the dead, or even to one's mother country. Tiger's newest tattoo, scrawled in English across his neck and the back of his shaven head, reads simply: "Asian Gangster."

Serving out a five-year prison sentence in California, Tiger often seems to be dealing rather well with his situation. He makes friends easily, not just among the very few Vietnamese in the prison but also with some of the black prisoners and others as well. Except for one brief interview with Tiger in his home during a few days' stint between prison sentences, and one jail visit, all my interviews with him were conducted by phone, taped in three-way connections with interpreters. The guards also taped Tiger's calls, as they routinely did all prisoner calls, which is one reason Tiger's answers were sometimes evasive and murky. However, his frequent letters (also read by guards) were in passable written English, and as months and years passed in prison, his English improved to a point where we could talk together without an interpreter.

Tiger speaks often of his dead mother, who died when he was four. "Sometimes when I sleep I dream of my mother, and feel her spirit talks to me, telling me to try harder to live a better life, and that hardships will soon be over. Her spirit looks very sad and sickly, very fragile and hungry, as she looked when she died," he says. Yet Tiger's family doesn't believe he truly remembers her. They say he was too young when she died. But sometimes when he speaks of her, his voice quavers, and he cries quietly. Of all the people who appear in these pages, Tiger is the one whose memories are most difficult to untangle from myth and confabulation, the one whose past is most difficult to trace.

Miss Dao (The Buddhist Nun, Chi Lien)

"For years, I have been hoping and praying to find some way to communicate a message to Americans," says Miss Dao, her expression both worried and earnest. Miss Dao is her American name. Her true name, as a Vietnamese Buddhist nun, is Chi Lien. In her late sixties, she has an honest, open face, short neat dark hair, and she dresses in plain American-style clothing. She no longer wears orange nun's robes, nor shaves her head, although she continues to lead a religious life in America, helping at her Buddhist temple especially on religious holidays, following a vegetarian diet, and observing religious rules.

Speaking through a Vietnamese interpreter—after several years in America her English is still mostly nonexistent—Miss Dao continues: "Of course I really appreciate the Americans who brought the Amerasians to the United States. That was really kind of them. But for a long time I have wanted to cry out as loudly as I could that the Amerasians need help, but no one has been willing to listen. I have wanted to scream out that Americans need to understand about Amerasians—the discrimination against them in Vietnam, the fact that they weren't allowed an education there, and so now they can't better their futures.

"Each Amerasian is different, although all have a good heart. But there are so many, many Amerasians with emotional and mental problems and complexes, who feel lonely and unconnected. The black ones especially suffered, because they were treated the worst."

Miss Dao has a serene and poised manner that causes you to respect her even before you hear her story. As she talks, she is often quietly working at the same time—preparing tea for a visitor, straightening a cushion. Mostly she is busy holding a squirming baby on her lap or comforting a toddler, one of several children she cares for in the modest home she shares with one of the now-adult orphans who came with her to America from Vietnam under the 1987 Amerasian Homecoming Act.

Looking earnest yet firm, Miss Dao continues: "This is something I want to tell to Americans: that the Amerasians were treated very badly in Vietnam, and that America should treat them better now, so they can have some good memories instead of all the bad, unhappy ones. And although no one can take all of them in and love all at the same time, maybe somewhere there is an American heart that can open to one of them. It makes me very sad to see so many Amerasians struggling and suffering in America, just as they did in Vietnam."

Miss Dao began on her spiritual path as a follower of the Buddhist monk Minh-Dang Quang and the well-known late nun Ni Su Huynh Lien of the Giao Thap Khac Si order. Minh-Dang Quang had founded the order in which nuns and monks went barefoot each morning to the market to collect alms and small donations of food. But in 1953 Minh-Dang Quang was kidnapped and murdered by a general in the religious army of the Hao Hoa order. The nun Huynh Lien was one of his nine most outstanding nun disciples; some Vietnamese describe her as a sort of female Martin Luther King Jr. because of her active involvement in social programs such as opening orphanages and schools, and for her courageous dedication to human rights.

Caring for orphans was not the path Miss Dao had chosen for herself when, as a serious, pretty sixteen-year-old, she first became a nun. She had planned to live a sheltered life, praying, meditating, and studying her religion. But the chaotic events shaping Vietnam over the years made such a choice impossible. More and more during the war and in its traumatic aftermath, she dedicated herself to saving orphans and abandoned children, both Vietnamese and Amerasian.

Sara Phuong

The first thing anyone notices about Sara Phuong is how pretty she is, with her smooth, coffee-colored skin, flashing dark eyes, and slender figure. On the dance floors of one or another of the Vietnamese night-clubs in Little Saigon in Orange County, California, she has often turned heads and attracted many suitors. To see her, you might not know how hard her life has been. For many years after arriving in America, she worked long hours several days a week in a Vietnamese sewing factory to help support her three children; now she works six days a week as a manicurist. During the days, her children were mostly cared for by Miss Dao, who raised Sara in the orphanage in Vietnam. Sara's two oldest children have now started school in America.

During the years of hardship growing up in Vietnam, Sara often went hungry, and as a half-black Amerasian was taunted and mistreated. But it was after she came to the United States that Sara suffered some of the worst mistreatment of her life, during a long, difficult marriage to an American Caucasian when she was still mostly obedient and intimidated. Finally, Sara stood up for herself, showing resolution and courage to escape the marriage and the man who had fathered her three children. Sara is a complex and courageous person, who often displays a sunny manner even when she is most discouraged.

Sara was too young to remember much about the war. The memories of Miss Dao, some a bit blurry but others sharp and clear, offer the only knowledge of Sara's early childhood in Vietnam, when abandoned babies and children — both Amerasian and Vietnamese — were common. Even when a mother wanted to keep her baby, even if she could care for it, family members often insisted it be abandoned, especially if it was Amerasian, and especially if it was black. In fact, only one baby was ever brought openly to Miss Dao's orphanage by her real mother, and that baby was Sara, who was born in 1972 — the year President Richard Nixon was reelected partly because of his promises to end the war. All her life Sara has been proud of the fact that she was the only child brought by her real mother.

Miss Dao closes her eyes a moment to remember the details of that day. "It was about 11 A.M.," she says, "and I remember Sara's mother wore black slacks with a white tunic, and was carrying Sara in a basket. Sara was seven days old, when usually the babies brought to us were just born. The mother was about twenty, very pretty, looking a lot like Sara looks now, except Sara is black. She said she was a student from Saigon who couldn't tell her family about Sara. Sara looked very, very dark then, as black as her mother's black slacks, although as she grew up she became much lighter. The mother was concerned she wouldn't be able to raise Sara because she was so black. I tried to convince her to raise her baby herself, and she became very frightened that we wouldn't accept it. I remember it was cold that day, and she said she wanted to run down for a moment to the cigarette vendor near the temple gate and buy cigarettes to warm herself. But when I looked out the window I saw her running quickly away down the street, until she disappeared.

"Baby Sara's little toes were all hurt, nibbled by rat bites, so I put medicine on them. And then I raised her." Sara's mother put her own name in a letter in the basket with Sara. It was one of many precious documents about the orphans apparently later lost in the chaos of the war and its aftermath.

Son Chau

"My American dad really cared for me, he had concern for me. And he was very crazy in love with my mom," says the Amerasian Son Chau, moving restlessly about his mother Du Chau's small, colorful apartment in Little Saigon. Son is always on the move, not just within a room but traveling from state to state, living first in one city and then another. At the same time he is often juggling several tasks at once—phone calls, paperwork, visitors. His English is fluent, if not yet perfect grammatically, and he needs no interpreter to talk to Americans.

The living room of Du Chau's apartment is partly used as a bedroom by an older sister, Aunt #9 (Vietnamese carry the title of their birth order throughout their lives) who is visiting from Vietnam. The room is filled with bright-colored ornaments and objects. Red and gold paper decorations dangle from the ceiling, purple and orange silk flowers crowd a bowl, photos and other objects adorn the walls. A large bowl of fruit sits before the photographs on the small family altar, and there is a telephone shaped like a motorcycle. Du loves such knickknacks, including a Christmas tree made of lighted pink roses that Son bought for her.

Du, now middle-aged, wearing thick glasses, is bubbly and talkative. Like Son, she is a fascinating storyteller, and she has earned a reputation among friends and neighbors as a fortune-teller with strong psychic powers. Scorned and mistreated for years in Vietnam as the mother of two Amerasians—Son and a half-sister two years younger by another American soldier—Du now seems secure and happy. Her fortune telling has developed a small side income supplementing her Social Security disability payments because of her near-blindness.

She brings out special candies to offer guests, along with the precious faded black-and-white photos she kept hidden from the new North Vietnamese regime after the war, as well as new color photos of Son and his family. In the old photos are one or two of his American father, then twenty years old. You can see that Son definitely resembles him— both men are handsome, slightly built with dark hair and intense eyes.

Social scientists and others who have studied the Vietnamese Amerasians often comment about their ability to survive, referring to them in reports and articles as "survivors." And some, like Son Chau, do seem to be born survivors, rare individuals who understand almost from childhood what it takes to "make it" in the world. Son has always been independent and adventurous, always thinking, figuring, looking for angles. When he recounts some of the tales from his life, one can see how he smoothly deals with many kinds of people, from a hardened Communist interrogator to an American resettlement worker. Stubborn, smart, generous, and hardworking, Son continually built a network of contacts and close friends. His "cool" demeanor drew friends and intimidated enemies. Son also has a flair for making money. Since coming to the United States, he has started and then sold or abandoned several mostly successful small businesses. Yet like many Amerasians, he has an inner restlessness. He often returns to visit Vietnam, and is subject to the periodic depressions that attack most Amerasians.

Although often labeled "survivors," many Amerasians of course did *not* survive. Victims of the war, and later of the diseases and near-starvation that swept Vietnam for years afterward, during an era when the United States blocked most international aid to the devastated nation, the Amerasians, among the most impoverished in the country, had a very high death rate. As they grew older, many committed suicide. And not every Amerasian who survived physically survived psychologically and emotionally. Those who did often tell of a parent or caretaker who once loved them, protected them as best they could, and/or validated their worth.

Sometimes that person was someone they met only in their mind. Son, for example, has carried an image of a loving American father he never met throughout all the hard years of his life. Son's mother's lifelong effort to persuade Son of a concerned father helped create his inner belief in himself.

Louis Nguyen (The Singer Luu Quoc Viet)

Louis Nguyen sorts through his stack of CDs, most of them of Vietnamese American pop songs, beside the stereo in his Little Saigon living room. He chooses a Michael Bolton CD and puts it on. On the wall behind him is a 4' × 5' poster of himself, carrying his stage name, Luu Quoc Viet (which roughly translates as "Remembering Vietnamese Homeland"), announcing one of Louis's recent concerts in a large Little Saigon nightclub. Louis enjoys the poster, but certainly the poster and fans have not made him lose the groundedness that is such a basic part of his personality.

As the oldest son in his family, Louis has been boss of his household since boyhood, responsible and hardworking. Half-black, he is quite handsome, with chocolate-colored skin, black wavy hair (which he sometimes wears in shoulder-length extension braids), and dark, compelling eyes. A singer whose talent was first recognized in Vietnamese elementary school, where he was otherwise harassed as an Amerasian, Louis has developed a kind of star quality. Hundreds of fans crowd his concerts to hear him sing Vietnamese pop love songs—usually tragic—to dance to his faster cha-chas, and to buy his CDs, in the thriving music world of Little Saigon, sometimes called the "Vietnamese Motown." When he sings, young girls sometimes approach him on stage to present him with single red roses, or to plant shy kisses on his cheek.

Louis's mother, Luc, who came with him to America, moves silently around the apartment she shares with him. Older than most of the mothers of Amerasians, she is still attractive. Like Louis, she has become a U.S. citizen, although she can speak almost no English.

Although a singer, Louis is a very serious person. Only a tiny minority of the Amerasians left behind after the war attended school in Vietnam for any length of time, and many never attended at all. Yet because of the support and love of his Vietnamese grandmother and of his mother, Louis attended school in Vietnam until he was fourteen, and was determined to graduate from college in the United States. This dream cost him almost unimaginable struggles.

Painfully aware of the Vietnamese stereotype of Amerasians as troublemakers, Louis tries constantly to live in a way to disprove that prejudice, declaring: "I have rules for myself. That is why some people say I am not a fun guy." Often he seems to be distancing himself from other Amerasians. Blunt and honest to a fault, when he speaks of Amerasians and his own experiences he makes certain to try to give "both sides."

"Vietnamese in Vietnam and in the U.S. treat Amerasians bad because 50 to 60 percent of the Amerasians were very bad," he says. "Often they didn't have moms, or their moms didn't know how to raise them in a good way. They let them steal food or beg, and they had trouble in school, and everyone picked on them. The Vietnamese are very scared of Amerasians. They think they will always steal or fight, but there are 1,000 things that happen in an Amerasian's life to make them become a bad person. People *make* Amerasians become a bad person."

But Louis also shows flashes of loyalty to other Amerasians. He makes a special point of attending weddings of Amerasian friends, where he sings without charge. And he has donated singing performances to fund-raisers for St. Anselm's Cross-Cultural Community Center, the Amerasian services center in Little Saigon that helped him and other Amerasians when they first came to the United States.

The mainstream Vietnamese community in Little Saigon, like Vietnamese back in Vietnam, often looks down on Amerasians, especially those who are half-black like Louis. Here in the United States he deals with prejudice within the Vietnamese community "about 30 percent of the time," a Vietnamese friend estimates, explaining: "Younger Vietnamese don't feel it, but in Vietnamese restaurants and when he visits homes of his friends and deals with their parents, he does face prejudice because of his color."

"When some Vietnamese see me, it reminds them of something bad that happened, maybe a relative killed by an American, and they hate me, and that's why they treat me bad. And I accept that," says Louis. He hesitates a moment, then adds: "Also, many Vietnamese say that people who have black blood like me are usually very wild, and that African American blood like my father's makes a person violent and bad." He looks closely at me as he tells me this, to read my reaction.

Here in America, Louis has become a Christian. He is deeply involved in the Vietnamese-language church where he often sings. He seldom talks about the many problems he has encountered in America. "When God is with you, you are never alone," he says.

Nan Bui (Not Her Real Name)

"If my nun who raised me had still been alive I would never have left Vietnam, I would have stayed with her," says Nan Bui, a small, slender Amerasian with pretty cocoa-colored skin and light Vietnamese-shaped eyes. "My nun didn't want to go to America, because she said it was a stranger land with stranger people."

The origins of Amerasians are often shrouded in mystery and confusion because there is no one alive who knows the facts. Separating reality from lies or fantasy is often impossible, not just for outsiders but for the Amerasians themselves. Contradictory stories arise from shame around the conception and birth, or the abandonment, or the need to hide the secret of the birth from the mother's family, or because of fear of Communist retaliation for connections to Americans, or because records have been destroyed or lost, or to romanticize or exaggerate ugly or tragic truths. In stories about Amerasian births and adoptions, there is often a mysterious "woman at the hospital" who gives up her Amerasian baby, a woman perhaps related to, or at least well-known, to the person who raises the child. Other times the mothers or relatives simply sold the baby. And sometimes a woman appeared after many years, claiming to be an Amerasian's long-lost birth mother, but who was actually a stranger hoping to use the child to get to the United States. The truth, if it is known, is often impossible to unravel.

This sort of mystery surrounded the birth and early life of Nan Bui. Nan has the same restlessness as many other Amerasians. She moves frequently from apartment to apartment in the Little Saigon area, usually sharing her homes with other Vietnamese, sometimes living alone. Nan can move easily because she has few possessions other than a highly valued "entertainment center" with a large-screen TV, and a precious book of photographs. A lesbian, or perhaps bisexual like many Amerasians, Nan had the same woman partner for several years, although their relationship was stormy. Her girlfriend, Terri (not her real name), is a white Amerasian who sometimes became violent when she was drinking, and beat Nan, taunting her because she is half-black. "She was very prejudiced against black Amerasians," Nan says.

Unlike many Amerasians, Nan has often held steady jobs like factory assembly work for years at a time. Yet she accumulates little. Partly this is because she likes to gamble, as do many Vietnamese; but partly it is because she is so generous. She frequently sends several hundred dollars at a time back to her former orphanage, and at least once a year buys plane tickets for her "orphanage sister" Joan, who now lives in North Carolina, so Joan can visit her in California. Joan is the orphan two years younger who grew up with Nan and came with her to the United States under the Amerasian Homecoming Act when both were teenagers.

How It Began

Although the U.S. government and American people were not yet paying real attention to Vietnam, there were U.S. military "advisers" and intelligence officers in Vietnam even before 1950. And between 1950 and 1954, when the French colonial rulers and the Viet Minh nationalist (but Communist-led) resistance organization battled bitterly for control of the country, the United States helped fund French efforts. In May 1954 the French were decisively defeated by the Vietnamese in a two-month-long battle at Dien Bien Phu. As the beaten French withdrew from Vietnam, they faced the problem of thousands of children, legitimate and illegitimate, of mixed French and Vietnamese parentage. France arranged to evacuate some 25,000 French-Vietnamese children and some of their relatives to France, and, according to some reports, paid subsidies to some children who stayed in Vietnam until they reached the age of eight. All the children were given French citizenship, but could choose at age eighteen to adopt Vietnamese citizenship instead.

But soon a new crop of mixed children—half-Vietnamese and half-American—was born. In 1961 newly elected U.S. President John Kennedy increased aid to Vietnam's U.S.-backed Diem regime and sent more American "advisers," increasing their number until it had swollen to 12,000. By the early 1960s, they were not only "advising" the South Vietnamese but also fighting, dying, killing, and playing the roles of soldiers in other ways.

Of course most of the increasing numbers of American troops sent to Vietnam during these years were young men eager for female company—from brief, meaningless moments with prostitutes, to real love affairs, to rapes, to regular girlfriends, and even, rarely, to legal Vietnamese wives. As the numbers of troops and American civilians increased, so did the number of Amerasian births. U.S. policy was that each member of the military spend only twelve to thirteen months in Vietnam, and as more and more troops were rotated home so were more Amerasian babies left fatherless.

"If a Vietnamese woman lived in a long-term relationship with a man, the Vietnamese referred to him as her husband, and a child would not be hidden," a Vietnamese woman from Central Vietnam who had a child by an American during the war says. "But if the man left, who would take care of that baby? And if the baby was half-black, it was very hard for the woman to find a white American boyfriend or Vietnamese husband after that. Mothers may have loved their Amerasian children, but worried very much about what would happen to them, and about how disgraceful those children were to their ancestors. If there was someone with an open mind, or someone who could swallow his pride, the child maybe could be accepted, but if the family had very much hatred for Americans, they would never see that baby.

"So the woman knew that it would be very difficult for her and any baby she brought into life, and believed it was better to have an abortion or to give up the child. Many times the woman gave up or even sold the baby before she left the birthing hospital. Hospital workers would take the babies to orphanages, mostly Catholic orphanages because those got more aid money from the United States than the Buddhist ones. And sometimes nuns or others would come to the hospitals looking for babies to take."

Throngs of half-American children, many of them abandoned, began to appear in Vietnam. A *Los Angeles Times* article reported how an American Catholic Relief Service nun at Go Vap Orphanage near Saigon in the early 1960s borrowed pickup trucks and drivers from the U.S. Air Force, "gathering up Amerasian children nobody wanted," and "begging" the U.S. Army for food for them. After three years, she returned to America with two abandoned Amerasian toddlers whom she hoped would be adopted.

More than fifteen years later, January 1, 1962, would be chosen under the Amerasian Homecoming Act of 1987 as the first date on which a mixed Vietnamese American child could be born to be eligible to emigrate to America. Thus, a normal nine-months-long pregnancy of a Vietnamese woman by an American man would have begun in March 1961.

The racial prejudice and discrimination present in all countries is amplified in Vietnam by the homogenous appearance of the Vietnamese population; anyone who looks "different" is quickly noticed. The powerful Vietnamese emphasis on the family as a whole, rather than on its individual members, means that a mixed child can stigmatize not only his or her immediate and extended family, but its ancestors and all future family members, including those not yet born. It is not only a problem of racial mixture, or political considerations; having a father who can validate a child and link him to past and future family members (as well as present ones) is of great importance in Vietnamese culture.

Still Searching, Still Hoping

Although many fathers who know they left a child in Vietnam may have convinced themselves of many reasons why they would not or could not look for the child or even agree to meet a child who tried to see them, there are at least some fathers still apparently tortured by memories and thoughts of long-ago girlfriends left behind pregnant, or of babies they saw once or never saw, and what happened to them. I learned of a few such stories—one, for example, on my visit twenty-five years after the war to the big Catholic cathedral in the Central Vietnam city of Qui Nhon.

"Tomorrow," a Vietnamese nun there told me, handing me a half-page letter written in English that she had translated into Vietnamese, "we will run this advertisement in Vietnamese on the radio and television and in the newspaper. The American veteran who wrote this letter sent the money to pay for the ads."

The letter read in part: "I am looking for a [Vietnamese Amerasian] baby girl born October 15, 1973 and left by her mother on the steps of the Catholic orphanage in Qui Nhon in 1973 or 1974 with a U.S. soldier's dog tag around her neck carrying the first name of 'John.'"

The letter was from an African American veteran living in a small Georgia town. He also had written a year earlier, asking the orphanage to place the same ads, saying he had tried for years to find the baby or her mother through various U.S. organizations without success. No one answered the first set of ads. And a few weeks later, no one had answered the second set either. So far, no one had been able to say what became of that Amerasian child born thirty years ago—one of perhaps more than 100,000 such children conceived or born during America's long involvement in Vietnam.

In the final weeks of the war, this large Catholic cathedral, with its fenced complex of interconnected courtyards, had held some 250 orphans—most of them Vietnamese and children of Vietnam's tribal minorities, but also many Amerasians. On my visit I found it almost empty. Like the once-bustling resettlement sites for Amerasians belatedly brought to the United States as teenagers more than thirteen years after the war's end, most Vietnamese orphanages are "out of business," and without a war to keep supplying them.

At another, smaller Qui Nhon Catholic convent and former orphanage, I first learned of adult Amerasians still in Vietnam and still hoping to go to the United States. "I seldom see any Amerasians now," Sister Mai, a Vietnamese Catholic nun there told me. "Most have gone to America. But a few months ago, two who lived here as orphans when they were small children—one black and one white—came together to ask me to help them get to the United States." Middle-aged now, Sister Mai seems calm and capable, with the chaos and strife of the war years and subsequent hard times now past. During the war, as the number of orphans and lost or abandoned children of all backgrounds expanded, often an orphanage would be too full to take another child, and would ask a different orphanage to take it in. Sometimes, despite the traditional tensions between Catholics and Buddhists in Vietnam, the Catholic nun Sister Mai and the Buddhist nun Chi Lien—Miss Dao—who had become friends, would share food given by American and other aid agencies when supplies ran low at one orphanage or the other. At the war's end, Sister Mai's larger temple held 200 orphans compared to the 70 crowded inside Miss Dao's smaller temple.

In the final weeks of the war, Sister Mai brought together orphans from three different large Catholic orphanages, and managed to send forty-six of them, including a dozen Amerasians, out of Vietnam through an American aid organization. "Amerasians are different," Sister Mai says, echoing a phrase I heard repeated again and again, in both Vietnam and America. "When they were little, they didn't react the same as other children. They were quieter, more simple, and more honest, and usually very obedient because they had such low self-esteem. They were teased by other children so much that they didn't like to interact with them. They had very little self-confidence, and when they grew up, they remained the same.

"Nowadays, most people in Vietnam treat them like any other Vietnamese. They have the same rights, and the government treats them the same. But they see themselves as different, recognizing the two different bloods within themselves. Most have always wanted to go to America but have no money to do so. Generally, Amerasians have always been very poor." The two Amerasians asking Sister Mai's help told her that their lives had been "very difficult," she says. "The black Amerasian was bought by a fake family but the government caught them, so then he didn't have enough money to go to America, although he truly is an Amerasian," she says.

The two Amerasians asked Sister Mai to refile for them as orphans. "But I had already done that in several other cases and there were many complications, and nothing worked. So I told them I couldn't help them because I knew it was no use. It's too late now. They went away quietly. But they were very sad." Like the nun who showed me the letter at the other Catholic cathedral, Sister Mai still hears occasionally from someone seeking a long-lost child. "Just last month," she says, "a Vietnamese family came looking for their baby lost in the war. But they didn't find it through here."

Meanwhile, Americans have been going to Vietnam to adopt Vietnamese babies. It is a growing industry. In May 1999 *Reuters* reported that a court in southern Vietnam had begun hearing charges against eleven people, including the former director of Long Xuyen orphanage, accused of trafficking 199 children through an illegal adoption ring. The same year, another paper reported that since 1955, 141,000 Korean children—many the mixed children of Korean mothers and American GIs—had been adopted and raised in North America, Europe, and Australia.

The grinding poverty still existing among Vietnam's poorest sector is a major reason Amerasians and many other Vietnamese have wanted to go to America, where they believe life will be much easier. But the Amerasians have a greater claim and a greater dream. Many still yearn to find their American fathers.

Myths, Memories, and Lies of War

Lying, myth-making, self-delusion, distortion, and denial cross all boundaries of race, class, and power. The lies Amerasians and Vietnamese told to be able to go to the United States were necessary, and the myths and the comforting self-delusions Amerasians told themselves about their missing fathers and mothers in the midst of rejection and loss were also crucial. Their stories are reflected in the myths, lies, and comforting self-delusions some American leaders told themselves and the rest of us about the war. Many struggled to alter, distort, and deny facts, to make up patriotic or justifying tales and labels for some of their decisions and actions. Nations also must make up a story about themselves that they can live with. Perhaps the main reason America cannot "get over" its war with Vietnam is that Americans cannot fit what happened into its earlier myth of itself—that we had always been "the good guys," conquering injustice around the world. The tens of thousands of mistreated half-American children born in Vietnam are one untidy fact we have been unable to fit into that myth.

When we place the lives of the Amerasians next to the laws, policies, agency guidelines, and government rules that affected and controlled them, we see one of the ways history and destiny can be created by bureaucracies and legal edicts. How did some Amerasians manage to survive twice, first in Vietnam and a second time in the strange new land of America? And what has become of those Amerasians still living in Vietnam? The story of the Vietnamese Amerasians is still unfolding. To understand it, we must go back to the time before the Amerasians were born.

2

Romances, Rapes, and Casual Encounters, 1960–75

[In the firefight] our whole orphanage was destroyed, except for one wall. All the nuns and orphans tried to crouch down and hide behind it, but another shell hit and the wall collapsed, falling on us. Nine of the fifteen orphans, some of whom were Amerasian like me, were killed.

—Amerasian Nan Bui

The war affected different parts of Vietnam in different ways at different times. Whereas some areas in both the North and South were crushed by bombings, suffering, and death, in other parts of the South, where large numbers of Americans were stationed, life often was like a mammoth out-of-control party. Drugs and prostitution were everywhere, and there were vast amounts of money to be made by Vietnamese and some foreign civilians, through bribery and corruption as well as through increased business. Many poorer Vietnamese were drafted into the military like young Americans were. Other Vietnamese were driven by war in the countryside into the cities, where some found jobs working for the Americans as cooks, servants, and clerks, and others became destitute and homeless. Some Vietnamese women, many in their teens, often became prostitutes because there was no other way for them to earn a living.

In the southern cities of Vietnam, particularly in Saigon, bars, dance clubs, and brothels quickly sprang up to serve the growing number of

Americans entering the country, as well as the large number of Vietnamese military, officials, and others enriched by American spending and aid. Prostitutes crowded streets and alleys, especially in the Ton Dan area of Saigon, soon famous for its pleasures. Bars tended to become known as "black" or "white," drawing almost entirely one or the other racial group of American troops. Vietnamese women who worked in "black" bars often were looked down on by other Vietnamese, including other prostitutes.

"When you are homeless, with your village destroyed by war, what do you do?" says a former Vietnamese prostitute. "In the rural areas you probably would not go hungry, but once you were driven into the city, there were hundreds like you." Brothel madams would go to bus stations and other sites where refugees gathered to offer newly arrived country girls food and shelter in exchange for work as brothel maids. Most eventually "graduated" to prostitution, sometimes because they were not allowed to leave.

"Even if you got a babysitter or maid job, the man of the house almost always abused you, but the more you ran away the worse it got," says the same Vietnamese woman. "There were a few factories, but for every job, ten people wanted it. Most of the prostitutes then were between fifteen and twenty years old. They had to make a living, and many were supporting their families, too. The American men were also very young, most just teenagers themselves. But Vietnamese girls didn't consider them young because we ourselves had matured early and grown up fast. The Americans' bodies were so gigantic and they looked so powerful in their uniforms that we assumed they were also smart. But actually, they knew nothing about life."

Most of the Americans treated the Vietnamese women "very well," she says, able to buy gifts and take them to restaurants and clubs — things most Vietnamese men couldn't afford. "The American guys were young and lonely, and death was so nearby. Often the women they lived with were like moms to them, because the women, even young, were more mature. I think most of the young soldiers were looking for a relationship, but when they had one, they still went fooling around, because there were so many, many women out there."

Most of the fancy brothels then were owned by the wives of very high Vietnamese officers or officials, says a Vietnamese woman who lived in Saigon during that time. "Wives of a Vietnamese captain or lieutenant might have a smaller, poorer brothel. Brothels weren't licensed, but the bars and restaurants they operated from were, so

Vietnamese government and military connections were important. All the brothels had to pay off not only the Vietnamese government, but also gangster organizations."

Tu Do Street in Saigon was lined with whorehouses, and in many areas in Vietnam pimps on motorcycles would carry Americans to prostitutes and back. The women cost about $3–$5. According to "The XY Factor: Sex in the Vietnam War," a 2003 documentary on the History Channel, at many U.S. bases prostitutes sold hashish, heroin, and blow jobs through base fences. The tens of thousands of U.S. construction workers in Vietnam during the war made five times the salary of GIs, and frequently had long-term relationships and families because they stayed for years at a time. Americans could also get "rent-a-girls," paying a woman a flat rate to live with them for a week, month, or year. Vietnamese women who spoke some English could earn as much as $11 per day, or $50 for five days.

The same source reported an example of "Disneyland East," a twenty-five-acre compound near the U.S. base at An Khe in the Central Highlands where the U.S. First Cavalry was stationed. After one-third of the GIs there contracted venereal diseases, the compound, patrolled by military police and enclosing forty concrete whorehouses behind barbed wire, was established. There, a "quickie" cost $2.50–$5, and prostitutes were required to carry "entertainers' cards" and were given regular health checkups by U.S. doctors to ensure disease-free sex for U.S. troops. The system appeared to be modeled on one the military had used for years in the Philippines, and which had produced thousands of fatherless half-American, half-Filipino children, most also left abandoned and destitute. Male Vietnamese officials helped establish the compound.

Venereal disease rates were so high during the Vietnam War— twenty-eight cases for every 100 men serving there—that several strains became resistant to the usual quick-cure shot, said the documentary. A slang term arose among GIs—P.C.O.D., for "Pussy Cut-Off Date." Because no one was allowed to leave Vietnam for America until their VD was cured, men would try to abstain from sex for several weeks beforehand.

American military personnel didn't own brothels, "but some American civilians did," a Vietnamese woman says. "I knew one who operated a hotel and bar where prostitutes worked. He bought out a certain Vietnamese prostitute from her madam and made her his business partner, because this prostitute knew some very tough Vietnamese Special

Forces guys, gangster types, who would protect the business. In those times there were many very gorgeous prostitutes. An American could buy one out of prostitution by getting the madam to calculate how much she would have made if the prostitute kept working. I remember one, the most beautiful girl I ever saw. An American bought her out, but her customers, military South Vietnamese, continued to visit her at the American's home. She had at least five kids, both Vietnamese and Amerasian. Two she gave away at birth at the hospital, and one was by a Vietnamese captain who was her boyfriend on the side. This woman had a very serious gambling habit, and any money she didn't lose, she gave to him."

Although the battlefields were still mostly far from Saigon, an undercurrent of violence crept into the city and into other areas near American bases. "I remember another prostitute whose father, brother, and sister lived with her," the same Vietnamese woman says. "She supported them and sent her brother and sister through school. One day she was in bed with an American major and someone threw a grenade into her house and killed both her and the major. I don't know if the grenade thrower was Viet Cong, or a former lover, or a gangster, or what."

In Vietnamese culture premarital chastity for women had always been strictly enforced. Little was known there then about birth control, and there were none of the modern birth control pills and devices that began appearing in America in the late 1960s and the 1970s. As for condoms, most men were unwilling to use them, especially with prostitutes. When Tiger's mother became a prostitute at seventeen, unwanted pregnancies were common. "If a woman had a baby, she had to hide it somehow and pretend that nothing had happened," says a former Vietnamese prostitute. "Otherwise, she couldn't work."

So as with all wars and occupations throughout the history of the world, mixed babies kept being born and were often abandoned. But not all mixed pregnancies were the result of prostitution or of relationships. Out in the countryside, there were sometimes brutal rapes during village burnings and massacres, some of which must have resulted in births. A. J. Langguth, in his book *Our Vietnam: The War, 1954–75*, recounts the March 1968 massacres at My Lai and area villages when U.S. troops under Lt. William Calley burned, killed, or raped entire populations. At one point, writes Langguth, as U.S. troops marauded raping and murdering through nearby Binh Tay, a soldier named Gary Roschevitz "lined up seven women between the ages of eighteen and thirty-five and ordered them to strip," intending to rape them all, "but the first woman became hysterical, the others screamed and Roschevitz opened fire on their naked bodies with his M-79 grenade launcher."

The American government, American military, American media, American aid workers, and American soldiers themselves were well aware of the growing number of homeless, hungry Amerasian children. The U.S. military sometimes gave food or medical care to Amerasians and their mothers. A few private and religious American institutions and individuals operated orphanages and sometimes sent babies out of the country to be adopted, and also sometimes contributed food and medical care for Vietnamese and Amerasian children. A Vietnamese woman who went to live in Saigon when her own village was attacked during the war claims that "Americans didn't build those orphanages just for Amerasian children, they built them for the Vietnamese orphans they created when they destroyed their villages in the countryside. After they killed many people and burned a village, there would be all these children left, and the Americans would bring them to the cities."

In the United States, Americans were becoming ever more sick of the Vietnam War, and protests against it were beginning to spread into mainstream America. In early 1969 newly elected President Richard Nixon announced a plan to "Vietnamize" the war by gradually withdrawing American troops so Vietnamese troops would do most of the actual fighting. In June 1969, as secret peace talks were held in Paris, Nixon announced the first withdrawal of American troops—25,000 soldiers. By December 60,000 U.S. troops had been brought out, some of whom probably had already fathered or conceived Amerasian children. By December 1970 only 280,000 U.S. troops remained in Vietnam. In 1970, faced with media reports of up to 100,000 Amerasian children (mostly abandoned) in Vietnam, the U.S. Department of Defense issued this statement: "The care and welfare of these unfortunate children . . . has never been and is not now considered an area of government responsibility, nor an appropriate mission for the DOD to assume."

Alan "Tiger" Hoa

It was into the world of bars, brothels, loud music drifting from doorways, and prostitutes in sexy outfits calling out to passing soldiers that Tiger's eighteen-year-old mother, working partly to support her family, met and became pregnant by a black American sergeant in about 1971. Her family was poor, and all its members were expected under Vietnamese tradition to work hard and contribute to the family's survival. If that included working as a prostitute, then so be it.

Tiger's family was comprised of his grandfather, his mother, an aunt—seven years younger than his mother—and six brothers. Two of the brothers were disabled, one unable to walk but intelligent and able to contribute to the family by sewing piece work, and the other, who died as a young adult, mentally impaired. Khue, the oldest brother, had all the privileges and responsibilities the Vietnamese give to the senior male child, who is expected to help the parents supervise and protect the younger siblings. They in turn are expected to respect and obey him. The other brothers, in order of age, were Lam, Binh, and the "baby," Truong. Tiger's mother began work as a bar girl as a young teenager. Her family says she lived with the U.S. sergeant for a time, and that her oldest brother Khue once even went to meet him. The family says the sergeant was "very in love" with Tiger's mother.

Throughout the war, geopolitical events and policies of various governments were affecting thousands of Amerasian children. For example, the U.S. policy of assigning most soldiers to Vietnam for only twelve or thirteen months meant that relationships would be brief. After Tiger's teenaged mother became pregnant, her family says the sergeant asked her to go to the United States with him, but that while she went back to Hoc Mon to tell her family goodbye, his ship was "called away." She returned to find him already gone, and never heard from him again. "She was very sad," says her eldest brother Khue.

Eleven years after arriving in America with his wife, their three children, and Tiger, Tiger's Uncle Khue lives in a small but comfortable rent-subsidized apartment in Little Saigon. After Tiger's mother's death, the responsibility for Tiger's welfare fell to her extended family, which could have abandoned him, but instead took over his care. In 1990 Khue used his special position as oldest surviving male to win a bitter family quarrel over who would get to accompany Tiger to America. Now in his early sixties, Khue has the appearance of a man who has lived a rough life. He is a devout Buddhist, who manages to send money from the United States not only to family members but also to the temple near the family home. Khue has always worked hard and still does, spending hours each day sewing piece work. He even developed a side income driving neighbors to the airport or on other errands. His family's income is supplemented by food stamps and Aid to

Families with Dependent Children (his two youngest children were born in America, so were automatically citizens).

The family responsibility that comes with being the oldest brother is a heavy one. From America, Khue must send money to his wife's ten-member family in Vietnam as well. He also sends small sums of money to Tiger in prison, so Tiger can buy cheap cigarettes and toiletries. Tough and perceptive, Khue seems more realistic and open than his siblings; or perhaps he feels he can talk more freely in America than they can talk in Vietnam. Khue spent long hours on the road as a truck driver during the postwar years in Vietnam, and bartered for food and other goods with scarce salt, the way richer men might barter with gold. He has a detailed knowledge of the names and spellings of towns throughout many parts of Vietnam, as well as the new names and spellings given them after the new government came into power in 1975.

Closing his eyes a moment to summon old memories, Khue says: "When Tiger was born, in 1972, his mother gave him to her older brother Lam and his wife to raise." The couple was childless, and took Tiger so his mother could return to work as a prostitute. Khue maintains that despite whispers from neighbors and other problems that came with having a half-black child, the family never considered abandoning Tiger. "No one tried to make Tiger's mother give him up," Khue states somewhat toughly. "In the family we loved him, but his mother loved him the most, very much, so she kept him and raised him, unlike other families where he would have been thrown away because of his blackness. She loved him because he was the first son, the first grandchild [a very important role in Vietnamese culture] and also because he was fatherless. People can say what they want, but our family keeps our children. We raise our children, and they can say whatever they want to say." Yet Tiger says he always felt left out and unloved by his family.

A year after Tiger was born, his mother had a little girl by a Vietnamese man. This daughter was also turned over to Lam to raise. Not long afterward, Tiger's mother had a son by a Vietnamese man who left her. Tiger was only a toddler when his mother died of malaria at the age of twenty-three.

Nan Bui

Nan believes she was born in 1972, although her birth certificate says she was born in 1970. The nun who took her in as a baby had no real certificate, so simply used the certificate of one of many children who had died. Nan had several brushes with death during the war. She was a tiny three-month-old and very frail when her grandmother brought her to a Saigon hospital, dying of malnutrition, dysentery, and a high fever, probably caused by drinking polluted water. Nan's mother, she said, had left the infant with her. A nun visiting the hospital urged the grandmother to let her take Nan in hopes of saving her life. Nothing was learned at that time about Nan's American father, except that he was African American.

The nun took Nan to a small Buddhist orphanage at Binh Long. "There was a firefight near our orphanage when I was about three years old," says Nan, "and our whole orphanage was destroyed except for one wall. All of the nuns and orphans tried to crouch down and hide behind it. But another shell hit and that wall collapsed too, falling on us. Half the people in the orphanage were killed, including some nuns and nine of the fifteen orphans who lived there, some of whom were Amerasian like me. My nun carried a baby in her arms and one on her back, and the other nuns who survived—and the older orphans, aged four and five—each grabbed up and carried a smaller one. We were all running, running. . . . I remember running over many dead bodies." An American helicopter saw the children, "and swooped down very low to try to save us. I don't remember what happened next, but my nun told me when I was older that someone threw out a rope, and she lifted we children up into the helicopter one by one. Finally she threw the baby up to someone who caught it in the doorway, and then she was the last to climb aboard."

The six orphans who survived were eventually taken to Nhiet Chi Mai, a large Buddhist orphanage near Bien Hoa built by Americans. "Everyone passing on the highway between Saigon and Bien Hoa had to pass Nhiet Chi Mai," says Nan. At the time, it was crowded with about 200 orphans. Many of them—maybe half—were Amerasians.

Nan's most precious possession is the box of old photographs and a small black-and-white photo of the Buddhist nun who protected and loved her until the nun's death when Nan was ten. That photo is always the first thing Nan puts up in a new home.

Son Chau

Sometimes the stories of the Amerasians begin with a love story. Son Chau's mother Du has often told him of her romance with his American father—perhaps embellished, consciously or not. "I met Son's father in 1966 where I worked at the U.S. air base delivering papers to offices—I had met several American men, and one tried to match me up with others, but I was afraid of them," says Du. The twenty-year-old American sergeant apparently was in charge of the Vietnamese civilian food workers at Thap Cham air base at Thap Cham and Phan Rang when she met him. They lived together several months. "He was a very good man, very good to me," she says. "And he was good to the little boy I had then, who was about four." The boy, by a Vietnamese father from whom Du had separated, later died in an accident. Du's life before meeting Son's father was also sad—so much so that she had once sought to commit "suicide by tiger." Taking with her a baby daughter whom she could hardly feed and keep alive, she would spend hours sitting near the entrance of a tiger's cave near her home, hoping it would attack and kill her and her child and end their misery. The baby later died of a fever.

"My mom said when my dad first meet her, she was twenty-seven, he was twenty, and he have a lot of chances to look for the young, pretty girl," Son says as he looks through old photos. "Also, my mom is not smart. But she is sweet. So that's one thing I think my American dad did right."

Du became pregnant with the sergeant's baby. But before it was born, the sergeant was rotated back to the United States. "He wanted her to go to America with him, but my mom was too scared, and also he said she would have to leave behind her four-year-old son. My mom did not love my dad as much as he loved her, and she sometimes tried to run away and he would go after her. She worried that if she went to the U.S., she would not know how to ever get back to Vietnam. When he had to leave to go back to America, he cry and cry, he even try to run away from his base, and the military police had to come take him, arrest him. Also he had taken some little things from the base store for her to sell. And he said that maybe when he got back to the U.S. they would put him in jail."

Du went to see the sergeant off at the airport. She says he cried and that it was raining, and like in a scene from an American movie he put his coat around her shoulders while his fellow soldiers kept calling to him to hurry, and he took off his gold watch and made her swear to give it to their baby when it was born—especially if it was a boy. She says he gave her a $100 American bill, a large amount then, to use "if something happens." Six months later, on July 5, 1967, Son was born.

He was a handsome little boy who looked a lot like his father. At that time in South Vietnam, having a half-white Amerasian baby could be a status symbol in some circles. Sometimes such a baby even could be sold for as much as 10,000 dong (about $10 U.S.), a month's salary then, if it was "cute."

When Son was eight months old, Du "lost" the gold watch Son's father had left for him. She says someone "put a voodoo spell" on her and "made her give it to him." Some Vietnamese say such incidents are not uncommon, that voodoo practitioners—usually from one of Vietnam's tribal minorities—often approach people in the market, which is what Du says happened to her. "The voodoo man said he wanted to borrow the watch to wear to a wedding," she says. "Then he tapped me on the shoulder." Once that happened, she says, she "couldn't resist . . . because if a voodoo-spell person taps you on the shoulder you have to obey." She handed over the watch, and never saw it or the voodoo stranger again. Or maybe Du just sold the watch. Certainly, she needed money. Years later, when Son was a young boy taunted by other children because he was part American, he would sometimes reproach his mother for having been involved with an American, and reproach her for the loss of the watch, his father's gift to him.

One letter from the sergeant in the United States, living another life, far from the war, reached Du, she says, but she is illiterate and didn't answer. In any case, life was hard and she and her children needed to live. Du had met another American soldier, and in early 1969, when secret peace talks to end the war were being held in Paris, Du became pregnant with his baby. In October 1969 her second Amerasian baby was born—a girl, Linh, also born after the father had left Vietnam. Du says very little about Linh's father except that he was good to Son. Linh was born with her leg twisted, and Du took her to the American military base hospital where Linh was given a special shoe and treatments to straighten her leg. Apparently the hospital sometimes helped Amerasian babies and their mothers, especially once the fathers had gone. For most other help, Du offered prayers to Buddha.

One day in about 1971 when Son was four and his half-sister Linh was two, Du smoothed their hair and gathered their few belongings. The $100 left her by Son's father had long since disappeared. As Son now says simply: "Life was hard. She spent it to survive." The children were always hungry, and Du was distraught and exhausted. An American woman doctor at the U.S. military hospital was offering to pay Du a million dong to let her adopt the two children. "We had no money or food at that point," explains Du, "and this doctor said she would take the children to America and give them a good education and good future. But when I got to the hospital I changed my mind. I just couldn't bear to let them go."

The doctor and others tried to convince Du it would be best for everyone if she let the children be adopted. But Du cried and cried, and finally took Son and Linh back home. "I just couldn't bear to lose them," she says. "I was afraid they would grow up and come to look for me someday and not find me. I was afraid I would lose them forever, just because of money. So I decided I would rather suffer hunger and hard times than let my children be taken to America without me and never see them again." Du thinks that Son looks a lot like his American father and that his personality is also similar. "Son was always very stubborn and determined, but still always a good little boy, very brave, very smart, very adventurous, and friendly," she says.

Perhaps Du exaggerates her great love story with Son's father; but perhaps not. Certainly there were true love stories to be told from the war. An older Vietnamese woman who had her own love affair during the war says: "Looking back now, I think: The parents of the Amerasians, the soldiers and the women from both sides, Americans and Vietnamese, were very young, and both groups came from generations that had children born in earlier wars—in the case of the Vietnamese, the French babies, and in the case of the Americans, babies from World War II. Looking back I see so many beautiful things . . . the love between man and woman. . . . We created many babies and many beautiful moments, many loves, many heartaches too. That's why so many GIs want to go back to Vietnam. There are bonds between America and Vietnam; there is a major bond, like it or not.

"And when the war ended, that was happy news in many ways, but not for the love couples. To them the war was always secondary, the love was the primary thing, and the love couples were heartbroken. The women had first lost their families and villages and their ancestors' graves, then had come to the city as refugees and created new bonds and loves. And then one day the man took off and you never saw him again. He never even saw the baby you had by him, or knew if it was a boy or girl, if it was beautiful or a monster, if it had ten toes and fingers, nothing. But every American and every woman knew from the time the woman became pregnant that someday the man would leave, and the child would become fatherless. Usually the American dad would give the mother money when he left—but only a couple of hundred dollars, big deal.

"Still, although the war created a lot of sadness, without the war the love wouldn't have happened either, and the children wouldn't have happened. The Vietnamese woman and American man would never have met if there had not been a war, and in their memories now both should put the love first, so they don't regret so much the bad things they did, the ways they acted, things that still haunt them so much that they even commit suicide."

Another former Vietnamese prostitute now in America, after delivering a scholarly explanation of Vietnamese culture during the war, paused, then added shyly of American soldiers she had known then: "They were so sweet."

Yet sweet or brutal, lovers or rapists or casual customers of prostitutes or whatever they may have been, the soldiers were leaving, and leaving their children behind, almost always in terrible circumstances.

Louis Nguyen (Luu Quoc Viet)

Louis's father, a black American Army sergeant, met Louis's mother, Luc, in 1968 in Bien Hoa where she was working as a seamstress. He told her he already had a wife and daughter in the United States, but said they were separated. Luc liked the sergeant, who may have been in his twenties. The two lived together several months, but the sergeant was gone, probably rotated back to the States, when Louis was born in 1969. When Louis was about twenty months old in 1971 (the year the long-drawn-out Paris peace talks broke down temporarily) Louis's father returned to see him. "I don't remember that," says Louis, "but my mom says he loved me. I was his only son. She says he wanted her to come back to the United States with him, but she didn't want to go, and he asked her to give me to him to take back, but she said no again. That was the last she heard from him. Maybe my mom and he got disconnected. We moved around a lot, and in Vietnam when that happens you can get lost to people—there's no telephone directories or those kinds of records. Maybe—maybe he tried to find us and couldn't."

Many Amerasians say their mothers were asked by the American fathers to go to the United States, or at least to let them take their Amerasian baby with them to America. But the ties of the mothers to their Vietnamese families, especially their parents, were very powerful and very culturally binding. Whether many fathers actually offered to take the mothers or children to America is uncertain, especially considering the difficulty, if not impossibility, of battling red tape and then resettling with a new family in America. Some fathers did try to take the mothers and children—some even succeeded, particularly in the last desperate days of the war as the country was collapsing, and rules were flaunted. Other fathers may have made the offer but were less than sincere. The Amerasians who say their fathers wanted to take them to America clearly find it comforting.

After his father's return visit, Louis and his mother never heard from him again. That year Luc had a second Amerasian son, two years younger than Louis. That father was a friend of Louis's father, another sergeant who had served with him in a motor pool. One day that man disappeared, and Luc never heard from him again, either. The war continued, with peace negotiations stalled. The treaty had been drawn up between U.S. and North Vietnamese negotiators, and the South Vietnamese leaders felt its terms were detrimental to their interests. But Nixon continued withdrawing U.S. soldiers, and by December 1971 only 140,000 were left in Vietnam.

Louis remembers a little about the war. When he was three, he and other neighborhood children would be herded into a space beneath a house when planes passed over. "We heard bombs—boom! boom! boom!" he says. "Afraid? Of course we were! Sometimes we would stay there all day, or sleep there all night. But mostly we children would behave very quiet. In Vietnam, if children don't mind, the parents hit right away!"

Sara Phuong and Miss Dao (Chi Lien)

In the early Vietnam War years, Miss Dao had not yet begun to take in orphans. In 1963 long-simmering resentments of the Vietnamese Buddhists—the religion of more than 80 percent of the population—came to a head over the Buddhists' belief that the nation's much smaller Catholic population was being given favored treatment by Vietnam's U.S.-supported Catholic president, Ngo Dinh Diem. When Diem refused to let the Buddhists display their flag as they had always done at an annual national event, the call went out to Buddhists all over the nation to protest. Miss Dao was one of thousands of nuns and monks who flocked to Saigon. Members of her order walked barefoot across the country to the demonstrations. She took part in lengthy fasts and silent nonviolent protests. She saw monks and nuns, including the nun Huynh Lien, beaten and jailed by government police. In one protest a monk, Quang Duc, burned himself alive in the first of a series of self-immolations by monks and nuns, including one elderly nun who later set herself afire and burned to death as Miss Dao watched.

"I was a young nun [during the demonstrations], just doing what my teachers told me to do," Miss Dao says, "although as time went by I came to have strong feelings about social injustice. I wanted to fight not just for humanitarian things, but for fairness and justice so people could have a better life. My feelings and understanding grew gradually as I studied, and the longer I did the more open-minded I became."

The suicides horrified the American public. Although the U.S. anti-war movement was still small, the suicides raised serious questions about the war in the minds of many Americans, and hastened the U.S.-sanctioned coup that brought down the Diem regime in November 1963. Diem and his brother Ngo Dinh Nhu fled, but were quickly found and immediately assassinated by South Vietnamese coup members.

But the war itself continued. Weeks after the coup, President Kennedy was assassinated, and Lyndon Johnson, his successor, increased U.S. "advisers" in Vietnam the following year. In March 1965 Johnson had sent in the first U.S. combat troops—25,000 Marines—to defend Danang airfield. By December of that year, 200,000 U.S. troops were in Vietnam, and by December 1966 there were 400,000 U.S. troops in Vietnam.

On January 31, 1968, the North Vietnamese and the Viet Cong (their supporters in the South) had launched the surprise Tet Offensive during Vietnam's New Year's holiday season, attacking almost every major city in the South. Miss Dao was then in her thirties and living in Quang Tri province. Each morning, her group of nuns made their regular barefoot walk through town to the market where they were given small donations of vegetarian foods. The donations were the only food that, under their vows, they were allowed to eat.

On those walks, Miss Dao saw many small children affected by the fighting. They were orphaned, injured, or simply lost or abandoned, sobbing with helpless sorrow and fear. One day in 1968 during a heavy bombing raid, Miss Dao rushed into a shelter with seven other people. Minutes later it was struck by a bomb and everyone else inside was killed. Rescuers digging through the wreckage found a three-month-old baby girl clutched in the arms of her dead mother. "I was the only one to help the baby," says Miss Dao. She took the child, whose real name she never knew, and named her My Duyen. The baby was wounded, and had a piece of shrapnel embedded in one ear. She needed much nursing to live, and was the first orphan Miss Dao adopted. Her temple was already crowded and facing a continuing shortage of food. "But if I didn't take the baby, who would? It was war, and no one took care of no one then," says Miss Dao.

As the fighting dragged on, intensifying, Miss Dao saw abandoned or orphaned babies and children everywhere. While the war lasted, the orphanages of Vietnam were packed. "During the war, I saw so many suffering, sad little children, and I just couldn't bear to leave them all alone in the streets," she says. "I took more and more and more orphans into the temple, and finally we established an orphanage there, and I was made head of it." Some temples refused to take crippled children or half-black Amerasians, but Miss Dao took in any child she was able to feed. "Doctors would bring us abandoned newborns, often crippled," says Miss Dao. "Or relatives or friends of the mother would bring babies, usually only hours old, after the temple gates were locked for the night, so no one could see them do it. The mothers were too ashamed to bring a baby themselves." But of the many orphans she took in, not all could be saved. A dozen, both Vietnamese and Amerasian, died. Some had malaria, polio, or infections. Some died crippled by their mothers' failed self-abortions. Others were just too weak to survive. One tiny girl baby, her umbilical cord still attached, was brought to the temple by a railroad worker who found her abandoned on the train tracks. Miss Dao nursed her for three months, "but she was just too weak to live," she says.

Miss Dao remembers a morning in Qui Nhon when she unlocked the gates and found a newborn baby in a small basket, brought in by someone during the dark night hours. But the baby was dead. Hungry pigs that roamed the neighborhood had killed it, and eaten away most of its face.

To raise money to care for the orphans, Miss Dao sought funds from the U.S., South Vietnamese, and British governments. Sometimes she got food from various aid agency warehouses or from well-off Vietnamese families. She formed a close friendship with the Catholic nun, Sister Mai, and the two shared food for their different broods of orphans whenever supplies fell short. But the long years of struggle brought almost unbearable strain. As the war spread, nuns and monks throughout Vietnam who were caring for orphans found it an increasingly difficult responsibility as the number of children soared. The war and its aftermath would repeatedly test the values, moral courage, and religious commitment of those who cared for them. "But I believed when I first became a nun at sixteen that I needed to sacrifice to help people less fortunate," Miss Dao says, "and today I still believe the same. I myself raised many orphans, although only eleven were Amerasian."

One day in 1972 a South Vietnamese soldier brought to Miss Dao's temple a baby boy about two months old. The baby was very weak, close to death, with a horrible infected open wound on his throat. The soldier wept. He told Miss Dao he had found the baby "hanging in a tree like a little naked baby bird," bleeding and near death, beside a house where no one else was left alive. From the bodies he saw strewn in pieces, it appeared that soldiers had tossed a grenade into the house while a family was having lunch, killing everyone but the baby, who was flung up into the tree. On some impulse the soldier had taken the child with him as he moved fighting from place to place. But now he was forced to face the fact that the baby would soon die unless he found help for it. And if it died, it would need a proper burial according to Buddhist beliefs, and regular remembrance ceremonies each year or its soul would wander lost and miserable throughout eternity. Other orphanages had already turned the baby away, refusing that responsibility. "The soldier cried and cried so hard, pleading with me to help the baby, so afraid it would die. He begged me to raise it if I could save it, and if I could not, then to see that it had a proper burial." Miss Dao protested; her already overburdened temple was not supposed to take in any more children, and was always short of food.

"But he reminded me of the Buddhist proverb that 'Saving one child is worth more than building nine temples,' and that Buddhism is more about caring for life than about worshiping Buddha. The soldier made me open up my understanding of Buddhism, to see that loving is everything, and that you have to make the effort to love." She took the tiny boy and miraculously nursed him back to health. But she never saw the soldier again. "I don't even know if he lived through the war," she says.

During more prosperous war days when American money was still pouring into Vietnam, some people even sought to buy white Amerasian orphans. But Miss Dao always refused their offers. She says one man from Europe or America who visited her orphanage wanted to buy Sara, then a toddler, who, although half-black, was quite appealing. Again Miss Dao refused. "Some orphanages did sell orphans, and a lot of people came to buy my orphans, but I would starve before I would allow it," Miss Dao says firmly. "I loved my orphans like my own children, and I would beg or steal or die before I would give them up."

But now the Americans were pulling out, and international political events that would greatly affect the little Amerasians were developing rapidly. On January 27, 1973, shortly after President Nixon's second-term inauguration, a cease-fire agreement was finally signed, partly achieved through secret promises by Nixon and Kissinger to the North Vietnamese to pay reparations once the war ended. In return, the Vietnamese agreed to make every effort to find and return the remains of 2,400 missing Americans, 800 of whom were listed as Missing in Action with the rest presumed dead. The American public and Congress knew nothing of Nixon and Kissinger's secret pledge, but the Vietnamese believed it would be honored. On March 29, as the Watergate scandal involving Nixon escalated back in Washington, the last U.S. troops departed Vietnam. On April 1, all U.S. prisoners of war were released to return to America. Now, with almost all the American fathers gone home, only about 6,000 American military and CIA and about 9,000 American civilians were left in Vietnam, mostly concentrated in Saigon.

Although America continued its halfhearted support of the South Vietnamese military regime, giving South Vietnamese President Thieu large amounts of U.S. military aid, much of which he apparently siphoned into his own pockets, no one was surprised when in early 1974 the civil war between North and South broke out again.

On August 9, 1974, a disgraced Nixon resigned the presidency as revelations about his involvement in the break-in and burglary of Democratic headquarters in the Watergate apartment complex and the White House cover-up afterward led to a congressional committee's vote to bring impeachment proceedings against him. That year Congress also voted not to extend any more money or aid to the South Vietnamese government. The demoralized troops of the corruption-riddled South Vietnamese regime were no match for the North Vietnamese military's dedicated, driven cadres. Although some South Vietnamese troops continued to fight on bravely, others gave up any pretense of true resistance in the final days of the war, and desertions were common. As final battles hit the central and southern parts of Vietnam where the Amerasians lived, people were now seeing some of their worst days of the war. As the 1974 fighting began, U.S. troops had been in Vietnam openly for nine years and American "advisers" and clandestine agents had been present for more than fourteen years. The Amerasians they left behind, still mostly infants and young children, were among the victims of the renewed bombing, shelling, and killing.

3

The War's End and Aftermath, 1975–84

[After the war], all the Amerasians were very poor, and on the street would be kicked and beaten, and their mothers called whores, or worse, if the kid was black.

—Vietnamese American man now living in the United States

The long years of war between North and South Vietnam were now racing toward the frantic final ending. By March 1975 it had become clear to most Americans still remaining in Vietnam, and to some of the better-connected Vietnamese, that these were the war's final days. Some 50,000 Americans and selected Vietnamese already had been quietly evacuated by the Americans to avoid a general panic, and thousands of other well-off Vietnamese had left on commercial flights for France and the United States. Still, most South Vietnamese clung to the belief that the Americans would return and save them from the Communists when a final showdown came. In the meantime, some U.S. aid groups had begun a desperate effort to fly as many orphans as possible from Vietnam to the United States and other Western countries.

In an interview with author Larry Engelmann in his outstanding account of the end of the war, *Tears Before the Rain: An Oral History of the Fall of South Vietnam*, Susan McDonald, an American nurse, tells of working at three Vietnamese orphanages in 1973, during a time when most American troops had left the country. One run by an Australian woman for fifty homeless toddlers in Phu My placed orphans for adoption in the United States, Australia, Canada, and several European nations. The orphanages received money from abroad and local donations of food and medicines, distributing any extra to orphanages in the Delta region, where most of the children had lost only one parent and weren't considered adoptable. Information on totally abandoned children was published regularly in the papers in case some relative would come forward to take them.

Children brought to orphanages were often suffering from cleft palates, malnutrition, tuberculosis, and other serious diseases. McDonald said she visited "outlying orphanages" where disease epidemics often attacked entire groups of children, causing many deaths. Clusters of orphans slated for adoption in the West were flown out "fairly frequently," said McDonald, but toward the end of 1974, a "dramatic change started to take place"—supplies were harder to get, and the Seventh-Day Adventist Hospital in Saigon, which provided medical care to the orphans, was shutting down. Orphanages responded by increasing the number of children flown out to be adopted.

In March 1975 President Gerald Ford announced a U.S. plan to evacuate 7,000 orphans, of whom "many," said the president, were Amerasians. Labeling the plan "Operation Babylift," 2,000 unaccompanied minors were hastily rounded up to be flown out on cargo planes. Children were gathered from several orphanages, including Nhiet Chi Mai, which had about 200 orphans, perhaps half of them Amerasians. Many Amerasians were included because of a rumor that the Communists would kill everyone ever associated with Americans. President Ford personally ordered red tape cut to a minimum.

At 4:45 P.M. on April 4, 1975, the first Operation Babylift flight, a C-5A Galaxy transport carrying 243 children and 62 adults, tried to turn back after reporting decompression problems. It crashed in a rice field eighteen miles out from Tan Son Nhut, skidding across paddies and breaking apart. The U.S. Air Force pilot and half the passengers survived, but dead and injured children were scattered everywhere. Seventy-eight children were among the 144 people who died. While helicopters took survivors to the Seventh-Day Adventist Hospital, Vietnamese soldiers and civilians gathered—some to help and some to loot from the dead.

An investigation that followed the crash revealed an ugly truth—

some of the children on the plane weren't orphans or abandoned at all, but simply children whose families had "connections" or gold enough to get them onto the flight. Others were children whose mothers hadn't given them up for adoption and came looking for them. And some of the women who accompanied the orphans were actually intelligence agency staffers that the United States hoped to spirit out of the country without alerting the Vietnamese. The corruption and fraud that were to haunt efforts to get the Amerasians out of Vietnam were present from the very beginning.

On March 25, 1975, the major Central Vietnam city of Hue fell to North Vietnamese troops. The South Vietnamese regime was collapsing. Panic and chaos were sweeping the southern half of Vietnam. Soon more than a million refugees were traveling south toward Danang, the port city in central Vietnam where ten years earlier the first U.S. troops had landed. Over the next days, Vietnamese overflowed Danang's docks and beaches. Thousands, including mothers clutching babies, waded into the sea and fought frantically to board small fishing boats taking people to larger ships offshore. People drowned or were trampled to death; some were shot by South Vietnamese soldiers making room for themselves.

By March 29 crowds jammed Danang's airport and runways. Edward Daley, the American president of World Airways, flew a jumbo jet into Danang to save refugees. Within ten minutes the plane was mobbed by 300 Vietnamese—most of them former South Vietnamese soldiers—who fought aboard, shooting and killing one another for a seat. Daley, himself attacked and clawed by soldiers desperate to get aboard, clubbed one man in the head with a gun after seeing him rip a woman backward out of the plane, then step on her to climb aboard and take her place. The man fell backward into the hysterical crowd. Later, says Engelmann, a flight attendant said she recognized the same man crawling up the plane aisle, his head smashed open, calling "Help me!" As the plane lifted into the air, another man's body was wedged in the rear door, and people clinging to the outside fell to their deaths. The plane was badly damaged by bullets fired by those left behind. Only eleven women and children made it onto the plane; the rest were men. The man whose head had been smashed lived through the flight.

With North Vietnamese troops moving ever southward, McDonald, the orphanage worker, told Engelmann that Vietnamese mothers began to appear at orphanage gates trying to hand over children to be taken

to safety, but most were turned away. She helped close down the orphanages where she worked and left with 250 orphans on a U.S. cargo
plane for the Philippines on April 26, four days before the war's end.
From there, she said, the United States began flying sixty orphans per
day to the United States. McDonald estimated that tens of thousands
of orphans remained in Vietnam, including about 24,000 in orphanages.
Later in the United States a class action suit was filed on behalf of
mothers of some children taken for overseas adoption, alleging the children had been kidnapped. The mothers maintained they had only
placed the children in the orphanages temporarily due to poverty, visiting them frequently and planning to reclaim them when they could.

Although race played a big part in much of the U.S. evacuation—all
Americans who "wanted" to leave were evacuated, according to CIA
chief Thomas Polgar—group bonds between Americans and Vietnamese were very powerful in cases where the two groups had close connections. By March 1975 15,000 Americans, mostly civilian workers
who earlier had served in the U.S. military, remained in Vietnam. Many
had Vietnamese wives or girlfriends and Amerasian children, and
around April 15 the United States began to airlift some of them out,
sometimes including their numerous Vietnamese in-laws. In the final
days, busloads of Americans and their families left daily for Tan Son
Nhut flights bound for America. The U.S. ambassador to Vietnam,
Graham Martin, a strange man who made many poor decisions in the
final weeks of the war, was, according to author A. J. Langguth, "very
rigid in defining which Vietnamese qualified as legitimate dependents
[of Americans]." Wrote Langguth in *Our Vietnam War: The War, 1954–
1975:* "Since Martin excluded common-law wives and their children,
many American civilians refused to leave." Bogus marriage licenses and
adoption certificates began to be sold on the black market at exorbitant
prices.

In addition to Vietnamese politicians, military, and their family members spirited out by the United States beginning in March, by late April
many individual Americans were committing desperate and often illegal
acts to save Vietnamese with whom they had bonded. These acts were
well-known to the Americans responsible for preventing them, but they
were either too sympathetic or too harassed in the final days to try to
stop them. As the magnitude of trying to take out Vietnamese along
with large numbers of Americans became more and more apparent, the
U.S. Embassy ruled that only Vietnamese who were dependents of
Americans could leave.

Dr. Bruce Branson, a doctor at Seventh-Day Adventist Hospital in Saigon, told Engelmann that some Americans then began formally adopting Vietnamese, including adults they'd never met. When Americans ran out of the thousands of forms copied in the final hours, on which Americans promised to support Vietnamese taken to the United States, some Americans began writing out pledges by hand and giving them to any Vietnamese who approached them.

In one chaotic last-minute scene, eight Americans Branson knew adopted fifty to sixty Vietnamese, promising to support them in the United States. Hospital staff sending out Medevac flights of U.S. patients put Vietnamese in the airport-bound ambulances with them, and wrapped orphans as patients to slip them out. On April 25 all remaining Adventist Hospital patients were transferred to other hospitals as hundreds of Vietnamese surrounded its gates, begging to be evacuated too. At the end, Branson told Engelmann, they piled their Vietnamese staff into eight ambulances and raced to the airport, where they were allowed inside as thousands of Vietnamese outside fought to get in.

Chuck Neil of Armed Forces Radio was an American civilian working in Vietnam since 1967. In the last days, the station's six Vietnamese employees brought their entire families to live there, afraid they'd otherwise be left behind—mothers, grandmothers, aunts, uncles, in-laws, and so on. There were more than 100 relatives, plus some friends and a few strangers who somehow managed to sneak inside. On April 29 Neil was ordered by the U.S. Embassy to evacuate himself and the three other American staffers. Following a prearranged signal to those chosen for evacuation, Neil played the song "White Christmas" over and over as he and his staff prepared to flee. Determined to take out as many Vietnamese as they could, says Engelmann, they hid some staffers and their family members in the station's van and drove to the nearby U.S. Embassy, where the van was one of the last vehicles allowed inside. Neil says Marines were pointing a 30-millimeter machine gun at crowds outside the reinforced Embassy gate, and some Americans inside were "looking over the wall and pulling up some of their buddies— Americans." Vietnamese stretching up their hands were left outside.

Langguth refers in his book to "the blatant racism that marked the panic at the embassy," when "even Vietnamese with U.S. passports were turned away at the gates while any white face [including other Westerners] was pulled inside." The Vietnamese conception of what constitutes "family" is much broader than that of Americans, and many

Vietnamese arrived with fifty to sixty assorted cousins, distant aunts and uncles and, no doubt, a few unrelated acquaintances and friends. They wept when told they could bring no more than ten or twelve relatives if they got out at all, and begged Americans to make those choices for them.

But examples of group bonding crossing racial lines continued. Engelmann related how John "Vietnam Johnny" Wahlburg, who'd been living in Vietnam since 1969 and had a Vietnamese wife and three Amerasian children, spent two days filling out forms and bribing guards at the airport to allow his family through the gate. When shelling broke out, the driver of a bus full of Vietnamese ran off, and Wahlburg convinced U.S. Marine guards to let the bus inside. "They said [only] I could come in because I was a U.S. citizen," recalled Wahlburg, "[but] no way I was going to leave my wife and kids and those other people on the bus." He commandeered the bus and blocked the gate until exasperated officers allowed everyone in. By then Wahlburg had bonded with the seventy Vietnamese strangers, and began referring to them as "our group." He managed to get them through the chaos and onto a helicopter, including two Vietnamese nurses he'd never met who clung to his wife screaming "Help me!" They were the last Vietnamese allowed to board the helicopter to safety.

On April 23, 1975, President Ford gave a speech in which he called the war "finished," and on April 25, South Vietnamese President Thieu fled to Taiwan in a U.S. transport plane. Reported to have taken with him massive amounts of corruption-derived loot—in fifteen tons of baggage, Marilyn Young reports in her book—just before leaving, he denounced the U.S. "abandonment" of his government.

By April 29 the potential victims of a Communist victory included the estimated few thousand Americans still in Vietnam and approximately 100,000 Vietnamese employed, or formerly employed, by American military and businesses, along with their families. Former CIA agent Frank Snepp, in his book *Decent Interval*, says that the United States eventually left behind several CIA "direct operatives" and as many as 30,000 Vietnamese who had been trained by the CIA for the Phoenix torture and assassination program, as well as 1.5 million police, soldiers, and civil servants of the U.S.-backed Thieu regime. Vietnamese women who'd worked as prostitutes or bar hostesses or had American boyfriends were also vulnerable, as were any half-American children. Finally, President Ford ordered all remaining Americans evacuated, adding: "This action ends a chapter in the American experience. I ask all Americans to close ranks, to avoid recrimination about the past, to look ahead to the many goals we share and to work together on the great tasks that remain to be accomplished."

Months earlier, top U.S. and South Vietnamese leaders had devised a secret evacuation plan for themselves, fearing that South Vietnamese troops might turn on them and attack them once they realized they were being abandoned. The plan, "Option IV," also called "Frequent Wind," involved sending buses to pick up designated Americans and Vietnamese and delivering them to specified helicopter pads to be transported to ships offshore. But the plan quickly disintegrated when hysterical crowds of Vietnamese blocked the buses and swarmed over the helicopter pick-up points, screaming to be allowed on. Meanwhile, seventy U.S. Marine choppers were lifting 1,000 Americans and 6,000 Vietnamese out of Saigon—2,000 of them from the U.S. Embassy compound. For eighteen hours they shuttled back and forth to aircraft carriers offshore. America's final humiliating moment came at 4:42 A.M. on April 30 when Ambassador Martin, with the American flag tucked under his arm, boarded a helicopter atop the embassy roof as frantic Vietnamese were held back by armed U.S. guards. The remaining Vietnamese were left behind when the last Americans barricaded the steps to the roof. At 7:35 A.M., a large U.S. Chinook helicopter accompanied by half a dozen black Cobra gunships picked up the last Marines atop the roof. The Americans had left Vietnam.

North Vietnamese troops—surprised by the speed and ease of their final victory—entered Saigon a few hours later and quietly took charge of the country. By 11:30 A.M. the North Vietnamese flag was flying over the palace. Later that day the new government broadcast a ten-point program promising "peaceful reunification, freedom of thought and worship, and sexual equality." It banned prostitution and "acting like Americans." A Vietnamese man from the South now in America was then a teenager. He speaks for millions of Vietnamese traumatized at the time, saying: "Our family barely managed to get out two weeks before the war ended, and went to a refugee camp in Guam. On April 30, the day the war ended, they announced over the camp loudspeaker: 'Vietnam is now Communist' and 10,000 Vietnamese people in our camp put white sheets of mourning over their heads and cried and cried. Until then, we had thought we'd be able to go back soon."

After the Americans had departed, quiet fell outside the embassy compound. Hours earlier, crowds of frightened Vietnamese had scurried through the streets, and hundreds of South Vietnamese soldiers had torn off their uniforms and tossed them onto the pavement. It was in those earlier hours of terror that an American journalist noted dozens of abandoned Amerasian children, some younger than two years old, wandering through the crowds or standing alone, quietly sobbing.

In Washington in May the U.S. Treasury Department froze all Vietnamese assets (about $150 million) in the United States and prohibited Americans from sending money to Vietnam—a disastrous restriction for Amerasian children left behind, as well as for family members of Vietnamese refugees. But the new Vietnamese government was counting on the secret U.S. promises of reparations made by Nixon and Kissinger, and on June 3 Vietnamese leader Pham Van Dong, in a speech to the Vietnamese national assembly barely a month after the war's end, called on the United States to normalize relations and pay the reparations Nixon and Kissinger had promised. The United States ignored the appeal.

Although the United States had given approval to bring out 35,000 Vietnamese if the country fell, except for the orphans official approval to begin evacuating was not given until April 25. In the end, Americans actually brought out 135,000 Vietnamese. "We got out every American who wanted to go, including seven American inmates serving time in Vietnamese prisons for crimes like rape and murder," embassy staffer Wolf Lehmann told Engelmann.

Sara Phuong and Miss Dao

Although few had realized that the day the war would end—April 30, 1975—was so close, it had become clear to some in the final weeks that the South was losing. The number of lost or abandoned children continued to swell, and mothers and families with Amerasian children were terrified. A Vietnamese woman who was in Saigon during the final days says: "People were panicking. There were so many rumors going around, including that the Communists would kill anyone ever involved with the Americans. Of course, that included anyone with an Amerasian in the family, and the Amerasians themselves."

Sara, not yet three, remembers nothing of that desperate time as the country was collapsing. Says Miss Dao: "There was an important American man at one agency or organization named—" she struggles to pronounce the English name, settling on: "Eng Oon." "He helped build orphanages, and when we were short of money or food we would tell 'Eng Oon,' and he would make sure we got what we needed." By the end of March 1975, Miss Dao and the six nuns at her temple had accumulated seventy orphans, including many Amerasians and one half-Korean child, fathered by one of the South Korean troops who fought alongside Americans during the war. Several orphans were crippled. The youngest orphan was an infant, and the oldest was three, except for two brothers, four and five, the only survivors of the shelling of a truckload of refugees. Their parents had been killed in the attack.

A South Vietnamese captain who had taken an interest in Miss Dao's orphanage warned her that she should move the children near the American base in Cam Ranh. He sent two trucks to pick them up, but when they arrived "there was so much bombing and shelling that the drivers fled," says Miss Dao. Desperately she tried to rent two replacement trucks.

"At that time everyone was very afraid of death," she says. "I myself was very afraid, and Sara and all the orphans were crying and frightened. As things reached the end, there were many frustrations and everyone was terrified, and I was going out of my mind. I tried to borrow money to rent other trucks but no one had it. I tried everywhere. And many, many people were fleeing."

Miss Dao couldn't bring herself to leave the orphans. Finally she scraped together enough to rent the trucks—800,000 dong, a very big sum at that time. The nuns packed the children's few belongings, giving Sara and each of the older children small bundles to carry. On March 29 the trucks arrived, and the nuns and children jounced off to Cam Ranh amidst a mob of panicking refugees. "The captain had told me to look for him when I got to Cam Ranh and he would help us," says Miss Dao, "but when we got there it was so chaotic I couldn't find him. I never saw him again."

As final battles were being fought all over the South, many orphans and nuns were experiencing the same traumatic situation as Miss Dao and Sara. Van, an Amerasian who was seven at the time and staying at an orphanage in Long Khanh, remembers her own frightening days. "On April 21, 1975 [nine days before the war ended] there was a big battle in Dinh Quan nearby," she says. "Our nun rented a truck to bring the smallest orphans back to our [regular] orphanage. But there wasn't enough money to rent one for us older orphans, so she gave each a small bag of rice to be our food during the trip, and we had to walk back through the jungle. In our group were also my older brother and sister.

"Our nun carried the Buddhist flag as we walked, in hopes it might protect us from the soldiers fighting all around. She wanted to get back to see my mother, who was dying of tuberculosis in a hospital. My mom had left we three children at the orphanage because she was too sick to take care of us. But I remember a lady who sometimes came outside the gates to see me and my brother and sister, who'd toss us a few coins through the gate. She could not come closer because of her tuberculosis. That same lady used to come and beg the nuns not to punish me if I made a mistake, and that lady was my mom. I was her only Amerasian child."

Van's nun managed to reach the mother's bedside just before she died, begging the nun to raise her children. Unable to bring the mother's body back to Bien Hoa because of heavy fighting, the nun let the hospital burn it along with five others. "But I had no concept then of what death meant," Van says. "When my older brother heard our mom had died, he ran to me and said, 'Mom is dead.' I said, 'Oh, she's dead? Can you buy me a candy?' After that, of course my mom never came back, and no one cared about me or protected me. When I realized I was alone I matured more than the other kids. As I grew up I felt ashamed I was Amerasian and I began to study harder, and learned how to play a musical instrument and write poetry. I tried to do everything better so the other kids wouldn't underestimate me because I was Amerasian."

Meanwhile, Miss Dao, Sara, and their group had managed to reach Cam Ranh around April 1, crowding into a temple with other refugees. But on April 5, Cam Ranh fell to the southward-moving North Vietnamese troops.

For four months after the war ended, Sara's group of nuns and orphans remained in Cam Ranh. When they were finally able to return to Qui Nhon, everything in the temple was gone—all the precious papers on the orphans, apparently including the letter and identification number Sara's mother had placed in Sara's baby basket. Soon the new government began closing the country's religious orphanages, partly to be able to use the buildings for badly needed housing of troops and others coming from the North. As someone who had taken foreign aid money and had harbored half-American children, Miss Dao, along with many other nuns and monks throughout southern Vietnam, was arrested and put on probation.

"It was a very hard time," says Miss Dao. "For a long time I had to go to the police station every day to be questioned." Many also underwent reeducation. This practice of the Communists led to Vietnamese lying and distorting their "stories" to conform to what would give them the least problems. And "truth" held little value when survival was the question. (This was the same conclusion some American leaders reached when confronted with questions about the U.S. involvement in the war.)

"During my interrogations the soldiers would be very angry," Miss Dao says. "They would try to scare me by shouting and hitting hard on the table. But I was not really afraid, because I felt I had done the right thing. Then, during the first six months after the war, our food supplies for the orphans dropped lower and lower and finally ran out, although we did all we could to raise money. It was a very difficult and painful time, very heartbreaking, because I had to deal with the children's hunger and my own hunger, and also because I was called an enemy. The government put a sign on every orphanage, announcing they were being closed and that people could come to look for their lost children, or to adopt." The new regime needed the work of every able-bodied person, including some of the bigger, stronger children, to rebuild the country. In Vietnam and most poor countries, children aged five and older have always been considered able to work.

"Every day at 7 A.M. the soldiers removed the adults from the orphanage until night," says Miss Dao, "and gave orphans to people who had supported the Communists. Most of the orphans were crying, screaming, begging to stay. The government could take any child it wanted; I had no way to protect them. I was heartbroken. Most of the children I never saw again, including the little six-year-old half-Korean boy. And I never had any idea what happened to any of them." A few of the healthier and "cuter" orphans were adopted by Vietnamese families who "might treat them very nice," says Miss Dao, "but times were very hard, and most people couldn't afford to take care of children. I saw people adopt them saying it was because they loved them, but actually they wanted ones five and older to work on their farms doing all kinds of hard work, almost as slaves. The government took the healthiest, strongest, good-looking orphans, most aged seven or eight, including two or three Amerasians, to work in the fields. Only Communists could take Amerasians because others were afraid to take them."

Several years later the *New York Times* carried a story about a seven-year-old half-black Amerasian orphan taken in 1980 to a government work camp where he was assigned to make bamboo baskets and clean a soldiers' graveyard, sleeping at night on the floor in a roomful of other children and subsisting on meager bowls of rice.

Sara, only three at the time, was not taken. "At the end of the war I had thirty-seven orphans left; after they took twenty-two away, fifteen were left," Miss Dao says. "Among them were six handicapped Vietnamese boys that nobody wanted. None was blind or had mental problems, although one had shrunken legs and couldn't walk. They were put out to work on the streets during the day." Like so many others in Vietnam at the time, they must have earned at least part of their living through begging. The oldest Amerasian who stayed with Miss Dao was born in 1968, the youngest in 1971 or 1972. In 1978 Miss Dao took in her last orphan, a two-day-old Vietnamese boy she named Vinh, found wrapped in a little torn shirt and with an infected umbilical cord.

"The most heartache," Miss Dao continues, "came in 1975 when everyone was so poor, and we had no food, no medicine, no clothes for the children, and when I was separated from so many of my orphans. I had raised them since they were so tiny and felt such a bond with them, but I couldn't keep them together, and I was so heartbroken and so sad. This was the most painful time of my life." Exhausted and poorly nourished, she was also experiencing the heart problems that would continue to plague her. "There was a time I felt I had lost all my energy, and couldn't go on anymore," she says, "but every time I looked at the children's little faces I could never bear to leave them all alone. I had to continue, to keep on, and try to support them."

As years passed, Miss Dao went to work on a farm, went to the forest and picked leaves to make incense to sell, cooked and sold rice cakes in the market, and helped grow beans to make tofu to sell. A few Vietnamese families contributed what little they could, but the Vietnamese government—also desperately poor in the years after 1975, when many in the country were facing starvation—contributed nothing. Totals of the war's damage to both sides were brutal, but the Vietnamese had suffered far more. Figures vary, but approximately 300,000 South Vietnamese had been killed in action along with 300,000 South Vietnamese civilians, 1.5 million North Vietnamese and Viet Cong soldiers, and 65,000 North Vietnamese civilians. Three million Vietnamese had been wounded, the infrastructure was shattered, countless Vietnamese were mentally and physically disabled, 300,000 Vietnamese were missing, and tens of thousands more had fled the country.

An estimated 200,000 prostitutes and bar girls listed by the government at the end of the war, including many mothers of Amerasians, lost their only means of making a living when the new regime, repulsed by the widespread prostitution and other forms of vice that flourished during the war, closed down all such establishments. Thousands of Vietnamese who had been connected with the Americans or who were accused of being corrupt were sent to reeducation camps or the so-called New Economic Zones where they were supposed to fight the country's food shortage by farming empty lands. Families were scattered or destroyed; physical wounds such as amputated limbs would last for a lifetime; mental wounds were incalculable, with both soldiers and civilians suffering post-traumatic stress disorder and other mental illnesses, and many turning to drugs or suicide.

Historian Marilyn B. Young says the war's aftermath included 879,000 orphans, 181,000 disabled people, 1 million widows, 1.5 million farm animals killed, and 25 million acres of farmland and 12 million acres of forest destroyed. Tons of still unexploded ordnance sowed everywhere guaranteed that killing and maiming would continue for decades. So did the 19 million gallons of herbicide sprayed on the South during the war, leaving vast swaths of chemically poisoned soil and foliage that would lead to multiple miscarriages, and, more than twenty-five years later, to continuing serious birth defects and cancers. All these carried the memories and damage of the war into the future. The young Amerasians, with their half-American features and their racially mixed backgrounds—already a taboo in Vietnam's racially homogenous culture—also represented reminders of that war. Like other children in postwar Vietnam, which for years continued to be one of the world's poorest nations, they suffered terribly. Vietnamese streets were filled with those maimed by war, including many Amerasians who had been wounded and lost arms, legs, or eyes. Others were crippled by polio or suffered from tuberculosis, malaria, malnutrition, and other conditions endemic to impoverished countries. The North Vietnamese officials of the new government moving into the South from the North needed housing and everything else. They ordered many families—especially the very wealthy—from their homes and confiscated their possessions.

Unofficially, the new regime's dislike and prejudice against the Amerasians was made clear from the start. The children's half-American faces were constant reminders of the Americans who had killed and maimed relatives and friends and destroyed much of the country, then abandoned it. The strong racial prejudice most Vietnamese feel toward "non-pure" Vietnamese was felt throughout both North and South. So was class prejudice, because most Vietnamese believed all Amerasians were children of prostitutes. As the Amerasians grew up they were seen as lower-class troublemakers.

Nan

Nan, the Amerasian taken to Nhiet Chi Mai orphanage after a firefight destroyed her orphanage at Bien Long years earlier, says that rescue workers for Operation Babylift "had tried to choose the cutest orphans to go, and I was not one of those picked." ("Cute Amerasians," she says, usually meant "white.") Among the "cute" babies whose body parts were strewn over the ground after the crash was one of Nan's "orphanage sisters" who, like her, was one of only nine survivors of the destruction of the first orphanage. "If that girl were still alive today, she would be thirty years old," says Nan. "Another of my orphanage sisters was adopted around that time by an American family, and now lives in Bangkok, working for the U.S. government. For years she sent back money to our orphanage. All the children brought to America in 1975 don't even remember how to speak Vietnamese now, because they came so young."

Thus, if Nan had been among those evacuated, she would have gone to American schools, would have received an American education, would now speak excellent English, and probably would be a college graduate. Instead, she was left in Vietnam for another fourteen years. She estimates that at least 100 other Amerasians had been living in her orphanage at the war's end as the final Operation Babylift flights continued, and as President Ford was photographed carrying a baby off one of the first flights to arrive.

After the war's end, Nan says, "When my orphanage was closed, some of the nuns were jailed for several weeks. The local officials allowed each nun to keep two orphans, one Vietnamese and one Amerasian. When people came to pick orphans, they would choose first the good-looking, strong Vietnamese kids; then the good-looking, healthy white Amerasians; and so on, until only the ugly, weak Vietnamese and, last of all, the black Amerasians would be left. But my nun really loved all her orphans, and was afraid anyone not adopted would be pushed into the streets. So she tried to save the less desirable ones by secretly asking some of the temple members to pretend they wanted them. That way she was able to bring the unwanted ones back together under her care.

"Our nun made and sold vegetarian food on the streets to support us. Everyone was always hungry, and if we ever had rice and the government learned about it, our nuns would be taken into the district office for questioning. It was really our nun who suffered most, sacrificing for us while she tried to raise us. She lived a very harsh life and had high blood pressure, and was more and more exhausted and ill. She died in 1980 when I was about ten." But, says Nan, "not all nuns are good, kind people. One nun I knew would take in only white Amerasians." As for Miss Dao, even some members of her own family questioned her devotion and sacrifices on behalf of her orphans. But despite the hardships, she still refused to abandon Sara and the others.

Son Chau

Son remembers a little about the war. When he was between four and six, U.S. soldiers from the nearby base sometimes gave him a ride on their trucks. "They liked me a lot," says Son, "and sometimes they would give me my favorite food then—fruit cocktail."

The day North Vietnamese troops captured the area where Son, then seven, lived, Communist soldiers occupied his small house while helicopters and planes circled overhead. Like other mothers of Amerasians throughout the South, Son's mother was hastily burning and hiding letters and photos of the children's American fathers. Unfortunately, she burned the only photo on which Son's father had written his U.S. address, but she did keep and hide another that showed his name tag, bearing his complete name.

Son remembers running with his mom to a hiding place under his house as North Vietnamese troops entered the town. For a long time Du kept Son hidden in a hole there with his Amerasian half-sister. "Then, after the Communists came, we all went to my aunt #9's house and lived together," says Son. "My aunt #9 was the wealthy one in our family. She had a little shop in her house." There, Son often played with Hung, his black Amerasian cousin one year younger. Although younger, under Vietnamese custom, because Hung was the son of Aunt #8 and Du is sister #11, Son called Hung "Older Brother." Says Son: "I teased Hung a lot about being 'Older Brother' when we were little." In Vietnam, Amerasians are quickly noticeable. Half-black Amerasians like Hung were hardest to disguise. Curly hair was cut off or greased back, but it was hard to lighten skin color. Hung and Son became close while living together at the aunt's, although Son was often mischievous. "I am the one who stole the cookies and coins from my aunt, but I told people Hung did it, and although he said, 'No,' they not believe him," says Son. "They trusted me, not him, and they hit him with a stick." Son laughs guiltily at this memory. "No one ever gave Hung strong teachings about life, but we loved each other always, because he was a good man."

When Son was nine, a friend convinced his mother, Du, to marry Hanh, a former Viet Cong soldier who'd fought with the famed 48th fighting division. In a culture where a man could simply claim an unprotected, unattached woman as his wife, Hanh basically forced Du to live with him. "We thought he would know all the Communist laws and ways, and would be a man around to help do the hard work," says Du. "But he was mean. He beat me and my children. Especially Son. He kept taunting Son about being Amerasian." Hanh would also taunt and beat Son's black Amerasian cousin Hung.

Du says Hanh "was so cruel that he wouldn't let Son go to school," and when Son, nine, was starting fifth grade, Hanh tore up Son's books and ordered him to go to work. Luckily, Son had always been energetic and adventurous. "Even at age nine," Du had said, "Son knew how to work and make money." He began going into the jungle to look for bamboo shoots for her to steam and sell in the market. And he chopped wood, staggering home with heavy armloads to sell.

Son remembers that time well. "In 1975, when the Communists came, my family had nothing. No one in Vietnam had enough to eat, and it was a very terrible time." Hanh also beat the little boy to keep him from sleeping at home. Du says Son often slept on the hard stone floor of the town's deserted Buddhist temple at the jungle's edge. The new government had removed all the Buddha statues, and soldiers were living in one section of the temple while another was used for school classes during the day. Son would catch colds, and often be half-sick. "He was always hungry, and I was afraid he would be taken by a ghost," Du says. "Sometimes he would try to hide and sleep in an empty barrel. He was always crying, and I was too." Often at night she would sneak out of the house to try to find him. But she was afraid of Hanh. "Even though it was usually Son who brought home food money, Hanh would chase him away from eating, and dump anything left over in the yard so Son would go hungry," says Du.

"People pushed me down a lot because I am Amerasian. When I was a very little boy about seven, I said bad things to my mother when I knew I had an American dad," says Son. "I knew because everyone called me the nickname 'Con My' [mixed blood half-American] and thought my mom was a bad woman for having had an American boyfriend. That's why Vietnamese don't like my mom, and don't like children from American fathers. It made me cry because everybody always thought the American people is really bad. I felt ashamed, not proud, to be part American."

More than twenty-five years later, Hung was still living in Vietnam, deeply marked by the hardships of his life. Son, who was busy working in America, arranged for me and an interpreter to talk with Hung and some of Son's friends on a trip there in 1999. Tall, and looking more African American than Vietnamese, Hung often walked or sat slightly apart, watching quietly rather than speaking despite attempts to draw him out. Sometimes he refused the offer of a small thing such as a soft drink, almost as if he did not deserve it. His hands were scarred from hard work. His manner conveyed both the loneliness of someone who had often been hurt and the dignity of someone who had come to depend solely on his own resources. After the war, little Hung and his mother were sent to one of the New Economic Zones, desolate jungle areas, some near the Cambodian border, where the government sent "undesirables," including an estimated 76 percent of all Amerasians. There, Hung told us, he grew up scouring the jungle for wood and bamboo shoots to sell at market so he could eat. "Everyone was hungry and in the same situation, so we just had to accept the hardships," Hung told us.

After some coaxing by Son's outgoing friend Kim, who had grown up with him, Hung did tell a few memories. "When Son's stepfather was drinking when we were little boys he would say things to us like, 'I'm fighting America to help my country!' and hit Son and me. He would hit Son's mother, hit everybody. When he came home drunk, we all would go flying off in every direction to get away from him. When Son came back from school, he would have to hide and eat in the chicken pen, and when Son was nine or ten, if the stepfather caught Son eating, he would beat him up." Most of the time the two boys were growing up, only five Amerasians were living around Song Pha. "But Hung was not as smart as Son," says Du, who likes to brag about Son but is also expressing the family's lifelong consensus comparing the two. "So over the years Son helped look out for Hung and his mom when he could."

"Many times Son's stepfather would say to us, 'You are sons of Americans! Who do you think your are to sit at the same level with me?'" said Hung.

"My stepdad had to have alcohol every day," says Son, "and when he was drunk he did very crazy violent things he don't remember. I didn't ever like him even in the beginning when I was a little boy. Even my mom not like him. In Vietnam they have no law, no rules, so if you're drunk you can do everything. He'd tear off the door of our house, force his way in, whatever. Nobody stopped him because I was a little boy and my mom, a woman, and no police came to help us. My stepdad was not really a Communist. Before the war he was in the Viet Minh, and later the Viet Cong. So he said sometimes he killed people, and he did this and that, so maybe it bothered him and that's why he was always drunk. I don't want to say bad about him, but he had many women. Many women in Vietnam were widows then with no husbands, and he kind of forced them. My mom didn't care. We had to survive with him, she had to stay with him, otherwise she would get into trouble."

Son remembers his mother talking to him about his American father as he grew older. "She said he was a very good man, crazy about my mom and about me. When I grew up a little more, maybe ten or twelve, I thought about him and missed him and wanted to look for him. After I understood their story, I loved him more and more, because he was a good man. But he was not a lucky man. That's why he met a woman in Vietnam and loved her a lot, and was concerned about her pregnancy but had to leave." Son says his mother "was kind of country, not fancy like some other girls. My dad liked to take care of her, do good things for us if he can." Son's father asked Du to go back to America with him, Son says, but "he was allowed to take only a wife, and nobody else. And at the time she had a little boy from another man, about four." That boy died later when he fell into a stream beside the nearby electric plant. (Du's seven-month-old baby girl had died of fever before she met Son's dad.) "My mom told my dad, 'No, I'm scared, I don't want to leave to go to the U.S. by myself.'" But Son began to dream that some-day he would go to America and find him. He carried the image of a caring father in his heart throughout all the bad times ahead. "I know that my real dad, my American dad, had concern for me," says Son.

Alan "Tiger" Hoa

Those first ten to fifteen years after the war were terrible for everyone in Vietnam. In addition to the deaths, injuries, and destruction left from the war, there was the problem of inexperienced officials trying to set up a government where tremendous enmity still existed between North and South. Tens of thousands of Vietnamese were sent to the re-education camps, where some considered to have committed more serious violations during the war remained for fifteen to twenty years. Approximately 1.5 million Vietnamese were sent to the New Economic Zones, inhabited at the time by one of Vietnam's many indigenous tribal minorities and by a handful of Communist troops guarding the area. The government policy to send "undesirables" included former prostitutes — many of whom were mothers of Amerasians. Most people sent to the NEZ were city people who knew nothing about farming, and the *Los Angeles Times* was later to label the program "such a disaster that Vietnam faced famine in 1986."

Tiger was three in 1975 when the government sent him to an NEZ area with his mother, his two-year-old sister, and a baby brother; Tiger's Uncle Lam and his wife, who'd raised Tiger since birth; and two of Tiger's other uncles, one retarded, one physically disabled. Tiger's Uncle Lam was among many required to sit through nightly reeducation meetings that included references to American transgressions. Lam had been a soldier in the South Vietnamese Army, and from 1972 to 1975 his unit was surrounded by Communist troops in the Binh Long and Loc Ninh areas. The troops captured Lam and his fellow soldiers and forced them to work for them. His wife is a gentle, kind woman whom Tiger admits was good to him when he was a small boy.

The spot where Tiger's family was sent was between Phuoc Long and Tay Ninh provinces, in a primitive section called Bu Dop by the tribal people who until then had been its only residents. The new government renamed it "Tan Loc," part of its practice of renaming many towns, streets, and districts, which contributed to problems people had finding one another after the war. In 1975 a dirt road to the area passed through little more than thick, desolate jungle. One Vietnamese man who lived through the hard postwar years says the new government "made it sound as if it would be a good life in the New Economic Zones, but actually it was terrible — just bare, hard land with no houses, no water, and jungle all around. Really the new government wanted to take over the houses of people sent to the NEZ for people moving down from the North. And also there was not enough food in the country, and they needed people to try to farm some of the worst land."

The NEZ area where Tiger and his uncle Lam's family hacked out a space to live was pure jungle, where dangerous animals, including snakes, elephants, and tigers, roamed. "To get there from Hoc Mon where we'd lived, you take Highway 13 all the way up to the Cambodian border, and walk the last five miles—farther in rainy season, when the road was nothing but thick mud—and Lam and Tiger lived at the very end of that road," says Khue. Their only neighbors were the few government soldiers stationed nearby, other city Vietnamese exiled to the NEZ, and members of one of Vietnam's more than seventy tribal minorities, each of which has its own customs and language.

The tribal people living near Tiger's new home hunted in the jungle for the many wild animals living there and bartered parts, skins, and wild rice to traders who ventured into the area to trade salt and other necessities. Tribal members, who believed elephants were sacred, wore few if any clothes, and had long, matted hair. They spoke a tribal dialect rather than Vietnamese. Tiger remembers being frightened by them and repelled by their dirtiness and strange ways when he first arrived in the NEZ as a three-year-old. He remembers watching a tribal man with wild, long hair, wearing only a dirty cloth sarong, reach down into the mud to snatch up a tiny, wriggling lizard, then pop its squirming body into his mouth, chew, and swallow. Tiger's Uncle Khue confirms: "They ate anything that moved, even insects, any creature they could get their hands on. But they had no salt, so we would bring in salt and dried fish to trade with them."

The family's closest neighbor, an elderly tribal man named Bay (which means "the fifth" or number-five child born in his family), raised elephants. He was kind to Tiger and Tiger has never forgotten him. "Tiger remembers so much about him because the old man came to our house very often to ask for salt or tobacco," says Khue. "At that time Tiger was an open, friendly person, and he used to joke around and play with that old man. He was very nice to Tiger." Because there was never enough food, before long Tiger too was eating the mud creatures, the lizards and insects. "I had to, to survive," he says now matter-of-factly. After reflecting a moment, he adds forcefully: "When people are hungry the only thing they do is fight for food. When I have been hungry in my life, all I worried about was looking for food, and I got it by stealing. In the jungle you don't steal from other people's hands, but people fight for the place where they can find roots or wild fruits, or any pond where they can catch fish, and whoever wins gets the food. Everyone was always hungry, so everyone invented ways to outdo each other, and if you got caught, you got in trouble. When people are hungry each just wants to hang onto his own portion and grab more if he can. That is true everywhere and always, even in prison, where people will fight for a small bag of rice."

Tiger's Uncle Lam plays down Tiger's suffering as a child. "Tiger was raised by me since he was born," Lam says. "Tiger's mother lived nearby in the NEZ because she was living with a Vietnamese man and had the younger sister of Tiger and a baby boy. She had her own family and had to protect their happiness. Life was really difficult. But Tiger wasn't affected at this time by anything." Some of the tribal people showed Lam how to find food and how to build a rough shelter. Life was so harsh that some Vietnamese who had been sent to the NEZ migrated illegally back to towns, where, unable to obtain proper government papers, their children could not attend school or be assigned housing or government rice rations, and often were forced to live homeless in the streets.

In the NEZ, hunger and sickness were even more serious and widespread than in the cities or small towns. The newcomers had little immunity against the virulent tropical diseases of the area—encephalitis, meningitis, hepatitis, and always malaria, which afflicted virtually every person there, including the tribal people. More than twenty-five years later Tiger's three oldest uncles—Khue, Binh, and Lam—all toughened by years of hardship, still weep when they speak of those terrible times. "There wasn't enough food to eat and we didn't get used to the new area, and life was horrible. It was hard just to stay alive. Many people got sick and there was no medicine, so they would just get sicker and sicker and die because of starvation and lack of medicine," says Lam. In the area around Bu Dop were mutant strains of malaria, probably including cerebral malaria, which affects the brain. "People who got that kind of malaria, or had lots of malaria attacks, become like robots or zombies," says Khue. "Malaria there is very vicious. By three o'clock every afternoon every person in the area would be shaking and shivering all over with chills and fever, including Tiger, although he got better after he moved back to Hoc Mon." Khue thinks it's possible that Tiger's mind was affected by the malaria. In America, Tiger still suffers from it occasionally, as well as from tuberculosis, and has been given medicine in prison to treat it.

To Vietnam's poor, especially in rural areas, illnesses came and went, undiagnosed, usually untreated, except by various folk remedies that included using insects and animals as medicines. A certain small lizard swallowed alive is used to cure asthma, and a certain poison caterpillar is swallowed to commit suicide. "My mother suffered a lot after she was sent to the NEZ, and was very sick a lot of the time," says Tiger. "When I was small I got sick a lot too, with fevers and other illnesses. I remember one time that was very terrible. No one helped save my life but Lam and the tribal man, Bay. They caught jungle creatures and leaves to make up remedies to cure me. Probably from frogs and lizards, they extracted some kind of liquid for me to drink. I remember one made of earthworms and frogs that the tribal man concocted. It tasted bitter and very, very gross. But my mom's blessing and God watching me from above saved my life."

"Tiger was a very lively, outgoing little boy then," says Khue. "The tribal man would always greet him, and sometimes take Tiger along with him. But he was already very old then, probably sixty, and he must be dead now." Tiger's twenty-three-year-old mother, already weak and fragile, was helpless against the serious malaria she contracted after only two months in the NEZ. A family member rented a bike and pedaled two days back to Hoc Mon to tell the rest of her family that she was ill. Tiger's Uncle Binh finally caught a ride on the back of a timber truck to the faraway area, bringing medicine to save her. But Binh says he knew she would probably be dead by the time he could get there. "The herbal medicine used to try to save Tiger's mother—Xuyen Tam Lien—no longer exists. It was given out for any kind of disease," Tiger's aunt, his mother's only sister, says sardonically. After Tiger's mother died, says Khue, "all our family went there with a document to bring back her body to bury it, but the government officials told us it had already decayed and been buried, and they wouldn't let us move her." Both Tiger and Lam remember that Bay helped bury Tiger's mother. "He gave us the materials to prepare a coffin and helped build it, and he came to her funeral," says Lam.

The differing accounts of Tiger's life offer a case study in the variations between recollections of the same events, and in the changing of memories over time. Sometimes painful memories are altered, or stored where they cannot be retrieved by the conscious mind but exert subterranean power. Tiger's family denies that he suffered much, but when Tiger tells his story, it is full of pain. At this very early point in Tiger's life, when his mother died, his memories and those of his family begin to diverge. Tiger has always insisted that he was ten when his mother died, but records show he was barely four. He also tells many stories about his mother and her loving treatment of him that simply cannot be true. He says she told him he could drop out of school in first grade when he was teased, and that she once gave him a special locket engraved with the name of his father. All his stories center around her love for him. Yet when Tiger's relatives insist he cannot possibly remember his mother at all, that, too, rings untrue. Says Lam: "Because I raised him, Tiger wasn't that affected when his mother died. He was just a little kid running around, innocent and carefree. When his mother died, he was too young to understand what pain is." But the age of four is not too young to form important memories.

The uncles, wracked with grief at the sudden death of their young sister, think Tiger hardly noted his mother's death. "He was too young to realize anything," says one. Says another uncle: "I hardly remember even seeing him during that time around her death, and when we buried her." But Tiger insists he does remember. He says that at first he thought his mother was only asleep, and that at one point he tried to lie down beside her body and snuggle up to her, a tale that has the ring of fantasy. Yet surely Tiger could have run about unnoticed and underfoot as grim, grieving adults sought to prepare and bury his mother, all of them too torn with sadness and worry to comfort the thin, small boy watching. "When my mother died we had no money for a coffin, so we had to just wrap her in bamboo reeds fastened around with string to bury her," says Tiger. Americans can hardly understand the significance for Vietnamese of a proper burial, but to them it is of overpowering importance. There were no Buddhist monks or nuns for many, many miles, so the family said its own prayers as they lowered her body into her grave. Maybe Bay, the tribal man, noticed Tiger and tried to comfort him. For a long time Tiger insisted to me that he lived with the tribal man rather than with his uncle. The rest of Tiger's family were surprised that Tiger even remembered him.

Khue remembers that when Tiger was seven or eight he often would look for a long time at his mother's picture, one taken when she was seventeen, and one of only two the family has. "But he did not ask me questions about her," says Khue. "Maybe he is remembering the image of her in his mind." A Vietnamese woman who knows Tiger, and who herself underwent much suffering during the war and its aftermath, explains: "People like Tiger who have had so much suffering have many fantasies. They draw a picture in their heads, and after awhile they are not sure what is true and what is not. When you are suffering too much, you tend to live in the fantasy even more—*much* more—because you draw deeper and deeper inside your fantasy in order to dispute the suffering in your real life."

Half-starved, often with a high fever, Tiger growing up in the NEZ was frequently dazed and disoriented. Most Vietnamese believe in ghosts and spirits, and Tiger began to believe his mother came to him. He says even now he sometimes sees her ghost, looking as she did near the end of her life—ill, thin, sickly, on the verge of death. But always her spirit lovingly encourages him. After his mother's death, Tiger says, Lam's wife was very kind to him. Yet his struggle to live became a desperate one. And soon Tiger would again be affected by geopolitical forces outside his control, as Cambodian Khmer Rouge troops began invading Vietnamese NEZ settlements near the Cambodian border. One day in 1977 when Tiger was six, a group of Khmer Rouge soldiers suddenly rampaged across the border, raping women, burning down the fragile huts, and slashing people to death with machetes. The Vietnamese Communists and the Khmer Rouge Communists of the two neighboring nations had been allies during the war and for a time after it, but there were centuries of suspicion between their countries. Perhaps the Khmer Rouge feared the NEZ settlements at their border were the first Vietnamese step in taking over Cambodian territory.

"I was sitting in our house," Tiger says, "and heard screaming. The Khmer Rouge soldiers had appeared and began slashing at people with machetes. I saw them kill people, stab them with knives, set houses on fire. I saw a naked woman screaming and running away, and the Khmer Rouge ran after her and chopped her to death with a machete. I didn't understand about rape then, but now I think she was raped." Tiger believes it was the tribal man, Bay, who saved him. But Lam says: "I had Tiger's little half-brother in my arms, my crippled brother on my back, and held my mentally ill brother by the hand." His wife carried Tiger's half-sister in a chest sling and held Tiger by his hand as all ran from the killers. "The Khmer Rouge burned down houses and were very cruel," says Lam. "They attacked every family, killed anyone they saw, and whoever cried or hid they would track down and kill right away, even children. The tribal man, Bay, and all the other tribal people and villagers were running along the road with us, about fifteen miles."

Lam is surprised that Tiger remembers enough to describe some of the terrain over which they fled, with the settlers and tribal people mixed together, running and crying. "I remember running over a ditch," Tiger says. "I remember running a long way to where the Vietnamese government troops were. We lived there until things settled down, and after someone investigated to make sure it was safe I was taken back to our settlement. When I got back it was horrible. I remember seeing all the dead bodies, and for a time I could still smell their blood when I ate." Lam says that the returning survivors helped bury the dead. At the small graveyard in Bu Dop, where Tiger's mother was already interred, most of the ten other bodies buried near her were strangers. "We didn't really know the other people buried there," says Lam. "No one knew one another then, because all of us had been sent there within the past year."

The Vietnamese government decided that the border area was too dangerous and moved Tiger's family and the others farther from the border to Bu Nho. There, they had to clear land all over again. Lam's eyes were injured when sap squirted in them while he was chopping down a poisonous tree.

"Life was very hectic and burdensome," says Tiger, "and everyone would be working very hard every day in the fields and jungle so we rarely talked with one another." The years of hunger in the NEZ and later in the Saigon streets haunt Tiger to this day, and have shaped his view of life. As for Bay, the elderly tribal man who befriended him as a child, Tiger repeatedly refers to him as the kindest person in his entire life, the one who loved him the most and treated him the best.

On December 25, 1978, the Vietnamese army invaded Cambodia and quickly drove the Khmer Rouge, under whose four-year reign 2 million people died of executions and starvation, up to the Thai border. From there the Khmer Rouge and its leader Pol Pot, along with two allied groups, in a coalition supported by the United States, would continue to battle the Vietnamese-backed government in Cambodia for more than ten years. In addition, the United States continued to vote to seat the Khmer Rouge–involved coalition in the United Nations as Cambodia's legitimate government. The main reason was the continuing U.S. punishment of Vietnam, which kept troops in Cambodia to battle the Khmer Rouge.

Louis Nguyen

Louis's mother Luc, trying to keep her two Amerasian children with her in Bien Hoa, went from house to house buying and selling old clothes and doing whatever else she could to survive. Even those mothers of Amerasians like Louis's who had not been prostitutes were finding that, partly out of fear of repercussions, no one wanted to hire anyone who had been connected to the Americans. Like other mothers of Amerasians, Luc was required to go the local police station several nights a week for reeducation. The mothers would be queried by stern women cadres about why they had become involved with the enemy Americans, and told repeatedly how bad the Americans were. The mothers wrote out their confessions over and over again. At first they were frightened, but eventually some of them began to joke secretly about some of the stiff, country-reared Communist women who operated the classes.

When Louis was seven, his mother took him and his younger brother back to her hometown Chon Thanh in Song Be province where they lived with Louis's grandmother, who was already in her seventies. Unlike grandparents of many Amerasians, she had strongly encouraged Louis's mother to keep both of her Amerasian babies, and now gave Louis, the oldest son, complete devotion. Deeply religious, she read to him each night for an hour from Buddhist teachings. Every day she walked him back and forth to the nearest school, six miles away. School in his district was free, although children had to buy their own books and supplies—an expense most Amerasians simply couldn't pay. In rural Vietnam, where most people lived by farming, and most were barely literate if at all, education was not considered very important.

But Louis's family believed in it. And although his classmates often treated him cruelly, as they did other Amerasians, his grandmother wouldn't let him quit school. "Our family was very poor, and sometimes we didn't have money for food, but my mom always found some jungle plant we could eat," says Louis. "Nowadays that stuff might make me almost sick, but as a kid, with no chance to ever eat meat or other good things, it seemed fine." Their house was tiny. Until Louis was seventeen, he slept each night with his grandmother in her bed. "Because my Mom had to be off working in the fields twelve hours every day, it was mostly my grandmother who raised me," says Louis. "She tried to live by Buddhist principles and teach me how also. So no matter how bad people treated us, I *know* my family had value."

Like other Amerasians, once he started first grade Louis was taunted, hit, and harassed by other children. In class the children were taught lessons and songs about the ugly role of Americans in the war. At first Louis would fight his tormentors, until teachers intervened. "A lot of Amerasians, when they went to school people called them something bad every single day, and they fought and got in trouble every single day, and the teachers called them troublemakers. They always blamed the Amerasian," says Louis. "So they got kicked out of school or just quit going. But my Buddhist grandmother teached me how to handle it. She said to never say anything bad back, because when someone gets you angry, they love it. So a lot of times I was really angry but I told myself, 'Calm down.'"

In the whole area lived only six or seven Amerasians, including Louis and his younger brother. "Some families wouldn't let me play with their children," Louis says. "People would say to me, 'Get out, black guy!' and in Vietnam, 'black' is a very heavy word. That word hurt. I would be quiet and then go. If you didn't leave, if you said something back, they would beat you. Some Amerasians tried to talk to people like that, but I would say to them, 'Why do that?' Many times Vietnamese boys hit me, but I didn't hit back. I remember one whose older brother hit me no matter what I did, right or wrong, and the teacher tried to stop him. When I was about eleven, he was seventeen, and he hit me very bad, and I ran to her and she told him he had no right to hit her students, and if he hit me again his brother would be kicked out of school. I did cry, but I didn't tell my family. I didn't want to upset my mom. And if I brought any trouble home my mom would hit me too. My younger [Amerasian] brother fought a lot, though. He got in more fights than me. I only got beat up one other time, when I was about ten. A guy said something bad like 'black' to me, so I hit him."

At school Louis had few friends. "I didn't get along with people. I was very unhappy," he says. He spent years during which he would wait to enter class only when the morning bell rang, and leave immediately at the end of the school day. "But now I am very proud of myself because of how I acted," he says. Vietnam had a youth organization for schoolchildren, the Young Pioneers, something like the Boy Scouts, known as the Ho Chi Minh Youth Brigades. Louis was allowed to join. "I was a Good Ho Chi Minh kid," he says. "I wore the red [neckerchief] and all when I was ten. To be a Ho Chi Minh kid you had to follow the five rules: no fighting, obey the school rules, be a good student, wear the school uniform—although some people were too poor to buy one—and volunteer to help around the school. When I got older, I didn't allow myself to hang out with gangbangers."

One happy part of Louis's life was that while he was still in grade school his talent as a singer was discovered and soon he became well-known locally, invited to sing at more and more school and district occasions and Tet celebrations. "They had me travel to other schools to

sing, too. Mostly the songs were about Ho Chi Minh. They have a thousand songs in Vietnam about Ho Chi Minh, and every child has to learn
them." Louis thinks he may have inherited his beautiful, soulful singing
voice from his black American father. "My mom can't sing, nor anyone
on her side of the family, so I think maybe I got my voice from my
American dad," he says shyly.

"For a long time I wouldn't quit school. I told myself I was going for
myself and my family, not for anybody else. So I couldn't let anyone
stop me. And also I really liked to learn. When I got older I promised
myself that someday, if I finally came to the United States, nobody
would ever treat me bad again."

The new Vietnamese government, seeking to unite a country torn by
civil war as well as foreign interference, and furious at those who had
opposed it, was dealing with terrible problems with almost no resources. The Vietnamese were the winners, but at a horrible cost, and
the damage done by the American enemy was not easily forgotten or
forgiven.

Gradually the new Vietnamese government settled into control of its
war-ravaged and enmity-plagued country. But many in the United
States were still furious at Vietnam, and continually sought ways to
punish it. For years the United States blocked most humanitarian aid
to Vietnam. And it blocked efforts that would have taken the Amerasians to the United States. It also refused to honor the secret promises
of postwar reparations. The resultant creation of severe hardships in
Vietnam disproportionately affected the Amerasians, since they were almost always in the poorest strata of society. As years passed, many Vietnamese were desperate, helpless to help others or themselves. Some
families abandoned their children on the streets, sometimes because
they simply were unable to feed them. Other children were turned out
when a mother died. And still others, with neither love nor food at home
to hold them, simply wandered away to live or die on their own. This
was the situation in which the little Amerasians were growing up.

Americans paid little attention to how U.S. actions would affect the
Amerasian children left in Vietnam, although the newly elected U.S.
president, Jimmy Carter, appeared to be seeking to heal the after-
effects of the war. In January 1977, the day after he was inaugurated,
he pardoned 10,000 American draft evaders. In March his administration began exploring the normalization of relations with Vietnam, sending a mission to resolve the question of 2,400 missing U.S. servicemen,
800 of whom were listed as missing in action. Already a Republican-

headed congressional committee had concluded that there were no U.S. prisoners alive in Vietnam and that a total accounting of the missing was "not possible and should not be expected." But an immediate stumbling block to the talks was discovered. The Vietnamese had been confident that America would honor Nixon's and Kissinger's promises in a secret protocol to the 1973 Peace Agreement that would have given Vietnam more than $3 billion in reconstruction and other aid after the war. The official language in the Paris Agreement (not the secret codicil) committed the Vietnamese "to facilitate the exhumation and repatriation of MIA remains," and committed the U.S. "to contribute to healing the wounds of war," but verbal promises had been made of much more aid. The Vietnamese were determined to discuss the reparations before talking about searching for missing Americans, and the Americans were determined to do the opposite, so the talks ended badly. (As the U.S. group was leaving Vietnam, it asked the Vietnamese to locate the fiancée of a U.S. veteran of the war who had come with the delegation, and arrange for her to leave the country to marry him. They did.)

Afterward, the United States extended its trade embargo on Vietnam. In June 1977 Congress even passed an amendment to a foreign aid bill explicitly renouncing any reparations and forbidding any funding, including indirect aid, to Vietnam. The United States also vetoed Vietnam's bid to join the United Nations, so Vietnam was barred from receiving aid from most international lending agencies such as the World Bank. These actions by the United States had a devastating effect on Vietnam—and the Amerasians—for many years. In early 1978 what one source labeled as "weak espionage indictments against some low-level Vietnamese . . . [were] used to justify the U.S. 'postponement' of so-called normalization," a postponement that would last almost twenty years. Vietnam would continue to be a pawn in the cold war, and the chances for Amerasians to leave Vietnam decreased. Thus they remained in a years-long limbo.

A Vietnamese man from a wealthy family who now lives in America says that in Vietnam he "grew up discriminating. In our family we called women who married or went with Americans 'bar girls,' and in school we made fun of Amerasians, saying 'Your mom is a whore.' All the Amerasians were very poor, and on the street would be kicked and beaten, and their mothers called whores—worse if the kid was black. Some tried to deny they were mixed—they'd say, 'Oh no, I just have darker skin,' or claim they had some French blood way back in the family. In the rural areas they were even crueler. Many Amerasians weren't allowed to go to school. One Amerasian girl told me that every day when she went to school people would line up along the road as she passed, saying 'Your mom is an ugly whore.' She said she'd just put her head down in shame.

"The old Vietnamese saying is that the dad is the foundation of the home. Without him, even if the mother is strong, you are not accepted in the culture. In Vietnam, the Amerasians were not accepted as Vietnamese. And in the U.S., they were not accepted as American."

4

Surviving Once, by Any Means, 1980–90

When I first ran away [to join a gang in 1982] I was ten, and people were starving and would steal food from one another everywhere. People were in rags, sleeping on the pavement.

—Amerasian Tiger Hoa

n February 1979 China, long a backer and supporter of the Khmer Rouge, briefly attacked and occupied the northern border of Vietnam, partly to "teach Vietnam a lesson" for invading China's client, Cambodia. Vietnam, ever-suspicious of its fellow Communist nation China since China's 1,000-year occupation of Vietnam centuries earlier, had already begun to repress its large ethnic Chinese minority. Tens of thousands of ethnic Chinese fled into China from Vietnam on foot, and over the next months tens of thousands more fled Vietnam by boat. By December of that year, the massive exodus of the Vietnamese "boat people," was well underway. At first the Vietnamese government secretly encouraged it, and refugees paid the Vietnamese government bribes to be allowed to leave.

But the toll on the boat people was horrible. Thousands drowned or were slaughtered by pirates; those who made it to land jammed refugee camps in nearby countries. Finally, forty countries under the umbrella of the United Nations established the Orderly Departure Program, or ODP, to stop the exodus. Amerasians were not mentioned among those to be admitted to the United States under the ODP, but after 1980, when Ronald Reagan was elected president, a very small number did leave under that program.

The Vietnamese government quickly cracked down on boat outflow, closing it down almost entirely, although boat escapes by Vietnamese continued throughout most of the 1980s. A young Vietnamese woman who escaped to the United States by boat in the mid-1980s as a twelve-year-old remembers the treatment of Amerasians while she was growing up. "Our neighbors had several children, and one was Amerasian. She was quite little when I first knew her, and I remember that they always made her eat in the kitchen with the cook and the nanny for the other children. I've since learned that her mother was a prostitute when the Amerasian was born, and that it was the grandmother who insisted the mother not give the child away. I think she was afraid that otherwise that mother would be punished in a future incarnation. But still they treated the Amerasian badly. It did seem a little strange to me, but I was just a child myself then so I didn't really think much about it. Often when I played with her sisters the Amerasian girl would stand apart watching. She didn't seem angry. I think she had just become used to the way things were."

As America tried—and failed—to forget its shame and defeat in Vietnam, relations between the two countries closed down completely. The United States forbade Americans to travel there and only a few representatives of private American aid agencies were still entering. Seeing the suffering of the Amerasians, some began making efforts to get them out of Vietnam. Their every attempt was blocked—mostly, they have charged, by the U.S. State Department. But the Amerasians like Louis, Son, Tiger, Nan, and Sara had not been entirely forgotten by everyone. In the early 1980s, according to Thomas Bass in his important book, *Vietnamerica: The War Comes Home*, aid workers stepped up their efforts to get at least some Amerasians out of Vietnam.

In 1980 the Vietnamese head of the Department of Social Welfare in Ho Chi Minh City, referring to the Amerasians, was quoted as saying: "Our society does not need these bad elements." That same year, says Bass, a paper on their plight was circulated by John Shade of the Pearl Buck Foundation, and "Rosie," the mother of an Amerasian, proposed that the United States follow the example of France, which had airlifted some 25,000 French-Vietnamese children and relatives to France at the end of its involvement. By 1981 Don Colin, then head of ODP, had gathered the names of 3,000 Amerasians. He began pressing the United

States to include them under ODP Category III, "people closely associated with the U.S. presence in Vietnam."

For years the law on Amerasians going to America continued to shift. Although word first filtered through Vietnam a few years after the war that there was some chance of Amerasians going to the United States, not everyone heard about it, and most people who did, didn't really believe it. One early law granted all Amerasians born since 1950 in Southeast Asia, including Cambodia and Laos, first visa preference, but the U.S. State Department refused to follow the law in Vietnam, saying that it contained no provisions for family members. At another stage a variation of the laws required mothers of Amerasians to sign an affidavit that they would not seek to join their child in America if the child was allowed to go. Apparently, U.S. policymakers didn't want former girlfriends showing up along with Amerasian offspring.

A 1982 Amerasian Immigration Act included mixed children in Vietnam, Cambodia, and Laos, but the U.S. State Department said the act couldn't be applied in Vietnam because the United States had no diplomatic relations with that nation, and thus had no consular officials there to conduct exit interviews. The United States offered no third-party back channels, such as negotiating through another country's embassy, as was often done in similar situations. That year David Guyer, head of Save the Children, drew up an agreement with the Vietnamese government to take out Amerasians, but the U.S. State Department vetoed it. Bass writes that half-American children, or "HACs" as the consular cables called them, were considered Vietnamese except for the few hundred with American birth certificates or passports who happened to have been in Vietnam when the government collapsed. Those were called "PAMs," presumed Americans, or "AMCITS," American citizens. (Human Rights Advocates International, a U.S. public interest law firm, was contending without success at that time that all Amerasians should have automatic citizenship.) The Vietnamese government was insisting that Amerasians were not refugees but either emigrants or U.S. citizens. It hoped to leverage the Amerasian issue to force direct negotiations with the United States on other matters.

By 1983 the situation of Amerasians was drawing a small amount of attention in the American media, and *Newsweek* magazine, grossly underestimating the number of Amerasians in Vietnam at only 8,000–15,000, said Vietnam claimed it would "let every Amerasian leave immediately," but that the United States refused to have any bilateral negotiations with Vietnam which would involve discussing any other issues. The Amerasians' fate, said *Newsweek*, "remains mired in bureau-cratic tangles and fickle relations of two nations that treat their common offspring as little better than political pawns."

The Reagan administration had begun accepting a few Amerasians under the UN Orderly Departure Program, looking for proof of Ameri-can fathers in old photos and letters along with a child's physical ap-pearance. Entries in the Ho Khau, the traditional Vietnamese family register, were accepted as proof, but many Amerasians were never reg-istered, said *Newsweek*, "lest they taint the family name." One real prob-lem was Vietnam's lack of computerized records, which meant the Vietnamese had to sort through mountains of papers and old photo-graphs by hand. The few Vietnamese Amerasians who emigrated alone as "unaccompanied minors" were placed with American foster families through religious agencies. In the meantime, as they grew older many Amerasians had become problems in the streets of Vietnam, and seemed destined to become problems in the streets of America. A Vietnamese man who fled Vietnam in 1983 reported that at least 100 Amerasians aged eight to fourteen, most of them homeless street children, were in-carcerated in Chi Hoa prison on Le Van Duyet Street in Ho Chi Minh City, where several died every week of malnutrition and disease.

Meanwhile, Colin was reporting serious symptoms of protein defi-ciency in many Amerasians, and most had long since found ways to help support themselves, through subsistance work, begging, prostitution, or crime. As for those still alive, life-changing chances were quickly be-coming lost forever.

Son Chau

After Son left for America many years later, he kept in touch with a few special friends who had gone through the hard years with him in Viet-nam when he was mostly despised and mistreated by others. Busy working in the United States, he had arranged for me and an inter-preter to meet in Vietnam with his friends Kim, Hai, and Tieng, who'd once searched the jungles for frankincense with him. Along with Son's black Amerasian cousin, Hung, we visited the area around Song Pha, Son's hometown. Kim is small and wiry, and more talkative and outgo-ing than either Hai or Tieng. In many ways he seems a lot like Son—a good storyteller, who can be quite funny, acting out many of his tales.

Song Pha is surrounded by steep mountains covered with trees and vines, so thickly interwoven that once in the jungle one can see only a few inches ahead, and must laboriously hack a narrow passage to push through. It is the kind of town where everyone knows everyone else and all their family histories, where it is the *only* world they really know, and where people become friends or enemies over a lifetime.

When Son was ten, Hai, then one of the teenagers who worked drawing sap from the rubber trees in the mountain jungles surrounding Song Pha, chose him from among all the village boys to accompany his small crew of workers. It was 1978. "I took Son along to cook for us and do general kinds of work," remembers Hai, a tall, striking-looking Vietnamese man now in his thirties whom we met at the tiny store he operated in a tribal village near Song Pha. "A lot of boys wanted to go, but I chose Son because he was smart, and knew how to listen and learn and follow instructions." Like Son, Hai, Kim, and Tieng have the competent, self-assured manner of men who have faced and overcome incredible hardships and dangers—who perhaps even relish such challenges. "Son isn't brave, but he is willing to take risks," Hai says, leaning forward a bit. "Even when Son knows something is dangerous he will do it anyway. Over the years he became like a godbrother to me. Son has always wanted to stand out. He never gives up, and even when something seems impossible, he will keep persevering, trying to do it."

The jungle was, and is, full of wild creatures including tigers, monkeys, venomous snakes, leeches, exotic poisonous insects, and malaria-bearing mosquitoes. Fatal illnesses lurked in the streams the hunters were sometimes forced to drink from when their own supplies ran out. The hunters used machetes to slash their way through the thick jungle foliage. Occasionally they would discover a slight, dim pathway, made by some tribal group. But such a path might lead to a dangerous encounter with the tribal people themselves, including armed tribal guerillas who had served with the Front Unifié de Lutte des Races Opprimées (FULRO), the United Front for the Struggle of the Oppressed Races, and other organizations. The guerillas had been armed and trained first by the French and later by the American CIA as anti-Communist resistance fighters during the war. "Many had kept their guns and might shoot you, because they were afraid when you came out of the jungle the government soldiers might question you about who you saw there," Son had told us. And there were a thousand other dangers. Son claims he once even encountered a group of headhunters.

When Son was fourteen, some traders came to Song Pha from Ho

Chi Minh City. They were frankincense hunters and dealers, tracking down the illusive, and illegal, scented and hardened sap sought as a valuable ingredient in Chinese perfumes and medicines. "At that time," says Kim, "nobody even knew what frankincense was. The dealers told us how it came from a tree called the wind tree, and showed us how to recognize a tree with frankincense inside and to take the black part back to a hut in the jungle to be processed." Hai explains: "The tribal people call it the wind tree because they believe it can prevent the wind from destroying their village, so it has special value and meaning." Yet hunting frankincense was extremely perilous, not only because of the dangers of the jungle, but because it was illegal to hunt it or sell it. Government soldiers guarded most of the passages into the jungle. "Frankincense was like gold," Son had told us, "but if you were caught, you went to prison."

Nonetheless, finding and smuggling frankincense out to traders was a way to stay alive in those years when starvation still stalked Vietnam. The hunters traveled in groups of two or three, so if one was injured or became ill the others could go for help. They took with them food and water to last for several days. Son was never injured, but sometimes fell so ill with fever he had to return home.

"We often started walking towards the jungles by 4 A.M.," says Kim, "and once Son and I walked two days just to get to the base of that mountain there." He points to a faraway peak covered with heavy jungle. Kim, Hai, and Tieng say that they, like Son, do not believe the many tales about the jungle being filled with ghosts—lost souls of those killed in the Vietnam War or earlier battles, and doomed to wander forever. Like Son, they also insist that they didn't believe in evil jungle spirits who could be called down on them through voodoo curses placed by the tribal people. Yet at the start of each trek, they performed a special ritual. Each carved his name and date of birth into a large tree. Kim says this "was like presenting your papers to the police," or one's credentials to whatever spirits ruled the jungle. Next they made a stack of rocks, a sort of altar representing the mountain they were about to climb, and another rock altar for the spirits and ancestors who protected the jungle. They would burn incense and pray for a safe journey and for help in finding frankincense. "Yet we really couldn't think about ghosts or other dangers," says Hai, stressing once again their hunger and desperation at that time. "We needed the frankincense just to stay alive."

Before we left for Vietnam, Son had told us many harrowing stories of his days looking for frankincense, and we repeated some of them to the three hunters, triggering memories of their own. "On one trip, a big tree fell on two hunters and when it was lifted off, one had no head at all, just a body and neck, because his head had been completely crushed," recalls Hai. The other two men nod, remembering. They estimate that as many as twenty searchers for frankincense were killed during those years after the war.

Although Son and his friends never found unexploded bombs or shells in the jungle, they did find other remnants from the war—a grenade case, and, once, a box that they dared to open. It was empty except for some papers they couldn't read. Once or twice, they had passed the rusted ruins of a crashed airplane, the tattered clothes of the dead pilot and crew dangling rotting in the moist jungle heat. But they saw no bodies or skeletons. In some parts of Vietnam a person daring to enter the jungle's deeper recesses, like one man who ventured in to trade Western medicines for gold, brought back strange stories of having seen two or three American deserters living among the isolated tribes. They said the Americans had long beards and hair, wore tribal clothing and spoke the tribal language. But perhaps they actually were half-French, or even Amerasians born long before the Vietnam War, fathered by Americans who began entering Vietnam on secret U.S. missions as early as 1950.

Gradually Son became expert at spotting the frankincense-bearing trees. "It takes a very long time to learn how, depending on how smart they are," Son had told us. "You have to recognize a tree with frankincense from among a thousand other trees, then cut down a big, big tree and find inside it a little, little bit of frankincense. When the Chinese conquered Vietnam maybe a thousand years ago, they planted these trees. But before 1975 people were afraid to go into the jungle to find them. Then times got so hard that they went anyway." Says Kim: "I remember the first time I ever put step into the jungle at night, I couldn't sleep at all. It is completely silent there, so you can hear even an insect or worm when it crawls in the leaves. When night passes and day comes, then you concentrate only on getting frankincense or something to sell, so you and your family can eat.

"At first," continues Kim, "we were not very successful, but we helped each other, growing up together looking for the frankincense. Because Son was Amerasian he could get in more trouble if the police caught us, so he would worry more than most. I remember one time they caught us and Son hid his face because he was Amerasian, and

knew they would punish him worse." On those long trips the two
friends would talk for hours, and Kim remembers Son speaking of his
dream of someday finding his American father, even years before there
was a law allowing Amerasians to go to the United States. "Son and I
were very close, like in the Vietnamese saying 'ate from the same bowl
and slept in the same bed,'" says Kim. "When there were just the two
of us working together during times we were waiting with nothing to
do, sometimes Son would be sad, and talk a lot very openly about how
he hoped one day to find his real dad. He would give a physical descrip-
tion of his American dad, based on what his mother had told him. He
would say that his real dad looked like him. His mom told him things
like when his dad left, he gave her a necklace for Son to wear so he
could recognize Son some day, and a cloth of some kind. Sometimes
Son cried when he talked about this, talking with a kind of hope he
would someday see his dad but with a hopelessness around it. He wondered what his dad's reaction would be once he found him, and how it
would turn out when they finally met—whether Son would end up crying or happy. And he couldn't predict whether his dad would be happy
or sad."

Son had told us, "Even with my first girlfriend, we were in love very
good, but I told her I could never marry her because someday I would
go to the U.S. and find my dad." In his mind he was preparing himself
to meet that American father, so different from Son's drunken, brutal
stepfather Hanh. Left to face the world on his own, Son was developing
his natural skill for dealing with all kinds of people. Sometimes direct,
sometimes diplomatic, sometimes offering gifts or favors, and always
using courage and smarts, Son trusted himself and his own instincts
above any outside counsel.

When he was fifteen, he began going into the jungle less often. Instead, he began buying frankincense from other hunters and smuggling
it out to sell. It was still very dangerous, but he could make more money
that way. "I knew if I was caught I would be sent to prison," he had
told us. "In my village the police knew me, and I could bribe many of
them, but not in other places. Still, I am lucky. I traveled all over Vietnam and was never stopped. I hid the frankincense in hollowed-out
stacks of rice cakes, or I would get some lady to hide it tied to her legs
or under her clothes as if she were pregnant."

But his hometown officials knew he was smuggling, and had begun
watching his every move. Some were angry that an Amerasian was
doing better financially than many Vietnamese in the area. Son began

sleeping at different friends' houses on different nights, but sometimes the police would hunt him down, wake, and interrogate him. Yet they still couldn't pin anything on him. Son's Amerasian cousin, Hung, went on the frankincense trips only once. "When I was seventeen and my cousin Hung was sixteen, once just before the Tet holiday he came and asked me, 'Son, can you take me on your next trip? I want to make some money for Tet.' Hung was very poor then, and we took him, the fifth in our group. He had no skills for the jungle so he stayed in camp and cooked for us.

"On our last day, when we had been in the jungle a week, Hung stayed in camp cooking. When we came back for lunch he was done. We sat down to eat when two guys ran into our camp shouting: 'Run, run! The Communists are coming, they will shoot you!' We all jumped up to run, but then someone said: 'No, if you run they will surely shoot you!' But me and another guy ran anyway, and the police were shooting right at us. Rather we die than go in jail! So we kept running down hill with four or five police following, shooting. We came to a small river and jumped from big rock to big rock. The police shot a big rocket at us and we heard its scary sound, so we ran under a big rock and hid until night. Then we went back to our camp. Everyone was gone, and all the food Hung had cooked was burned up.

"That day the cops had arrested forty people, but no one from my group except Hung and two others. There was no punishment, the cops just warned everyone. Because me and the other guy were gone so long, everyone in the village thought we were dead—but not my mom, because she is psychic. Anyway, we never got money from that trip, and of course Hung got no money for Tet."

Meanwhile, Son's stepfather Hanh was a growing problem. As Son reached teenhood he felt less fear and more anger toward his drunken and abusive stepfather. Once Hanh, drunk as usual, smashed Son on the head with a board so hard that he knocked the teenager unconscious. "I thought Son was dead," recalls Du. But when Son regained consciousness he chased down his stepfather and struck him back. Although the value of filial piety—of respecting, obeying, and revering one's elders, and particularly one's father or stepfather, as well as all older male relatives including uncles and brothers—is perhaps the most deeply engrained and strictly enforced of all Vietnamese cultural values, Son became less and less deferential to Hanh and tolerated him less and less. In Son's mind he had begun to pay that respect to his American birth father instead.

"By the time I was fifteen," he says, "I sometimes hired friends to come to my house and help clean the frankincense to make it look better, so we could sell it for more. One day I knew I would need the house for that the next day, so I told my mom: 'As soon as Hanh goes off tomorrow morning, cook him a nice dinner and have it ready when he comes home, and do everything to make him happy so he will not make trouble. Try to talk nice to him if he's drunk, then let him go away, because I will need the house.' So about twelve o'clock he came home and Mom had everything ready. I tried to talk very nice to Hanh to convince him to just eat his lunch, then go take a nap or whatever. I asked him to please not talk about politics or the police. That's what he would do when he was drunk. Then he don't know how to think, and he always would keep talking and talking loud about how he served the Communists, and now they not treat him good, and how the police were stupid. Sometimes he would even go down to the police station to say it." Here the customs of a small town came in handy. "The police could not take him to jail because they knew him, and knew when he drunk he would lose control and say bad things and hit people," says Son. "And almost ten years I spent with that man!

"So I say to him: 'I know you are drunk, but I put out a lot of money for this frankincense laid out in our house, and you got to be careful, not talk loud bad about the police, because maybe they will just walk by and hear you, and come to check on you and see this frankincense.' But my stepdad just kept talking louder, louder—until I say, 'I cannot stand no more, you got to get away from here!' And I kick him one, and he fell unconscious over the table and the lunch." Son's resentment of Hanh had become unbearable. Son says by this point in his life he was "always thinking of leaving Vietnam and coming to America, and thinking about leaving made me crazy at the time. I began to think America was a very good country, I never think Vietnam was my country. I just wanted to find my American dad."

Son began trying to leave Vietnam as early as 1983, when word first began going around Vietnam that Amerasians might be able to emigrate under the continually changing U.S. laws. His mother, Du, tried three times to file papers for Son and her family to go to the United States, but local government officials kept turning down her application. The town's police chief and Son hated one another, and the chief would block any application by Son. "Everybody in our village hated that chief," says Son. "He was so hateful, so impolite, so a bully. Even when he would see the older people he would say to them: 'Fuck you.' He would do bad things to everybody, and nobody could beat him." Du agrees. "That policeman was very strict, but also very corrupt and wanted bribes. But he was sneaky so he wouldn't get caught. That policeman was always picking on Son because he was Amerasian, trying to find some reason to arrest him. There were some other Amerasians in the area, and all were treated badly. But Son was a little bit different because, for one thing, he was making that money from the frankincense. So the police kept bothering him." Secretly believing he would soon be able to go to the United States, Son decided to confront the chief. "There was a big electric plant nearby with a special place for enjoyment, a swimming pool and other things," says Son, "but I was not allowed in there. It was special and only for the high-class, the Communist, but I was just the normal person.

"I was with some friends and the big chief came by with several police carrying guns, and I asked him if we could go in the enjoyment place and enjoy it too. This chief did bad things to everybody, and nobody can beat him. But I wanted to see how strong he was. So I say: 'It's nice in there, we want to be in there. I am asking this favor and need only a yes or no answer. Will you let us in, yes or no?' And he tried to explain to me, 'I cannot give you this favor, not to you or anybody, it is not the law.' He tried to explain this way and that way, so I said: 'I don't have time to talk to you so long, I just need you right now to say yes or no.' And I knew for sure he would say 'No.' And he did say 'No.' So when he did, I hit him right in the face, and it broke his tooth and he fell unconscious. I *wanted* to hit him, because he think he was the big policeman and can say 'Fuck you,' and tell people 'Do this, do that.' Everybody hate him. And also, already I had the paper to leave Vietnam someday. Then right away I ran away from my village to Dalat for five months. There was a nice family there with a son my age. During those five months I don't have much money, but that family, they love me, and they put money out so me and their son can go around to other farms, and in one week buy up twenty-five to twenty-six cows and water buffaloes, and put them in a big truck to take to Ho Chi Minh City to sell to make meat. The government didn't allow this, so we paid bribes.

"After five months I came back to my village. I thought maybe they would forget about how I hit the big cop, but right away the police taked me in the police office and made me write out my history. Sometimes the Communists make you do that—write down how you are Amerasian, and all the ways you belong to South Vietnam or North

Vietnam, and all that kind of thing. And I tell them how the big police guy made me feel bad in public, so I could not control myself and lost my temper and had to hit him. And finally they let me go." Small-town customs and relations again were working in Son's favor—this time. Over the next few years, waiting to go to America, Son moved in and out of his home village, constantly traveling around Vietnam. Mostly he was smuggling frankincense and doing other money-making schemes, with varying success. Once or twice he got his now teenaged Amerasian cousin Hung, who was very poor and often hungry and homeless, to help him sell incense to earn money for Hung's mom. "Hung lived nearby in the mountains in the NEZ area, working as a laborer whenever he had the chance. He made bricks from mud," says Son. "He had scars on his hands and legs from hard work and doing dangerous things, and never paid attention to himself or took care of himself."

Mostly because frankincense hunting was illegal, Son has only one photograph from his frankincense-hunting days. (See photo insert.) It was taken in February 1985, when Son was eighteen and avoiding authorities in Song Pha while wandering throughout Vietnam, in the village of Nhi Ha in Ninh Thuan province. Son says he felt it was safe to take the picture because his aunt #9, Lieu Chau, was "a women's rights person," chosen by the Nhi Ha village women as their leader. "We left right after the picture was taken. We had rented a [buffalo] to pull us on a wagon for two days, through the flat foothills up to a very tall mountain. On the way we saw many deep, burned-out bomb holes all around us, made by U.S. bombs during the war."

Alan "Tiger" Hoa

When Tiger was seven, a year after the Khmer Rouge attack, he and the rest of his family moved back to Hoc Mon. It was still a very terrible time in Vietnam. Tiger was put under the supervision of his uncles Binh and Khue. Khue got a job driving trucks for the government, and when he registered the family with the government, he purposely did not list Tiger as an Amerasian. And so, he says, the government "didn't really know" about Tiger. "Neighbors said bad things about Tiger, but he was our family," Khue says firmly. Although Tiger's neighborhood in Hoc Mon has been swallowed up now by the edges of Ho Chi Minh City, it still has the same "village" feeling as do the small towns where Son and Louis grew up. All the neighbors know everyone's business and never hesitate to offer advice and opinions on every detail of one another's behavior. As one Vietnamese woman says, "In Vietnam everybody knows every single thing about you, and they gossip all day, and people care very, very much what others think."

Sitting in the living room of his small subsidized apartment in Little Saigon in California, Khue leans back wearily in his chair as he speaks. After Tiger and the other family members moved back to Hoc Mon from the NEZ, "those were still very hard times in Vietnam, and some days all of us in our family would be hungry," says Khue. "Everyone in the country then was just struggling to survive. During the time I was a truck driver, I would leave at 7 A.M. and work until 7 P.M. or be gone overnight, just coming home to eat dinner." Therefore, neither Khue nor anyone in the family had much time to give attention to Tiger — except for Tiger's widowed grandfather. "That's who Tiger usually talked with," Khue says, eyes half shut as more memories began coming back to him. "Tiger was the only grandchild then, and the grandfather really loved him."

Tiger says he only went to school ten days. Others in his family, perhaps embarrassed, say vaguely they think he went for two or three years, but because they were able to give him so little supervision during the postwar years they may not know if he went to class or not. "Because he was teased at school by the other kids and called 'black kid' he got embarrassed and quit," says Khue. "Then he was just hanging around." It was during this time, Khue remembers, that Tiger "would look and look at his mother's picture. But he didn't ask questions about her."

Only Khue among all of Tiger's many relatives knows that Tiger has spent most of his life in America in prison. Tiger has asked him not to tell the others back home, and, in a situation that does not seem odd to Vietnamese, Khue has agreed and kept the secret. Still, it has caused much bitterness toward Tiger from his family in Vietnam who do not understand why he has never sent back money to them as other Vietnamese in America do for their families, nor why Tiger has almost never written or called them over many years. A letter from prison, of course, would bear the prison's name stamped on the envelope.

Tiger has always insisted that Khue's wife hated and mistreated him, even as a child, and certainly now she seems quite cold toward him. "Maybe my Uncle Khue really loved me, but his wife really hated me, and I suffered a lot," says Tiger. "She made me cook and clean the house, and also scrub the family laundry by hand every day in a big tub." To Vietnamese boys, being made to do family laundry is a punishment, and having to wash women's pants and underwear is considered highly degrading. Tiger has always insisted Khue's wife felt revulsion toward him because he was Amerasian. At the same time, Tiger might not have been the easiest child to raise for someone also overburdened by the severe stresses in the years after the war.

On one thing everyone agrees—Tiger was given many beatings by family in the Vietnamese child-rearing tradition, to try to straighten him out. "I remember once my Uncle Binh made me kneel on the peel of a Jackfruit, and [he] hit me with an electric wire in the afternoon sun, and I will never forget it," says Tiger. Such beatings, sometimes serious enough to leave scars, were more the norm than the exception in raising Vietnamese children and teens in those days, especially in rural areas. Tiger's Uncle Binh is proud when he tells people: "I was the only one who could control Tiger. Whenever he went out and got in trouble I had to hit him so he would stop 'doing stupid things.' There were times I was yelling at Tiger and times I was begging him to stay out of trouble. But regular beating wouldn't work—he would just run away and we couldn't catch him because he ran too fast."

Khue says Tiger's grandfather died when Tiger was nine, "and that's when Tiger started getting into trouble." Tiger says that one morning when he was ten, feeling especially bitter and lonely, "I woke up and just decided I was going to leave home. When I first ran away to Ho Chi Minh City, I had no place to go and knew nobody. I slept in a corner of the market and ate the leftover food at the restaurants. Sometimes I would go back and sleep behind my Uncle Khue's house. His wife knew I was there but didn't call me in."

When Tiger ran away in 1982, times in Vietnam were horrible. Many children already had been on their own since age five, earning their own living doing farm work, acting as servants for food, or living as homeless abandoned street children, begging and stealing. "When I first ran away, people were starving, and would steal food from one another everywhere," says Tiger. "People were in rags, sleeping on the pavement. Everyone was very poor." Tattered, starving homeless people, elderly people, prostitutes, gangsters, people who were dying (some from war injuries), people crippled or maimed in the war, drug addicts and drunks, and people mentally scarred by the war—among them many veterans—all were living then on the streets. Thousands slept on the pavement outside the markets, or in cardboard tents leaning against the outside walls of houses, or in cemeteries. Babies were born on the sidewalks; sometimes people dropped down in the street and died there.

Sometimes funeral services were conducted right there over their bodies.

While Son Chau was struggling to survive in the jungles around Song Pha, youths like Tiger were in the urban-jungle streets of Ho Chi Minh City and various former U.S. military-base towns like Bien Hoa, where they kept barely alive by sweeping restaurants, begging, or crime or child prostitution. "There were pimps who made young girls and boys do prostitution. I had to do this also," says Tiger. "I understood, I had to accept that hardship, and yet I felt bad for young girls who had to put up with it. But as a boy I could put up with it."

Occasionally Amerasians bore physical scars from being hit or kicked on the streets, or having dogs sicked on them. As years passed, some Amerasians committed suicide, and a great many other half-American children simply were unable to survive. "During those years I knew people who died, killed themselves, or got ill, or got tortured and beaten by gangsters," says Tiger. "Of Amerasians, I knew of one beaten to death by gangsters, two others who killed themselves." Tiger's relatives admit that he often stayed away for weeks or months at a time. "Yes, sometimes we were hungry," says Khue, who remembers Tiger wandering in and out of home a lot, sometimes cadging a meal at other people's houses. "But usually he came home to eat or sleep, because who could take on another child in those hard times?" Lam, who tries to play down Tiger's difficulties and the struggle the family endured, says: "We were too poor, so Tiger had to go out and find some way to survive. It was not really like he was robbing. But he would get in trouble when people teased him, like fighting, and he was also sometimes gambling." Tiger says some gang members "were trying to bring food to their family's table without telling their families how they got it. Others did gang things just for the thrill."

Tiger says he ran home crying one day when he was about eight, after other children chased him, and a woman who sold tofu on the street near his house comforted him, told him she had known his mother, and told him that he was Amerasian. Sometime afterward he began to dream of an American father who would protect him, never beat him. He was very unhappy. "Most people don't want to get involved with a half-breed like me. When I was a child I wasn't a bad boy until they mistreated me. Before I ran away and turned real bad I did steal food sometimes, but that was for survival," he says. With little love or food or other comforts to hold poor children at home, many simply found the streets more able to provide food and more exciting, and some families were too exhausted and desperate, too poor and broken, to do much to stop them. No doubt some families felt special bitterness toward Amerasian members, who attracted so much gossip and problems from neighbors and officials. Says one young Vietnamese man who immigrated to America: "For an Amerasian in Vietnam, even your own family didn't love you."

"I met other Amerasians when we were all living in the streets, and some would share with me," Tiger says. Some had run away; others had been put out by their families. Soon Tiger was hanging out with three particular Amerasian friends, one eleven like him and two older, fifteen or sixteen. "The older ones were put into the street when they were very young and had lived there most of their lives. They didn't know their parents at all," he says. Tiger joined the crowds of skinny, homeless children who would stand for hours hungrily watching people eating at the small sidewalk food stalls—usually just a table with one or two chairs in front of someone's home—waiting to eat anything left over on their plates. "Some people hated to have those beggars around waiting for them to finish, and they would ruin any leftover food by spitting into their bowls so the kids couldn't eat. But when the kids were too hungry and desperate, they would eat it anyway," a Vietnamese woman told me.

Says Tiger: "The people who had these restaurants did not allow beggars, and sometimes I would just run over and grab food from a table and run. Then the restaurant people would get angry, and chase and beat me." He and his friends also picked food from garbage, and stole things to sell or trade for food. A Vietnamese woman who lived in Ho Chi Minh City during that time remembers eating at a restaurant in front of someone's home. "Three little kids came up and circled around and around our table," she says. "Rich people eating at such places would be afraid they'd be robbed, and would get up and leave. That kind of little poor kids all carried these tall aluminum silver cans that said 'Legal Milk' on the side in English. They'd grab leftover food and put it in the cans and run before they were caught, or just stuff the food in their mouths on the spot."

It didn't take long before some of the gang members in the area noticed ten-year-old Tiger. "They saw me hanging around and said, 'Do you want to join us?' So I did. Street people recognize each other, we are drawn to each other." One day Tiger saw The Eagle, the gang boss for the section of the city where Tiger lived. The Eagle dressed in expensive suits, and "looked like an attorney," says Tiger. "He looked like

Asian mafia. And he always had a lot of money." Although The Eagle was not tall, there was something powerful and important in his every gesture. Wearing a diamond ring and a thick gold chain with a heavy golden Buddha pendant, The Eagle rode on a fine motorcycle, followed by two bodyguards also on motorcycles "with long Chinese knives under their jackets," says Tiger, perhaps stealing a bit from a kung fu movie.

Tiger was thrilled when he was about eleven and The Eagle began to look out for him along with other street children. "He often gave us food or money, something we could not get at home," says Tiger. The Eagle was following the Asian "Big Brother" gang tradition of providing protection and material rewards for younger gang members, the "Little Brothers," in return for snatching purses, stealing, and child prostitution to bring money to the group. The Eagle sometimes helped them crowd into motels or crash houses at night, gave them part of the money they earned committing crimes for him, keeping most, however, for himself. Charismatic, confident, powerful, The Eagle was good to Tiger, and more than a big brother or even a father figure—more like a god. "When I met The Eagle," says Tiger. "I was very poor and I saw all his money and motorbikes and food, and how he and the other gang members were so nice to me at first. I went into gang life step by step.

"When The Eagle asked me if I would do a lot of work and share with him, he was very nice. He taught me how to steal things, and at first my work was also mostly as a child prostitute. There are two kinds of gangs. One of them's sole purpose is to do mean things—kidnap girls and turn them into prostitutes and kill people and do all kinds of cruel things. But my kind of gang was a bad nomad kind of group. In those days we were poor, we were hungry, we couldn't find jobs to make money. Maybe we had a sweetheart we wanted to give some gifts, so therefore we robbed and stole, although that was not our essence. We did kill people and burn houses and such. We did bad things, but good things too. If you were poor we loaned you cash with interest, if you didn't pay us back or didn't respect us and wanted to pick on us, we got revenge in our own way.

"As a kid, after I understood my mom had died," says Tiger. "I didn't care about nothing. I was confused and sad, and I became stubborn and hard. That is when I gradually began to hurt myself and also to hurt others." Tiger tells what led him to inflict the first of more than thirty self-mutilating cuts he now bears all over his arms. One night when he was about thirteen, he was drunk, and had just been rejected by a girl he liked. "I felt I had nobody to take care of me, no food, and my mommy had died. I took out my knife and cut my left arm," he says. "I was crying. One Vietnamese friend took me to his home nearby and his mom was there. She kept asking what was the matter. Finally I said I was sad and wanted to die. His mom said 'OK, I'll take care of you.' She gave me money to buy more beer and fixed up my arm. I cried all night and she told me, 'It's over now.'"

When he first left home at age ten, Tiger's choices were either to stay with his family where there was little food, money, attention, or affection, or to roam free in the excitement and independence of the junglelike streets of Saigon, close to the power and comradeship of his gang, with a chance to share in any food, drinks, and shelter.

As Tiger grew older The Eagle asked him to do more serious crimes, like robbing whorehouses and beating up people who wouldn't pay "protection" money—common gang practices. "Our gang didn't have a permanent place to stay, but sometimes we rented a temporary place. We still lived like street kids and mostly stayed different places at night. The worst part was having no real place to sleep, no comfort of a blanket, and all the time we were cold and bitten by mosquitoes. We hung around bus stops to rob people—life was dirty. Sometimes I slept on a straw mat in front of the market or on the bus station floor."

The gang house where Tiger sometimes stayed was used to store weapons and stolen loot. "Whoever needed a place to crash could go there. We drank, we gambled, and sometimes when we got older we brought girls there. The songs we sang were like rap songs, describing what we had done, and telling sentimental things and feelings about gang life." At age eleven Tiger was drinking heavily, a habit that would cause trouble for him all his life. He usually denies using drugs except for hallucinogens when he grew older, but this is doubtful, especially because he supposedly dealt cocaine and Ecstasy in America. "I drink as a way to forget everything," says Tiger, "and because so many people drink I went along with them."

A Vietnamese woman who lived as a child during this time a block from a gang house—maybe Tiger's—on Ton Dan street says such houses looked like any other, "except there were no adults there, just children and teens and a few people in their twenties hanging around, some in rags. Lots of times electricity would go out in the whole area, and in the dark the gangsters would steal from anyone nearby. They'd pull your bike away from under you, grab and touch girls, tear your ears to get gold earrings or scratch your neck grabbing for gold chains.

Sometimes gang people would kidnap little kids and dress them in rags and send them out to beg. And sometimes they would hold one for ransom. They'd choose a kid whose family they had watched, and send him home sometimes with an arm or leg missing because the gang people would be angry at the kid for not begging right. Even two-year-olds—you'd see them crying and begging for money. And sometimes groups of gang kids would stand outside the market and sing gang songs set to popular tunes. Like, 'Life sucks . . . pretty girls on the street, look and don't touch . . . fuck life . . . life is terrible. . . .' They'd sing as if upset, kids aged five up to teens, both boys and girls, orphans with no one to take care of them. It was scary to pass by them—they might rob you or grab you. I remember one song that was sort of upbeat and optimistic, like, 'We're homeless, but our lives might be better than yours—we have no bills to pay—and so on.'"

Tiger sent me the words to one of the gang songs or gang poems, part of which went like this:

> "Before the law I am a gangster
> Among the streets I am a dissipate
> Nothing hurts me but the change of hearts of my friends.
> I would rather be a gangster than a Communist
> the gangsters' rule is to choose death over snitching
> If you tell, your life is over—it's up to you!
>
> In heaven I'm considered a sinner
> Down here on earth I am a loner
> If anyone asks me if I am angry at my life
> I just bow my head and accept my pain and misery.
> in prison I dream of the uncertain past and future,
>
> The night is so still—the light bulb is too weak to show the future's path
> Lying here in the night my heart is miserable
> Forgotten past love tastes sadly bitter on my lips"

The police targeted the gang members, and just as police in America sometimes target certain racial groups, police in Vietnam tended to target Amerasians. The *Los Angeles Times* reported that when in April 1985 Vietnam celebrated the tenth anniversary of the fall of Saigon, police "swept the [Amerasian] youngsters from the streets [of Saigon], removing a reminder of another era that they didn't want to mar the event."

Other "undesirables"—such as homeless and beggars—would also be rounded up and swept out of sight at times of important events that might draw foreign visitors. Another big sweep took place in November 1990.

When Tiger was fourteen he was sent to jail for the first time. The reason is unclear. He gives several different explanations, all for minor crimes like stealing food, and Tiger himself may not be sure why he was arrested. Many other Amerasians were among the prisoners, he says, all of whom worked from 7 A.M. to 7 P.M. and received only a small amount of food each day. But this was not just for punishment—outside the jail, throughout Vietnam, people were starving and often working to exhaustion for only a small amount of food. Tiger's uncles brought food to him every few days, and after a few months paid bribes or fees to free him. Here again, memories diverge. Tiger says the jail head-knocker—the type of dominant prisoner apparently found in every jail and prison around the world, who doles out both beatings and favors to the other prisoners—beat Tiger so badly that he couldn't walk for days. Tiger's Uncle Lam says "the beating wasn't that bad. There is always an old prison leader who rules the other prisoners. It was just a 'greeting thing.'"

Tiger's more detailed and emotional version seems truer. "They beat me so bad I lost my mind. The first month I could only sit in a corner and cry and cry. I hated the headknocker so much I wanted to kill him, but I couldn't move. I couldn't walk, couldn't eat, and the other prisoners took my rice. I was so sick that when I stood up I fell down. When I was first released I couldn't see, everything looked upside down." Tiger is quiet for a moment. He usually denies strongly that he has ever had any kind of mental problem, but now he continues his earlier thoughts. "More than once family and society have put me into losing my mind," he says soberly. "I have to keep my mind busy, because if I start to cry or think of things, I could go crazy." Even now, years later, he says, he can't watch a movie or TV show that has to do with family or love because it makes him cry, and feel angry, guilty, and lonely, and go out and "do stupid, crazy things." Tiger can spend hours watching children's cartoons like Tom and Jerry, or Sylvester and Tweety Bird. And like many Vietnamese, he is addicted to endless martial arts movies.

When Tiger returned to the streets several months later, after his first time in jail, they still were full of ragged, starving children and adults. Many had become addicts, craving cocaine and heroin, going in and out of dilapidated drug houses, the children starting dope at about thirteen. Tiger says the addicts' faces were "frightening," twisted with desperation and the kind of paranoia Tiger himself was beginning to feel constantly as he grew older.

Yet there was a part of Tiger's life where he could partially escape his problems, at the big dance club in District One, near Ven Tan market and Dam Sen Park. With its flashing lights, live bands, and well-dressed patrons, the club seemed magical to him. Opened after 1975, it was run by a "very famous" dancing teacher, Uncle Tan, who had been in the South Vietnamese Army and later went to America. "I began going there when I first left home. Most of the people living in nearby Dam Sen Park then were street kids and female prostitutes, but not yet many Amerasians," says Tiger. "I always loved music, but they would kick me out of the club because of the way I dressed, in old dirty clothes."

When he grew older Tiger borrowed or rented dancing clothes for $1 per night, including dancing shoes that were painfully small. The Vietnamese are master dancers, and Tiger learned slow dancing, mambos, cha-chas, waltzes, be-bop, everything—even the lambada. He was also approached at the club as a male prostitute. "By the time I was fourteen, I made money as a prostitute and through crime, bought myself several chic outfits, and every weekend I got all dressed up and went dancing," Tiger says. The Eagle, in his "Big Brother" role, offered occasional guidance. "He watched out for me sometimes and gave me advice. He said it was OK to go dancing, but don't 'do stupid things.' Dance with your own girlfriend and don't get involved with others." The expression "doing stupid things" is a Vietnamese phrase for doing anything bad. The assumption seems to be that everyone knows not to do wrong things, so doing them is simply stupid. This advice followed an occasion when Tiger danced with a girl who he says flirted with him, and whose boyfriend "jumped me, and I hit him with a bottle of beer and he had to go to the hospital—but it wasn't my fault because she flirted with me."

In the meantime, Tiger was becoming quite a good dancer. "Sometimes after I learned a dance routine I created extra steps, and Uncle Tan, seeing my fancy steps, was impressed. I became very famous on the dance floor. I liked all the beats, but especially the cha-cha. That rhythm relaxed me, and brought me to heaven." His skill at dancing, and the blissful moments on the dance floor, are among the happiest and proudest of Tiger's memories.

But as Tiger committed more and more serious crimes, he had begun accumulating more enemies and more problems with the police. Gang life had become much more dangerous for him. "The gangs in Vietnam were much, much tougher than gangs in the United States," says Tiger, "because in Vietnam people were so poor and had so little that many were willing to die just to keep what little they had. Therefore gangs had to be tougher to get those things from them, and had to threaten people with more deadly threats, threaten their lives. True, gangs there did not have guns, but they had knives and machetes and other killing weapons. And a gang person had to be very, very tough to do those things. When I grew older and I realized what it involved to be in a gang, I became very scared, but it was too late.

"When you are in a gang there are ups and downs. And you get used to having money, so on days you are short you tend to be upset. You like to have money, you need to have money. But then gradually you realize you cannot get out of a gang. The Eagle, so nice when you come in, says he will kill you and all your family if you try to leave. And I know of cases where that happened to the person. And you develop enemies. So after awhile I began to always worry that someone would sneak behind me on the street and stab and kill me." Tiger tells varying stories about how he and three Amerasian friends confronted The Eagle and broke with him. Sometimes he says he chopped off The Eagle's arm—a story that closely parallels a scenario from a martial arts movie. Sometimes he says he broke with The Eagle after he ordered Tiger to kill some people who hadn't paid extortion fees, and Tiger refused, saying, "Couldn't I just beat them up?"

The Amerasian orphan Nan came to know Tiger when he was living in the streets and she was staying in a nearby temple. She says of him: "Tiger is chicken. In Vietnam he did not intentionally hurt people. His gang stole but didn't really hurt people." But some of the things Tiger did and saw during those years must be part of the memories that came to haunt him later. The Vietnamese call such obsessive memories *am anh*, and they mean haunting, unrelenting memories of things one has done wrong, harmful, painful things done to oneself, evil acts one has committed, cruel actions one deeply regrets, but cannot block from one's mind. Thus, emotional scars were mounting, matching the physical scars that Tiger sometimes made with his self-mutilations. And this was true for other Amerasians as well.

Sara Phuong and Miss Dao (Chi Lien)

"When I was little, I didn't know I was Amerasian. I just knew my skin was very dark," Sara says. "I thought the nuns and monks were my real family, and asked them 'Why did you birth me so dark? Can you give me something to peel off my dark skin?' I even wanted to pour boiling water on myself to peel off my skin. They would answer things like: 'You are skinny, try to eat a lot, stay out of the sun whenever possible, maybe you will get whiter.' And when I got older they would say it was because in an earlier life I hadn't wanted to study to become a nun, I had not lived a good religious life, so being born dark was my karma." This typically Buddhist explanation was meant to comfort, as well as warn, removing any blame for one's present life and offering at least some explanation. "Then," Sara adds, "as I grew up, I came to understand where I came from."

As Sara grew older, the prejudice began to affect her deeply. "The teachers didn't look at me the same way they looked at other Vietnamese kids, and kids at school called me 'black girl.'" Being called black in Vietnam is not the same as in America, where it simply describes an ethnic background. In Vietnam, "black" is like being called "nigger" in America. "It implies savage, dirty, and stupid," one Vietnamese man told me. Says Sara: "People said things that hurt me, but I ignored them all. I'd rather study hard and improve my knowledge than listen to those things. The teachers from the south and central areas of Vietnam were nice to me, but the ones from the North treated me unfairly. I knew they didn't like me so I tried harder to improve my grades and make them see I was really a good student. But they graded me unfairly, like my math teacher, who pretended that I never existed in her class and wouldn't help me." Some lessons and songs were taught at schools throughout Vietnam about the cruelty and injustice of Americans during the war. A Vietnamese man who now lives in America sang one of the milder of these for me, acting it out with the dramatic, triumphant type of gestures one sees in Communist movies of that era:

The Song of Talu

From the top of the mountain floating
I proudly sing this echoing song

Follow the footsteps of the soldiers
Accompanied by the Song of Talu!

Tinh, Tinh, Tinh, Tang [bird song notes]
the rhythm of the song to which I'm proudly marching
Hello, revolutionary comrades!
I follow you to fight the American invaders

Look at those wicked American troops!
They left their corpses behind in the jungle!
We are marching to your courage
Bravo to you for your skills!

"Sometimes a group of women would sing and dance to that song in public performances, carrying Communist banners," he says. "It was played constantly on the radio after 1975, and when I was eleven years old and wearing my red neckerchief as a Ho Chi Minh kid, I knew all those songs by heart, and I thought Ho Chi Minh was wonderful."

It's not hard to understand why political feeling against Amerasians still ran high in many hearts. Miss Dao claims that "just because some Amerasians attended school doesn't mean they got an education. The Amerasians weren't given enough books or teacher attention, and not allowed to express an opinion in class. They were not treated as equals. They were given harder questions on tests, and given worse grades even when they did well. Sometimes a teacher even made sure they stayed behind. And any Amerasian who finished twelfth grade would still never get a high school diploma, because the school wouldn't pass them." Taunted and even attacked physically by the other children, unable to afford books and fees, and living where literacy had doubtful value during that difficult time, most Amerasians solved the problem by dropping out of school. Sara, like Louis, was an exception. She could be secure in the love and protection of Miss Dao. Others were not so lucky. Van, a white Amerasian born in 1967 and raised in a Buddhist orphanage in Central Vietnam, remembers a black Amerasian girl at her orphanage who "felt very bad about" her skin color. "The love we received from the nuns was a religious love, different from the love of parents," says Van. But with so many children in the orphanage, she says, it was hard for any child to receive individual and personal love.

"Visitors to our temple sometimes gave each child a small amount of money to buy candy, and that Amerasian girl began to save what she was given," Van says. "When she was fourteen, she bought sleeping pills in the market, and took them all and went to sleep. Next morning she was dead. She already had her papers to go to America, but she must have been planning about the pills for a long time. There was a time when I too thought of suicide, but I learned in temple that if you kill yourself, over your next 500 lives you cannot be reincarnated as a human. Otherwise I would probably have killed myself long ago."

Even those Amerasians brought up by their mothers were often crushed by the pressures of their lives, especially when the mother was too desperate herself to offer much emotional support. A Vietnamese college student born in Vietnam shortly after the war into a prominent Vietnamese family tells of the suicide of an Amerasian girl who lived in her neighborhood. "Outside the area where we lived the situation was very desperate, full of drug addicts and very poor people," she says. "One of them was the noodle woman, who sold noodles on the street. She had two black Amerasian children, a boy and a girl. I often heard other kids in the neighborhood calling them 'Xi Den' (ugly black kid). The noodle son ran off and joined the 'dust of life' in the streets when he was young. The daughter was a fully developed woman at age fourteen, with huge eyes she would roll when she was angry, and she was angry a lot! When little kids teased her she would turn around and roll her eyes at them, and the kids would squeal and run off. I thought, 'Wow! That girl is really violent!'"

When the student was ten, the fourteen-year-old noodle daughter committed suicide. "I heard the kids in the neighborhood run screaming, 'The daughter of the noodle lady just hung herself! She's dead!' My mom would not let me out of our house but I heard the noodle lady wailing and wailing, saying how unfair her kids were, crying: 'They didn't help me, they either just ran off or committed suicide!' After the suicide I couldn't face the noodle woman, so I skipped buying her noodles for a long time. In Vietnam when you are freshly mourning, people don't want to associate with you, because it's bad luck."

Miss Dao says: "The black Amerasians always suffered the most, although all the Amerasians eventually developed many emotional problems and complexes. So many Amerasians were abandoned in the streets, without any family or friends, no opportunity for education or a future, teased, with no one to care for them, so they came to feel lonely and unconnected. All these things affected their feelings about themselves as they grew up. Inside our temple all children were accepted, no matter what color. But the children themselves noticed how some got adopted and some did not. And some would say to the darker children: 'Why not use hot water to wash your skin?'"

Nguyen Ba Chung, of the Boston-based William Joiner Center for the Study of War and Social Consequences, came to America in 1972 as a student. Born in the North, he grew up in the South after migrating there with his mother, a Catholic, in 1954 when some 800,000 Vietnamese, mostly Catholics, came South after the country was divided into two parts. He says the Communists tried to change societal prejudice against dark skin, conducting a sort of "Black Is Beautiful" educational campaign much like the one carried out in the United States during the same era. Says Nguyen: "In Vietnamese culture the concept of beauty is white skin, especially for women. It's something very ancient, and we don't know where it came from, except that only the well-to-do who didn't have to work in the fields had lighter skin. The Communists tried to change that idea, saying that one who labors is more beautiful than a princess. Everyone understood that meant that darker skin is more beautiful."

But the prejudice was difficult to change, just as it was in America. Another Vietnamese man who came to America in 1978 in his late teens says: "When I was about seven, growing up in Vietnam, my own parents believed, and still believe, that the lighter your skin, the closer you are to goodness. I remember a woman who worked in our neighborhood as a maid, who had a half-white Amerasian boy about my age. I used to taunt him all the time. There was an idea that there was dirtiness associated with being Amerasian, that all mixed blood—even white blood—is dirty. Thinking back about that little boy, I feel so mean. He was such a sweet little kid, with very white skin, freckles, blonde hair. When we played games he would ask if he could play with us, but we never let him. We'd call him names and hint that his mother wasn't a good woman. Finally he would go away crying to his mother, but she was a servant, she couldn't do anything to us. After I came to America my Vietnamese perceptions changed. In Vietnam everyone looks alike, but in America a common first impression is of everyone looking different."

Problems with school and with racial insults were not as serious as the unrelenting hunger and poverty of the postwar years, when nuns and children still at the orphanage often went without eating. As years passed and Miss Dao was moved out of the orphanage by the new regime, she lived in a nearby house, keeping with her the few orphans she could. As time passed two small black Amerasian boys who had been taken away ran off from a government work camp and returned, as did one of the crippled orphans. Sara also remembers one older orphan in his twenties, a deaf mute, who wanted to come back. Miss Dao had no place for him to live, but let him sleep outside their crowded house at night. In the mornings he would go to beg all day in the bus station. Almost always kept together with Miss Dao were My Duyen, the first orphan adopted from the bomb shelter; Sara; and little Vinh.

"Miss Dao was like a real mother to me," says Sara. "And I always helped care for all the younger orphans, like Vinh. I remember the morning when I was five years old and another nun saw a bag hanging on our orphanage gate, and my nun looked inside and saw the newborn baby, Vinh." Feeding him would be a problem. "But my nun knew a lady who had just had a baby and was nursing it, and that lady nursed Vinh too. A lot of people came to see Vinh. I think his parents must have been very poor, and that was why they had to leave him."

When Sara was nine, Miss Dao brought home a baby girl who had been abandoned at a train station. "The baby was very cute," says Sara. "My nun took care of it and I helped. We didn't have much to eat, but I remember feeding it rice soup with a little spoon." But the baby was too weak to live. After two months it died. Sara and other orphans and nuns in the orphanage "sat and watched the baby while my nun had to go get an official paper to bury her. We were very sad. It was raining outside so bad, and we were very poor with nothing to eat. They took the baby very far away to bury it." The shortage of food continued for years, sometimes reaching famine proportions throughout the country. When Sara was twelve, she and Miss Dao would ride borrowed bicycles together far out into the mountains to pick a certain kind of tree leaf to bring back and dry on the orphanage roof. "We would then take it to this place with a big machine where it would be ground into powder, and all of us would roll it into incense sticks to sell," says Sara. "We were hungry a lot, oh yeah! I remember one day we didn't have rice or anything at all to eat for a long time and when we went to the mountains we were sick because we had had nothing to eat. We picked some thick beans off a tree and cooked and ate them for several days. It was all we had to eat and we got so sick that one day my nun fainted in the street. Everyone came out to help her."

People tried to help, says Sara, by coining, a Vietnamese folk medicine practice that involves raking the edge of a coin over areas of the body until red welts arise. Miss Dao recovered, but remained sickly, and so did Sara, who for two years was diagnosed with blood in her stomach caused by malnutrition and other hardships. Sara remembers one good thing that happened. In 1986 Miss Dao somehow learned how to make ice cream. Sara, her eyes lighting up at that memory, says, "I would help her make it and sell it at the market."

Louis Nguyen

Most of Louis Nguyen's life was one long struggle of school and hard work in a setting of poverty and discrimination. But when he was fourteen, something happened that made him very happy and excited. Despite the bullying from some of his classmates, he had become a top student and his school's best singer. He and a girl classmate were chosen to represent their school at a national singing contest.

Chong Son, the small town outside Bien Hoa where Louis's mother had taken him and his brother to live with Louis's grandmother years earlier, was in many ways like the faraway small town where Son Chau was growing up. Researchers believe that Amerasians who grew up in small towns outside the NEZ areas often ended up the least damaged emotionally. But very few were like Louis, who, partly guided by his grandmother, tried to deal with prejudice by setting a strict course for himself that defied the stereotypes against him. "When I was growing up many people were mean to me, but some were nice," says Louis. "I had a Vietnamese girlfriend who always stood up for me, even though her family didn't like me. Whenever I didn't have money she would give it to me right away, and in one month, a month and a half, I would give it back.

"Every year the best students and singers from all over the country were chosen to go be in the national contest with their teachers and listen to Communist lectures, and the girl and I were chosen," says Louis. "I was excited, of course! The contest was being held miles away at Ben Tre. It's a very famous town in Vietnam. They call that town 'The Wall,' because the Communist soldiers went there early on and made the whole town love them. They had a Communist hero there who killed many American soldiers. They always talked about him, a guy who set himself on fire and ran into an American base and blew everything up!" The school provided food during the trip, although the students had to pay their own bus fare and sleep in a classroom. Louis packed a blanket, a few other small items, and the new clothes he kept only for special occasions—his school uniform, blue pants and a white

T-shirt required for all students. "All Vietnamese students got new clothes every year for Tet—in Vietnam you usually wear plain clothes of course, so I kept my new clothes only for something special," says Louis.

For weeks he practiced and prepared the song he would sing. But on the night of the big event, "the girl from our school sang, but at the last moment my teacher lied to me and said they didn't have enough time for my act too. Later, some people told me the real reason was that the contest people wouldn't allow an Amerasian to sing the song about Ho Chi Minh that all the contestants had to sing." Louis pauses, then adds: "Of course, I actually knew that anyway. My teachers loved me and picked me even though they knew I might not get to sing because I was Amerasian, but they never told me because they didn't want to make me disappointed. Amerasians could sing special patriotic songs about Ho Chi Minh at a local contest or school, but not at some ceremony where big important Communists came. Before I went to Ben Tre, I did think I might not get picked"—Louis says as if confessing—"but I didn't care. I went for fun. Of course! I was a little sad, but really I wasn't that disappointed." But his face still shows his hurt and disappointment, and when asked to repeat the words to any of the countless songs about Ho Chi Minh, he refuses. "I don't want to say the words of a song about Ho Chi Minh," he protests nervously. "I am in America now. Vietnamese people here don't like it, they might even try to do something to me. I don't want to talk about Ho Chi Minh anymore."

In this, Louis is like other Vietnamese in America, who also refuse to tell the words of the Ho Chi Minh songs. Virtually all of the Vietnamese living in America are virulently anti-Communist, most having fled that country either at the end of the war or later by boat, or under a U.S. law accepting former reeducation camp prisoners, or under family reunification. At least until 1995 it was dangerous for immigrant Vietnamese in America to return to their native country even to visit relatives, because the U.S. exile community would shun them, revile them, and in some cases commit violence against them. There had been assassinations in America of certain Vietnamese and one American professor believed to be "pro-Communist." As late as 2002 Vietnamese in the United States, especially of the older generation, were still demonstrating frequently against art shows or dance recitals that included anything or anyone from Communist-ruled Vietnam. And when former Vietnamese premier General Nguyen Cao Ky visited in 2003, death threats were made against him.

So it took me years of trying before I finally found one Vietnamese friend living in America who was willing to sing one Ho Chi Minh song for me. He explained it was a song about the renaming and transformation of Saigon into Ho Chi Minh City, thus symbolizing the achievement of revolutionary goals. "I knew that song by heart by the time I was ten years old, because it was taught in school along with many, many Ho Chi Minh songs," he told me. He then sang and acted it out with dramatic gestures:

Ho Chi Minh City Song

From this city the supreme Uncle [Ho] has departed
He took with him the hope that one day he will return
In this final victory he has come back with the proud soldiers
Uncle has arrived to each and every home with the soldiers
Uncle has come to each home and greeted the elders,
*   and asked after all the youngsters*
And started the rhythmic song of reconciliation
[between North and South Vietnam]

The shining City of Ho Chi Minh is always in each and every heart,
in each and every hope, in each and every smile, we always have Uncle
His committed, passionate teaching guiding us forever,
glorifying the name of thee, Ho Chi Minh!

Patrick Du Phuoc Long's book *The Dream Shattered*, quotes other Ho Chi Minh songs:

Ho Chi Minh, the man who disregards storms and snow, swords, guns, and
*   chains,*
makes himself a suicide pioneer, determined to win every battle.
Setbacks frustrate him,
But his soul remains youthful and full of love of mankind.

And:

Even though [Ho's] hands tremble, his knees weaken and his voice quavers,
His steel heart is still fired by his fighting spirit.
His voice said: Move onward and fight!

and the young rank and file after years of endurance,
brightened their eyes, with young arms raising their shining machetes, determined
  to kill and drink the blood of the oppressors.
What a pleasure!

The last-minute change in Louis's place on the program was not his only disappointment caused by prejudice against Amerasians. At about the same time a writing contest was held for students in the whole region. "And I should have won," he says. "I studied so hard, and should have gotten an award, but they gave it to another guy, and it hurt so bad. And I quit school." Older Vietnamese, themselves mostly illiterate, had long encouraged him to quit. They pointed out that the only likely job for an educated person would be with the Vietnamese government, which would never hire an Amerasian. Yet Louis maintains that his main reason for quitting school was economic. He says his mother's health had become so bad that he had to help out by doing more farm work for neighbors. "I was already working a lot, and the neighbors trusted me and didn't treat me bad because I worked hard and didn't steal. But I had always told them I still had to go to school in the afternoons. I'd work in the mornings and then walk an hour to school. In Vietnam everybody is so poor that of course everyone has to work. In Vietnam, you can't dare be lazy! Also I had a girlfriend, but I didn't have nice clothes, and I didn't feel right." His few clothes were worn and ragged. "When you have a girlfriend of course you need OK clothes, and at least *some* money," says Louis.

Louis says his grandmother, who had always insisted he stay in school no matter what, was very understanding when he finally decided to quit. "My grandmother knew I had worked very, very hard, and always pushed myself very hard. She was always there for me. When I quit school so I could work full time, of course I was more than very sad, but our family needed money for food. Also everyone told me if you didn't have money you couldn't go to America, so that's part of why I quit to earn more, but still I never made enough. My grandmother was not happy about my quitting school, but she loved me, she understood, she knew how hard I had worked, and told me: 'Don't be sad, we need you to go to work now because of the family situation. [In life], just be a good person! A lot of people have no education at all, but they are a good person.' That's what she said to me. And that is true." Louis gives me a sharp look to see whether I disagree.

A close friend of Louis says he and his grandmother "had an emotional link, a deep connection. Neither of them would ever kiss up to anyone even if they were starving. Both had a lot of pride, a strong belief in certain values that they wouldn't betray under any circumstances. And when you share those feelings, and also share so many hard times together and make it through — it means so much."

When Louis quit school his teacher came to his house to talk with him. He had been one of her best students. "She was a very special teacher," he says. "She always helped me study. I love her a lot, of course! She asked me why I was quitting. I said I didn't have enough money, and she said if I really wanted to stay in school she would try to help me get a scholarship. But I wanted to stop, and nobody can tell me what to do." Aside from the need for money, Louis's pride and sense of self had been gravely wounded. "But it wasn't because of a contest that I quit school," he insists. "In my life I been through a lot of disappointments, and the school contest was nothing!" Louis says his family first heard in 1983 that Amerasians might be able to go to the United States. "But people said if you applied to go, the Communists might send you away to some bad place. It might be a trick, so we were afraid. So we waited until some Amerasians sent back a letter from the United States, and my uncle in Saigon heard about that and said, 'It's OK, the government didn't kill them!' So we said, 'Let's file!' "

But as years passed he never had enough money to pay his way. "So I started thinking, 'Well, if I not ever get enough money to go to America, then I won't go.' When you have no one to stand for you, you have to stand for yourself. I don't allow myself to 'do stupid things.' I'm very careful. Like when I was fourteen or fifteen and other guys would buy wine to drink, I would say 'No,' I would not join in. They would say, 'Why not, Explain!' And I would say, 'No, I not explain, I have a rule for myself.' Some people say I'm not a fun guy. It's not been easy, but I keep the rule for myself. That's why I not get along well with some people. Why do I have the rule? You *know* why! Of course! Because I'm Amerasian, and I don't want to give people a chance to look down on me!"

While Amerasians like Louis were struggling to live year after year, over and over again their chances to emigrate were blocked, except in a few special cases. Only about 150 of the few Vietnamese Amerasians who had emigrated by 1983 through the Overseas Departure Program had U.S. fathers waiting and willing to guarantee them U.S. citizenship. That same year Human Rights Advocates International, a public-interest law firm, was contending that all the Amerasians should be recognized as citizens. But U.S. law said children born overseas first must have an "identifiable" American parent willing to legitimate him or her (in twenty-two states a father could do this without marrying the mother), but some veterans even put 'do not contact' notations into their service records. *Newsweek* magazine quoted one father who "described himself as a 'standard male shit,' explaining: 'I can't let anything intrude on [my present] happiness.'" The article appeared the same year Miss Dao fainted in the street and Sara was diagnosed with blood in her stomach after the two ate cooked tree pods. Those Amerasians who had managed to live through the early years and were now reaching their teens kept doing whatever they could to get by.

In 1984 a new Overseas Departure Program subprogram was announced to airlift out all Amerasians from Cambodia, Laos, and Vietnam within three years. But Vietnamese Amerasians were completely excluded by the U.S. State Department, which kept blaming the absence of diplomatic relations with Vietnam. It was still trying to pressure Vietnam on other issues.

In October 1985 Overseas Departure Program interviewers reported a backlog of more than 20,000 cases of Vietnamese already interviewed but "yet to be acted on" while awaiting their turn to leave Vietnam, with the number of applicants growing. Yet the United States had set a limit of only 1,000 per month total departures from Vietnam, a total including few Amerasians. To speed up the emigration of Amerasians, that year John Shade of the Pearl Buck Foundation managed to line up two luxury liners from Grace Lines, raise $2 million, and get Vietnamese government permission to take 8,000 Amerasians out of the country. But according to the author Thomas Bass, the U.S. State Department convinced the Buck Foundation Board to kill the plan, and Shade resigned in disgust.

Meanwhile, the Amerasian orphan Nan says when she was about ten and her nun was dying, "she called all us orphans together and told us that three of us had mothers still alive in Vietnam—the eldest orphan, one other, and myself. The eldest later found her mother, who was very wealthy, and they escaped to America together by boat. I myself felt very happy to know I had a real mother, and was very curious to see her. But I was still young, and besides I had no money to try to look for her. I just kept always hoping for some way to find her." But Nan's dream seemed impossible to achieve.

In January 1986 the Vietnamese government, seeing the giant backlog of cases interviewed but moving very sluggishly, accused the

Americans of acting in bad faith, expelled all ODP interviewers and closed the program. Many of the fake families who earlier had lined up Amerasians to use to escape from Vietnam kicked them out. That year an Irish woman visiting Vietnam reported ragged, homeless Amerasians eating ants off the pavements of Ho Chi Minh City. Some were selling sex; many were missing an arm, leg, or eye. Finally, in September 1986, more than eleven years after the end of the war, with almost all the Amerasians now in their teens or early twenties, the first direct talks on Amerasians began between the United States and Vietnam as part of secret meetings about a multitude of other issues.

5

Turning from Dust to Gold, 1988–93

[In 1987] ours was only the third of any American tour group to enter Vietnam after the war. Hundreds of ragged half-grown Amerasians were living in the streets [of Ho Chi Minh City]. . . . Some of the people on our tour were so moved that they went back and wrote their Congress members, demanding "Do something!"

—Gary Wintz, tour leader

Around 1986 a former Vietnamese commando who had worked for the CIA during the war and had just been released from prison camp took the 700-mile train trip from the North Vietnamese port of Vinh to his home in the South Vietnamese village of Vung Tau. After his train crossed the DMZ—the demilitarized zone that once split Vietnam into two halves—and pulled into the Central city of Hue, the man was amazed to see many, many Amerasian street youths, apparently homeless, selling fruits, cookies, and black market cigarettes in the streets. He saw this at every Southern stop along his trip.

Certainly most of the Amerasians still living had known little but suffering throughout their lifetimes. No one will ever know how many had already died, first in the war, then in the postwar epidemics and famines during an era when very few were untouched.

After 1975 and throughout the 1980s, the U.S. government forbid most Americans to travel to Vietnam, as it forbid travel to Cuba. But in the late 1980s a few Americans troubled by Vietnam's desperate post-war plight began going anyway, including some Vietnam War veterans who had an assortment of reasons for wanting to return.

One of the earliest American peace activists and advocates of reconciliation with Vietnam was John McAuliff, who by 2003 headed the Fund for Reconciliation, which, among other things, took delegations to Vietnam and Cuba and worked for better relations between those countries and the United States. In 1985 he had founded the Indochina Reconciliation Project, which worked for reconciliation and for lifting the U.S. trade and aid embargos against Vietnam. During the 1980s, McAuliff led some of the earliest tour groups, traveling as guests of the Vietnamese government. His organization also provided aid to several small projects there. McAuliff disputes allegations that the Amerasians were treated badly by the Vietnamese for political reasons, although he agrees they were mistreated on racial and class grounds.

"During the 1980s, some Amerasians were around, some begging," says McAuliff. "Some would approach you when you were walking through Ho Chi Minh City. In those days, there were beggars coached and run as teams, and if a kid came up to an American and said he was being treated [badly] because he was part American, it might not be true. The U.S. media was just discovering the Amerasians then. In America during the first half of the 1980s, there were two things happening after the war: There was the [American] guilt and there was the propaganda, where we had to say the Vietnamese were nasty and bad and deserved what we did to them. The Amerasian thing was part of this." McAuliff doubts the figure of 76 percent of Amerasians being sent to the NEZ. "People who didn't have jobs were sent there, and the propaganda line in the U.S. was that they were sent because they had connections to Americans," he says.

"In the U.S. it became a big hullabaloo [to take them to America]. If the U.S. only had put a tenth of the money into training programs in Vietnam [that it spent on the Homecoming Act program]. . . . Well, the act was a disaster from the beginning, and had to do with U.S. guilt as much as anything else." Other Americans, including veterans, who had opposed the U.S. involvement in the war and who generally believed in the new Vietnamese government's idealism, were appalled by postwar U.S. policies such as blocking most humanitarian aid.

While agitation was growing in the United States over bringing Amerasians into the country, says McAuliff, he saw no signs that Vietnamese officials or Communist Party leaders were mistreating them. People from the respected Vietnamese Women's Union "were very angry" at such reports by U.S. media, he says, "and one said to me: 'These are *our* kids, not kids for the United States to take away from us.' It's true that the Amerasians often did have special difficulties, because they were in fatherless families, especially if their mom had been a prostitute, or, like many prostitutes, had problems with drugs or alcohol, or had had a kid by an American. Vietnam is like every society—people have racial attitudes like they do here." In fact, he says, Vietnamese "used to say when accused of discrimination against Amerasians that with all the racism in the U.S., Americans hardly had clean hands [themselves].

"The Amerasians were one of the consequences of the war, and if the U.S. had wanted to help them it could have helped them in Vietnam with small businesses and schools. The U.S. could have recognized a 'special American responsibility' for them. My main point is that if [we] had looked at their situation with objectivity, the solution would not necessarily have been bringing them to the U.S." During the 1980s, McAuliff's organization was helping several Vietnamese projects, including the May 19 School, or "Loving School," run by a Catholic nun on a model by a Russian child development expert. It offered students both an income and an education and was quasi-governmental, says McAuliff. "There were 100 to 150 kids there, and 10 to 15 percent of them were Amerasian."

Another organization that helped the school was the William Joiner Center for the Study of War and Social Consequences based at the University of Massachusetts in Boston, at the time a center mainly for veterans of the Vietnam War still struggling with the war's after-effects. In January and June of 1987, Kevin Bowen, a Vietnam veteran and head of the Joiner Center, went to Vietnam on a Vietnamese government-sponsored tour arranged by McAuliff. "We were taken to many places dealing with social problems left from the war, like centers for disabled veterans and quadriplegics, a drug rehab center that included a lot of former South Vietnamese soldiers, some government orphanages including a big one outside Saigon with 200 older orphans and a very few Amerasians," says Bowen. "We asked about the Amerasians, and they took us to the May 19 School. We saw maybe 100 Amerasian kids there aged fourteen to twenty. We also saw a lot of Amerasians living in the streets, and a lot of disabled people crawling on their hands." Afterward the Joiner Center shipped medical supplies to Vietnam and sent people to do midwife training and to work with tuberculosis programs.

In late 1987 Gary Wintz, a tour leader for the large, respected

Linblad travel agency in Westport, Connecticut, named after its owner Lars Eric Linblad, took a group of fifteen Americans to Ho Chi Minh City. "Ours was only the third of any American tour group to enter Vietnam, although more than a dozen commercial groups planned trips there that winter," says Wintz. His tour members were shocked when, on the first day they stepped out of their hotel, they were swarmed by frantic, ragged half-grown Amerasians, hundreds of whom were living in the streets. "They would come up to our tour members, the first Americans they'd seen maybe ever, saying 'my father, my father,' in Vietnamese accents," says Wintz. "Some of the people on the tour were so moved that they spent their whole time with the kids, most of whom were living in a park. Then these people went back and wrote their Congress members, demanding 'Do something!' One woman even organized a write-in campaign."

Other returning tour groups also wrote their Congress members. Because Vietnam was one of the handful of countries covered by the U.S. Trading with the Enemy Act, the tours had to be licensed by the Treasury Department's Office of Foreign Assets Control, says Juan Fraim, then in charge of Linblad's Westport office. The U.S. government was furious over attempts by some returning tour members to publicize the plight of the Amerasians and promote reconciliation. It decided to put an end to the tours. The Linblad agency had run the tours to Vietnam legally for about two years, says another tour leader at the time, Tom Stanley, and had advertised future tours and applied for a new license not yet approved. In 1988 the government arranged a "sting" operation in which a woman agent booked and paid for one of the future tours. Soon afterward, armed FBI agents, local police, and Customs and Treasury officials burst into the agency, confiscated twelve to sixteen boxes of documents and some computers, closed the agency, and froze its bank accounts.

"I was sitting in my office when suddenly FBI agents and other government people, about fifteen to twenty in all, came in," says Fraim. "Some were armed. They allowed no one to leave, and were there five or six hours. I personally was not afraid because it was ridiculous.

"But it caused a lot of hardship to the company. [After that], there were several meetings with the Treasury Department, because the matter was to be brought before a grand jury, and Treasury threatened to indict the company and several employees. But in the end, we settled out of court. There were big legal fees. Mr. Linblad never felt he did anything wrong, but he didn't have the means to fight it to the end."

Another Linblad employee at the time, Donna Barfield, said Linblad was born Swedish, "but became a U.S. citizen who believed travel builds relations between countries by dealing with them on some level. . . . He had a heart attack and angioplasty while the case was going [on]." Linblad died the following year.

Fraim says one of the conditions of the settlement with Treasury was that, "we were not supposed to tell the media [or anyone] what happened, or what [fine, etc.] was paid. It was in the [settlement] order." Other sources say the fine may have been $75,000, the legal fees about $600,000 and the loss in business about $3 million.

In the meantime, publicity about the Amerasians was increasing in the U.S. media, and public pressure was mounting. In September a new program almost identical to the Overseas Departure Program (ODP) began alongside it. It mostly affected half-American children born in Cambodia and Laos. But the Vietnamese Amerasian issue had finally slipped out of U.S. government control. The breakthrough came when *Long Island Newsday* carried a photograph of a blond, blue-eyed fourteen-year-old Amerasian boy, Le Van Minh, who had been crippled by polio as a child and earned his living dragging himself on his hands and knees through the streets, begging. The photograph shocked many, including some students at Huntington High School in Long Island, who wrote to their congressman, Robert Mrazek, himself a Vietnam vet. He also was a member of the House Appropriations subcommittee that financed the ODP.

Mrazek did two things: He flew to Vietnam and brought Le Van Minh back to a foster home in Long Island, and, with another congressman and Vietnam veteran, Thomas Ridge (later head of the Department of Homeland Security), drafted and pushed through the 1987 Amerasian Homecoming Act, calling for all natural children of American soldiers and civilians who served in Vietnam to be airlifted to the United States along with their close relatives. The law was to go into effect in March 1988, and Mrazek was quoted as saying he thought it would result in a "massive airlift of all Amerasian children from Vietnam" and their resettlement in America within two years. The act covered any child born after January 1, 1962, and before January 1, 1976. It estimated that it would take out 8,000–12,000 Amerasians and 22,000 "close relatives."

"[The act] makes eligible virtually any child with black or Caucasian features [from] America's military involvement in Vietnam, which ended in late 1973," said Mrazek. The extension of the last covered birthdate to 1976 presumably covered children conceived up until April 30, 1975, the day Saigon fell. Some veterans' groups and individual veterans had opposed bringing Amerasians to the United States, perhaps dreading the opening of Pandora's boxes long closed. But a few anguished fathers hoped to be reunited with family left behind. Although the U.S. State Department fought the bill, it passed with little congressional opposition. Meanwhile, Le Van Minh's family—his mother, stepfather, and four half-brothers and sisters—had been left "almost starving" after losing their main source of support, Le Van Minh's income from begging. This at least was the claim made to author Thomas Bass by Nguyen Quang Phong, the Vietnamese official who brought the boy to Mrazek to go to America. Phong said the boy didn't want to leave his family, and "was crying." A year later Minh's family joined the boy in the United States.

The boat escapes from Vietnam had continued throughout the 1980s, although many fewer people—now mostly middle-class Vietnamese—were leaving. Thousands of those escaping were still being raped, killed, and robbed by pirates, drowned after the collapse of rickety, overcrowded boats, and turned away when they tried to land at neighboring nations. Some of the escape attempts included Amerasians. "There was an Amerasian girl in my school in Cam Ranh who was a very good student, but the teacher always made her feel bad," says a young Vietnamese man who came to the United States in 1990. "She was a straight-A student, and the more they were mean to her, the harder she worked. She was a white Amerasian—I think she was adopted. Her family had to pay a lot of money for her to go to school. It was terrible for her in Vietnam. When she was fourteen her family tried to escape by boat. But it flipped, and everyone on it died, including this girl. I went down to the water to see, and they had dragged forty-two dead bodies up onto the shore and laid them in rows."

The U.S. government, which still had no idea of the problems involved in bringing the Amerasians, allocated only $50 million U.S. to process and bring Amerasians to the United States, a sum that did not include their airfares. That was to be advanced by religious and aid agencies and later repaid by the Amerasians. The U.S. Office of Refugee Resettlement (ORR) provided a small amount to be used by Amerasian resettlement sites to facilitate resettlement in the United States (the number of sites eventually grew to fifty), and later a pittance of $1.5 million was set aside for that purpose. The American Council for

Voluntary International Action, called InterAction, contracted with ORR through September 30, 1990, to make subgrants of up to $35,000 per year for each agency administering one of the sites. The agencies were expected to raise additional funds from private and local government sources.

Originally the *total* of Amerasians *and* family members expected to arrive was estimated at as few as 30,000. The act projected that the Amerasians and their relatives could be processed and resettled during the two-year period beginning March 21, 1988. Because the U.S. government sets an annual total on the number of immigrants who can enter America each year, but sets virtually no limit on refugees, it wanted to categorize the Amerasians as refugees. This bureaucratic problem held up their emigration for years, because the Vietnamese government insisted they were not refugees at all, but children of Americans who should be considered U.S. citizens. The conflict was resolved by the United States calling them immigrants but giving them the same benefits as refugees, and using the resettlement process "normally used for refugees." It was an important ruling, because refugees received better benefits and protections.

When the Amerasian Homecoming Act went into effect in 1988, thirteen years had passed since the end of the war. The youngest Amerasian was thirteen, the oldest, under the parameters set by the act, was twenty-six. Some had children of their own. Aware of the terrible losses inflicted on those trying to escape Vietnam by boat, Vietnamese saw the act as an alternative. All they had to do was find an Amerasian who would claim them as relatives, and they could go with them to America by plane. Of course, usually they first had to buy the Amerasian from his real family or orphanage, or pay bribes and other costs of emigration. Overnight, the despised and mistreated Amerasians, formerly labeled "dust children" became "gold children." Soon fraud and corruption permeated every step of the new program. Because virtually every Amerasian was desperately poor, uneducated, and of a lower class, their real families, if they even had them, almost never could afford the costs of emigrating. Wealthy upper-class families, or poorer families sometimes using money sent by relatives already established in America, sought out Amerasians. The Amerasians found themselves prizes to be flattered, lavished with affection, and courted with gifts. And some were not above playing their own games.

Son Chau

One early morning during the rainy season of 1986, the year before the Amerasian Homecoming Act was passed, nineteen-year-old Son set out walking toward the cafe where he usually had his morning coffee. A few days earlier, Son's drunken stepfather Hanh had wandered off for a time, but the family was used to his disappearances. Son decided to stroll up to the abandoned Buddhist temple near his house where as a little boy he had often fled to sleep when his stepfather drove him from home. "It was a big temple they were building from before 1975, but after that nobody lived in there or taked care of it," says Son. "Sometimes you can go up there in the morning to breathe fresh air. With nobody around, you can be thinking. Around it, the wild grass grows very high."

A policeman neighbor and friend of Son's walked up toward the ruined temple too. Passing a large grass-surrounded hole, he saw in the puddled water "a big dead body," half-floating and bloated and disintegrating.

> "Hey, Son, LOOK! Somebody die in here!" he called.
> Son walked back and the two stared down into the water-filled hole.
> "The body was all swollen," says Son. "Then I say: 'Oh, you know who is that? That's my stepfather!'"
> "How can you know?"
> "You see his shirt? That's the shirt my U.S. cousin sent me, white with green stripes. I used to wear it and then I gave it to him."

Son says he felt "only a little bit" bad. "Hanh was a nice person except when he got drunk," he says, apparently hesitating to speak completely ill of the dead. "But when Hanh was drunk, which was most of the time, then he was a bad person. He don't think, and he hit people and say bad things. I looked at his body and saw he had blood on his forehead and worried maybe he'd been drunk and somebody hit him, or maybe he fell and no one knew, and the water make him die. I think now it was just an accident." But Son's bad relationship with his drunken stepfather was well-known in his village. "So I was 100 percent sure the police would question me and try to blame me, but 100 percent sure they would investigate and let me go. My police friend told me to go report what happened, but first I stopped by and told my mom. She cry and cry. I said 'Don't worry.' Then I went to the police."

Du says she cried because she was afraid Son was in serious trouble. "I was only worried for my children," she says. "I had no feeling for Hanh. He was cruel. When he was alive all of us were suffering and afraid of him; he beat all of us and was especially cruel to Son. After Hanh was dead things were better for all of us. Even Hai, my seven-year-old son by Hanh, was happy he was dead."

People in Son's village were electrified by the news of Hanh's death and Son's arrest, gossiping and debating Son's innocence or guilt. "The police were kind of afraid of Son. Regular people might be very afraid of Son," says Hai, Son's friend from frankincense-hunting days. "But he would never kill his stepfather. Wouldn't have and couldn't have, and in fact he didn't have time to do it. Because he was with me a few days before the body was found, and the night before, we came back late together." Son says he was kept at the police station all that day until they could perform an autopsy. "I told the big main cop, 'I know you got to question me, but I know for sure how he really must have died.' That cop said nothing, just smiled and smiled. They kept me over-night, and about 2:30 A.M. they woke me up to question me some more. I began to believe they would never release me. I said to the big cop, 'Can you just let me go home and help my mom with the funeral and things?' and he said, 'No, no,' and I read in his eyes he was 100 percent sure I killed my stepfather. So I was afraid they would put me in jail and shoot me."

Again the ways of a small town with its complex relationships held sway. Although Son had had many problems with some of the senior police officials, he was friends with several policemen. "I was lucky, because the cop who was guarding me in jail was a good friend I'd grown up with," says Son. "He kept telling me, 'Son, don't feel bad. If you killed your stepfather they will never let you get away with it. But if you didn't, they will let you go. Meanwhile, whatever you want, a cigarette, something to drink, we get it for you.'" As dinnertime approached, the guard took Son to the jail kitchen to eat with the police. "During those days in jail I didn't eat much, because I keep thinking, thinking," says Son. "I think about my mom, how my American dad left me, and all the stuff he left for me she didn't know how to keep, so when I was grown up I didn't have nothing. And then she remarried, and for ten years her new husband Hanh kept giving me a lot of trouble—first when he was alive and now when he died."

Although Son felt angry at Du in some ways, at the same time he worried about her. "Really I don't blame my mom, I understand my mom. She is not strong and intelligent like some other women, not responsible, that is not her nature, but she is kind and soft. Anyway, at dinner I sit there at the table worried, with all the cops eating, and I eat only one small bowl of food. And I have a cup of water and am smoking, thinking, and looking out the door, and finally I see the big cop coming back." The policeman was returning from the autopsy on Hanh. "It must have cleared me, and showed my stepfather drowned," says Son, "so the big cop told me I could go. I said 'Thanks,' but I hated him a lot because in his eyes I read he still believed I killed my stepfather. That cop was a real Commie, sixty-five to seventy years old, a North Vietnam person. And after that night I hated all cops. Some people misunderstand me, but that's what makes me a very strong man. I know 95 percent of the people in my village believe I killed my stepfather, but I never did it!"

Still dreaming constantly of finding his American father, and fearing if he stayed much longer in Vietnam his clashes with police might destroy his life, Son was one of the first Amerasians to apply under the new Amerasian Homecoming Act. Already, many fake families had approached Son, "but I always refused." One problem, he says, is that local officials kept blocking his applications. And no one in his small town was able to properly fill out the complicated paperwork. "But I knew this girl whose aunt was a schoolteacher before 1975, who knew how to help with the paperwork, and the aunt told me, 'Son, you have to get out of Song Pha, they will never approve you there. Also, you have to go to the U.S. alone.'" Once in America, he could bring the rest of his family over. So one day Son went secretly to Dalat, and filed an application there. He planned to pay the fees and bribes with his own money. "When I filed those papers I told no one in my village," says Son.

Secretly, he got together all of his family's important documents—birth certificates, photos of his father, letters, and official documents on each family member. Those kinds of papers frequently got "lost" during the application process, and had to be re-created or repurchased, sometimes more than once, with new bribes and fees. Son obtained a U.S. interview the same year the law went into effect, 1988. He and the other Amerasians knew nothing of various faraway policy arguments and decisions powerfully affecting their lives. They only sought to learn ways through and around the complicated procedures and restrictions. Son made his family swear to keep everything secret until he was safely out of the country, and just before he was to leave he secretly sold his family's house. As eldest son, he was legally entitled to do this. The purchaser was a Vietnamese man who had been kind to Son's family during their most impoverished days, sometimes even bringing Son and his Amerasian half-sister Linh toys at Tet. "This friend loved my mom, and I sold our house to him very cheap, so he could live there and watch out for her," says Son. "I didn't want her living by herself, where people could treat her bad, or bad people could push her down." At first Du cried and begged Son not to sell the house. "I was afraid we would end up homeless," she says. But Son finally convinced her that he needed the money to be able to leave Vietnam.

Then at the last minute, the schoolteacher who had been so helpful began to pressure Son. "She told me: 'Son, you can't take your family with you, so why don't you take my niece?' And even the girl's mom and dad wanted me to make a real marriage with her. At first I said, 'No, No,' but finally I had to agree. The aunt had kept some of my paperwork and she said she would throw it away if I didn't marry the girl. And I had already sold our house. I went away a day to think, then I came back and said OK. The niece was nice, but I not love her. She herself said nothing, just obeyed her parents. And so finally I had to marry her but not for money, they gave me no money." It was 1989. He returned briefly to tell his own family goodbye, again swearing them to secrecy. They learned he was safely out of Vietnam only when they received a note from him from the Philippines. "For awhile the officials in my hometown did not even know I had left Vietnam," says Son.

Nan Bui

Another Amerasian immediately affected by the new law was Nan, who'd been told several years earlier by her dying nun that her birth mother was alive somewhere in Vietnam. She'd heard vague rumors about the new act the year she turned fifteen, but at first it seemed like just another of the many fluctuations that had come and gone for years without real change. "Outside my Buddhist orphanage that year just before Tet, the whole world seemed happy, shopping and preparing for the big holiday," says Nan. "But after my nun died, our orphanage was so poor we often had no food or money at all. A kind nun from a different temple sometimes came by and gave us food when she saw how badly we needed it. That year, watching everyone outside so happy, I was feeling very sad and lonely because everyone looked down on us, and no one really cared about us. Then the kind nun came and asked what I wanted for Tet, and I said what I really wanted was to find my real mom, but I had no money. So this nun gave me money to travel with my orphanage sister Joan to Binh Duong where I had learned that my birth mother lived.

"When we arrived we went to a temple where a nun knew the true story. At first she wouldn't tell me anything, but finally said that since my nun who died had sent me, she would tell me where my mother lived. So next day I went there with my orphanage sister. I didn't know exactly where my mother's house was or what she looked like, and as we walked through town, people made fun of me because I was Amerasian, calling me names, even making their dogs chase me. But when I drew closer the whole neighborhood knew right away that I was my mother's daughter because I looked so much like her. There was whispering and murmuring, and the whole village ran ahead to tell my mother, 'Your daughter is coming!' So the first time I saw my mom she ran to me and gave me a big hug and was crying. And at first I felt happy. She told me she hadn't wanted to give me up, that she was sorry, and I was very touched and cried also. But then things changed. My mother had an older pure Vietnamese daughter, my half-sister. So I really hated my mother because she abandoned me but raised my sister. And I asked her, 'Why did you raise that other daughter and not me?'"

Nan's mother lived in a large house and was from a wealthy family. She'd met Nan's father through a brother who was a South Vietnamese army officer. "My mom showed me a picture of my dad wearing his name tag. He had skin lighter than mine, and his hair was not very curly," says Nan. "I am not sure of his last name, but sometimes in America I have seen ads for Camel cigarettes, and my dad's last name looked or sounded like that. But the truth is, my mom never raised me for even one day. She abandoned me to my grandmother, who gave me to my nun when I was dying as a baby. And what if I hadn't been raised by my own nun, and had grown up with no education? I wonder what my life would be. So I respect my mother because she gave birth to me, but I don't love her. If she really loved me she would have looked for me a long time before then. Where was she when I was really poor, and needed her help so desperately? She claimed she had come to the temple to look for me, but I don't believe she ever looked for me at all. *I* am the one who found *her*."

Under the Homecoming Act at that time (later modified) an Amerasian could bring only one "family" group to America—parents and siblings, or spouse and children. Nan's mother began pressuring her to bring her and her Vietnamese half-sister. "But my mom's brother told me about her selfishness, and it greatly cut down the feelings I had for her in the beginning, when I was so happy to find her. Still, I didn't truly know she was not a good person until she wouldn't give me the picture of my dad. So my orphanage sister Joan said, 'Get all the information you can about him and don't tell her she can't come to America with us. Then when you get there, you can bring her over.' I don't feel anything for my mother after what she did to me, and I don't think there is any love from my mom towards me, either. As for my half-sister, even though we share the same mother I feel no connection to her. The love I had for my orphanage sister Joan was much greater."

At first Nan's mother began coming to Nan's temple to visit her. "She brought me gold and jewelry because she thought she could use me. She wanted me to promise I would take her and my half-sister. Once she even brought a locket to carry her picture, but I gave it to my half-sister because I didn't want to wear it. My mom began nagging, 'Give me all your papers, let me go file them with ours, so we can get to America together quickly!' But I refused. I think she became suspicious. Meanwhile I knew I would leave soon, but didn't tell her because I feared she would make some kind of trouble. When she found out she couldn't come with me, she was so mad she said, 'Without me you can't have the picture! Without me, you're not going to go!'"

During one point in the long process of preparing to leave, Nan had all her papers together but not enough money to pay all the fees and bribes. Unexpected saviors stepped forward—two slightly older orphanage "graduates," young girls who had left the orphanage and become self-supporting by operating a tiny street stall. The two often came back to help the other children. They worked many exhausting hours, making countless sacrifices, even skipping meals, to provide for the orphans and raise money to pay for paperwork for America.

At last Nan and Joan were approved to go to America. They planned to take the two older Vietnamese orphanage sisters. But again at the last minute there was not enough money after all; perhaps some last-minute bribe or fee was needed. Then, says Nan, beginning to cry, a nun they didn't know from another temple offered to pay the rest of the money if they would bring her, a second nun, and eight orphans from the other temple. Nan, then sixteen, says she refused to leave the older sisters behind. "When we were struggling, that evil nun never helped us," she says through tears. "And nobody—nobody—nobody—but

those two sisters helped us or gave us a penny." Finally, the nun agreed
to include them. "But she was lying," says Nan. At the last minute the
nun secretly dropped them from the papers, and they were left behind.
"I still hate that nun so much," says Nan years later.

As for Nan's mother and half-sister, "I didn't need the jewelries my
mom gave me, not at all, and even though we are blood-related I still
felt I should bring the orphans instead. My mother and half-sister were
well-off enough to stay in Vietnam and be OK, but the orphans were
so poor, and really needed to go to America. I didn't feel right bringing
my mom and leaving all those children behind. Many people during
those days offered me gold to claim them as my family. If I were the
type who loves to be rich and greedy, I would have gone with them, but
I went with my orphan sisters instead, because I felt a connection between them and me. And also, they were the ones who really deserved
to come to America."

Alan "Tiger" Hoa

One day in 1988 when Tiger was fifteen, living on the streets of Ho Chi
Minh City, a white American named Tom came up and asked his name.
Tiger, who had thought all European-looking people were Russians,
says, "It was the first time I realized there was a difference between
Americans and Russians. I didn't understand English, so a Vietnamese
person who worked in the building came out and translated. Tom wrote
my uncle's name and address on a list. He asked if I wanted to go to
America and look for my dad. Later my family got a letter about going
to America."

In any case, Tiger was living in the park and involved in gang life the
day he was approached by Tom. In Tiger's story of the life-changing
events that led to him eventually coming to America, he says that Tom
was an American vet who had returned to Vietnam to look for his Vietnamese wife and Amerasian daughter. "He gave me new clothes he
brought from America and $1 the first week. The second week he gave
me $2," says Tiger. "I was very happy. But one day my Uncle Binh
came looking for me, and said the family had gotten a letter [from offi-
cials] about my going to America. He told me to go home, because some
of my family wanted to go to America with me. The thought of going to
America with new clothes, delicious food, and money in my pocket
made me very happy. I went home and stayed until the paperwork was

done, then left again." After Tom distributed small U.S. flags to some Amerasians, the Vietnamese government kicked Tom out of the country, says Tiger.

Before 1989 Dam Sen Park was occupied by ordinary homeless people and Vietnamese gangs as well as prostitutes. While the United States was building an Amerasian transit center there with $500,000 of State Department funds, hundreds of Amerasians began to gather, and Vietnamese hoping to go to the United States with them began to congregate there also. "We wanted the park for Amerasians only, and we totally took it over," says Tiger. "There was a great struggle, almost like a war, with people slashing and fighting every day. People had bruises and scars everywhere. Then when Vietnamese people came from all over and gave money to the Amerasians [after the Amerasian Homecoming Act was passed], we bought better weapons and longer knives, and we came to rule the park."

The transit center opened in January 1990, with dorms and classrooms for English and vocational classes in such skills as sewing. Homeless Amerasians, and Amerasians from distant rural areas awaiting their exit interviews, could stay in the dorm. The State Department paid the Vietnamese government $137 for each emigrating Amerasian and accompanying "relative" after they had been processed and left the country—an incentive to process as many as possible, real or fraudulent.

"Crowds of us Amerasians, most of us homeless, all gathered at Dam Sen Park near the transit center," says Tiger, excited at the memory. "The park was becoming like a fish market where people would bring gold to the Amerasians and also bring their daughters, saying we could marry them if we first would take their families to America. Everyone— even Chinese—practically fought over us like a supermarket sale." Chinese in Vietnam were looked on as especially wealthy and elite. "During that time many, many people would try anything to get me to go with them. All those people—even Chinese—even beautiful young girls— came to me out of nowhere offering me things!" Tiger didn't stay in the transit center because "we couldn't make any extra money there, we didn't have freedom to do what we wanted. And since it was next to the park with so much going on, that was more tempting. Every day we just came to the center and got $1 and left. And every day Vietnamese people came to the park offering me gold and gifts. But I didn't take it, it was not the right thing to do because they were just exploiting me.

The tribal man I knew as a child in the NEZ is the only person in my life who truly cared about me.

"These new people wanted to give me gold, and beautiful girls, and motorcycles, but honestly I would rather be on the street, my life up and down, together with my gang, stealing things together and sharing them. I would rather be a 'cowboy.'" Tiger does admit that he often would go home with people, "eat a delicious meal, put on new clothes they gave me, and then rush back to the dance place, where the dance teacher would tease me, saying, 'Now you're getting rich!'" Tiger was enjoying these heady new days of flattery, comfortable shoes, and a full stomach. And he may not have been as quick as he claims to turn down offers. Certainly he accepted many gifts from Nga, a woman ten to fifteen years older than Tiger with whom he often stayed for days at a time. "I called her 'auntie,'" he says. He at first wouldn't admit he ever promised to take her to America. He did say that Nga paid to be introduced to him by a middleman. "At that time people paid just to be introduced to Amerasians," says Tiger. Once he told me Nga had bought him with a $1,500 down payment and an additional $1,500 promised once they actually left for America together. Like many Amerasians, Tiger felt some cynicism toward the sudden outpouring of kindness and love from people who had formerly treated him with contempt and cruelty, although he seems to have genuinely cared for Nga at some level.

As the crowds of Amerasians and those who courted them continued to grow in Dam Sen Park, a mysterious person emerged in Tiger's life. Named Raymond (Tiger gives his name the French pronunciation of "Ramón"), he is sometimes mentioned in books and articles of that time. Half-black, he seemed to be in his thirties, and therefore too old to be a child of the war. Although he claimed to be half-American, he was rumored to be anything from a child of a black French Moorish soldier to an American deserter trying to get back into the United States by claiming to be Amerasian. Raymond said he learned his American English and ways as an abandoned child taken in by black American soldiers who raised him during the war. He was soon helping as an interpreter between the Americans and the Amerasians, filling out the complicated forms for a fee and explaining the procedures needed to pass the long exit process.

Tiger sometimes describes Raymond as a rival. "We didn't like him. He didn't live in the park like us, he just appeared from nowhere one day. He was aggressive and bossy, a slick person. Our gang was in a gang fight with him and almost killed him. We fought, we slashed each other with knives, there were many fights going on. I wanted to kill Raymond, but lucky for him one day he disappeared, so of course our side won." Tiger says an American vet gave Raymond $7 U.S. to give each Amerasian, and that Raymond kept $2 of each handout for himself. But at other times Tiger and Raymond may have been allies. Raymond was in the Philippines at least part of the time Tiger was, and Tiger mentions knowing him there. He says Raymond came to the United States about the same time he did with an older woman called Madame J, who also used the names Kathleen and Jacqueline. She was a well-known madam and gang boss in Vietnam. Tiger also may have spent time with Raymond when he later visited Madame J in New York. That is all Tiger will say about Raymond.

One of the Amerasians awaiting approval to leave for America was Nan, who stayed at a temple for several months while attending English classes at the transit center. "I saw the crowd of Amerasians hanging around outside—that's how I first met Tiger," Nan says. "He was very poor. He was not respected; he was living in the streets. I kind of liked him, and because he had no clothes and no food, sometimes I would give him a little food or money. I had a better life then than most Amerasians, because most were homeless and looked down upon, like Tiger. A lot of people tried to get him to sign papers to go to the U.S. Of course he was in a gang, but gangs in Vietnam didn't always mean they would kill people. Many were just hungry and had to steal to survive. Gangs in Vietnam are not as scary as gangs in the U.S. because they don't have guns, they only have instruments to cut throats and beat people. But gangs in the U.S. and Vietnam are connected, and some gang members who came to the U.S. were already important leaders in Vietnam." Later, some would reestablish gangs in America.

"Outside the immigration building there was always a crowd of Amerasians," says Nan, "and every day lots of Vietnamese would come and try to be nice to them. They would give the Amerasians gold, or give gold to a middleman to be introduced, and very often the middleman would keep most of the money. People would pay to take photos of themselves with the Amerasians, and then do fake papers. Most of the Amerasians were so poor they didn't know anything, they didn't even know they were getting cheated. Many had never seen gold before, and when some Vietnamese person took them for a good meal or bought them clothes, they'd never had anything like that or had anyone be nice to them before, so they would go home with them. A lot of Amerasians

even were kidnapped to rural villages far away, until time for the interviews. Many were so poor, and so not knowing anything, that they just
did whatever they were told. Sometimes a Vietnamese would claim to
be a long-lost relative of an Amerasian, and the Amerasian would actually believe they were a real family member. But other Amerasians
made money off fake families, going for exit interviews with several and
then canceling out or admitting in the interview that they weren't really
relatives. Then the fake family would be turned down, and lose its 'in-
vestment.'"

Sara Phuong and Miss Dao

Three times, Miss Dao says, the U.S. government sent papers to permit
her and some of her orphans to go to America, and three times the papers were "lost," or, she believes, torn up by Vietnamese officials wanting her to pay bribes she had no money to pay. "They wanted about
200,000 dong [$20 U.S.] for each paper," she says. An average Viet-
namese salary then was about $10 U.S. per month. "Because we had no
money to bribe local officials they never gave us the letters," says Sara.
Finally, taking sixteen-year-old Sara, who is clearly part African American, Miss Dao traveled to Ho Chi Minh City by overnight train. There
she made friends with an American official and also, she says, met with
Vietnamese officials "who knew I did good work" and helped arrange
matters "so that I did not have to do the bribery." A few months later
she was sent plane tickets for herself and four orphans. Like people at
orphanages throughout Vietnam she had divided up Amerasians with
other nuns and monks so several could go to America with an Amerasian and at the same time bring pure Vietnamese orphans as the Amerasians' "orphanage brothers and sisters." Miss Dao brought two half-
black Amerasians: Sara and Sara's orphanage sister two years younger,
who had been sent a few years earlier to another orphanage, and two
Vietnamese orphans, including twelve-year-old Vinh, left at the orphanage gate years earlier, wrapped in a little torn shirt and with an infected
umbilical cord.

Before leaving Vietnam, Miss Dao arranged the marriage of My
Duyen, the first orphan she adopted when she had taken her as a baby
from the arms of her dead mother after a bombing. "My Duyen fell in
love and wanted to stay," says Miss Dao. Another last-minute wedding
was the false marriage of Sara to the son of a family close to the temple.

Because under U.S. law at that time Amerasians could bring only one family set, the plan was for Sara to sponsor the son to come to America after she arrived. "Our temple had no money, but sometimes got donations from that one rich Vietnamese family," Sara explains. "Also, we borrowed money from them for such things as going to Saigon for interviews. Then this family said if I would marry their son, we would not owe them anything, and I could later bring their whole family to America. I didn't want to marry him—there was no chemistry or inner connection—but he was nice enough, so we were legally married, but without a wedding. We never lived together." Her attempt to live up to the agreement to bring the son to America would later cause a serious problem for everyone involved, including Miss Dao.

Although she had no hope of finding her American father, Sara often thought of him. "In my mind," says Sara, "I imagine my father as a black man, because I am half-black. I sometimes wondered why he didn't stay with my mother. If he had to go back to America, did he ever ask my mother to go with him? If my mother couldn't go, did he want to take me, his daughter, with him? Maybe he did ask my mother but she couldn't go because her parents still lived in Vietnam. My nun Miss Dao is very kind. She has always loved me and treated me just like I was her own child. However, my real mother must have loved me too. That's why she brought me to the temple instead of throwing me into a trash can, or leaving me on a street corner like some other people did with their children." Sara believed her new life in America would be very happy.

Alan "Tiger" Hoa

Tiger's family not only had to compete with outsiders who wanted to go with him to America; they competed among themselves. "My Uncle Binh promised if I would take him, he would never beat me again," says Tiger, "and he would take me shopping for new clothes, and help me find my dad. My Uncle Khue promised if I took *him*, he would buy me new clothes and a motorcycle once we got to the United States." Other relatives, like Uncle Lam, weighed in with reasons why *they* should be the ones to go. Tiger's family admits that "there was a lot of screaming around here [among us] for a time," although they tend to laugh now at that memory.

"But one time when they did not know I was listening," says Tiger, "they were all arguing about who would go. It started when my Uncle Lam told the family that *he* was the one who raised me, so *he* should be the one to go. Uncle Binh said he had partly raised me too. But Uncle Khue said: 'No, I am the oldest, I get to go. You all stay here and I'll send money home to take care of you.' Finally there was a big physical fight between my uncles. They had been drinking and they cussed and yelled and ranted and raved at each other. My aunt just sat watching and cried. I thought it was funny to see adults behave that way, but I went and hid at one of the neighbors. My uncles ended up fighting and were all bleeding—one had a bloody nose—and the neighbors had to come stop the fight. I heard my Uncle Khue finally say, 'I am the oldest in the family, and I am the one who has the right to go with him to America, so I am going.'

"No one else said a word after that. But three days before I left I saw sad faces around me because they were all jealous." As is usual in a Vietnamese neighborhood, everyone knew all of the family's business and never hesitated to express opinions and advice. Tiger recalls one elderly neighbor woman who tried to convince him to take his Uncle Lam, saying, "He has been the kindest to you. Don't you remember Khue's wife, your aunt, always beat you up? Don't you remember she doesn't like you and doesn't like Amerasians?" Tiger gave a typically Vietnamese neutral reply, saying that the paperwork was already completed. "But," he adds, "I didn't think Khue's wife would yell at me anymore, because when I got to America I would make a beautiful life and go to school and be good."

Khue says Lam's poor eyesight would have made it impossible for him to handle the difficult responsibility of supporting a family in the United States while constantly sending money back to Vietnam, and this is surely true. Nowadays, too, the family insists that *they* chose Khue to go because he already had children, and they were thinking of those children's future. In any case, work began on papers for Tiger to go with Khue. Tiger's family says all of them chipped in money over time to pay for the papers. Tiger says *he* had the money. Maybe it came from Nga. Then, when he was eighteen, Tiger was jailed again, and again he gives various vague reasons for why. He actually may not know. Possibly he was arrested in Vietnam's 1990 crackdown on "undesirables," during a period the government arrested and jailed many street people. But finally Tiger's papers were approved. This time being half-black was lucky for him, because black Amerasians were approved more quickly.

While Tiger was waiting to go to America, he was living a mixed existence of gang life in Dam Sen Park and occasional good times when he was being courted by some Vietnamese person, and sometimes staying with Nga. But he had decided to take his own family instead, and kept this secret from her as the time to leave drew closer. It is clear that Tiger feels some guilt about the way he treated Nga. "She was always very nice and loving to me," he says. When he finally told her he would not take her with him to America, they quarreled and Nga cried. "I told her I couldn't go with her because I had my family and was going with them. I apologized. I asked her, 'Why did you be so nice to me? Why didn't you treat me nicely before, when I was just like dirt? Where were you in the years when I needed you, when nobody really cared about me, until I got papers to go to the U.S. and all of a sudden everybody knowed where I live, and wanted to take care of me?'" Recalling how he had lived in the streets when he was eleven, he says he told Nga, "'I saw you almost every day and you never said "Hi" to me until I got papers to go to the U.S. Then you suddenly got friendly and concerned!'"

But in reality, Tiger finally admitted to me, this is a conversation with Nga that he had in his own mind, after he left Vietnam without her. In fact he never told her he was leaving. His family had long since taken her name off his exit papers. Tiger either returned her motorcycle to her or sold it and gave part of the money to a girlfriend, depending on which account he gives. When a "homie" of Tiger's told Nga that Tiger would be leaving in a few days, "She came looking for me," says Tiger. "I had to hide." Nonetheless, years later he regrets the way he left her. He had promised himself that once in America, when he was rich, he would send her money. But he never did.

As the date to depart drew closer, Tiger's family continued to be anxious. They seldom saw him, and according to Khue, Tiger had become so sought-after and had made so many promises to so many people that his family feared Tiger would leave his relatives behind at the last minute. "We had to beg him to stay around home, afraid he would just disappear or go with a girlfriend," says Khue. "Many times we were worried he wouldn't come back home. One Friday was the day we were to go for an exit interview with the Americans, and on Thursday Tiger was missing and we had no idea if he would show up in time. But he did. Tiger promised every girl he met he would take her to America. He has a really sweet tongue—he can melt anyone's heart." Tiger himself tells how he fell in love with a prostitute, Thom, promising to take her to America. "I saw Thom in a bar and said, 'You want to go to the U.S.

with me? Don't worry, if you get a baby with me I will take you both.'
But her papers weren't approved." Actually, her papers were probably
never submitted. In any case, Tiger left without her.

The night before they were to leave for America Tiger's family held
a good-bye party for him, "so Tiger *had* to be home. I was really nervous
and panicked a lot of the time that Tiger just might not come back,"
says Khue, "and worried that all the other people who tried to exploit
him and kept giving him money would persuade him to take *them*, because he was getting used to that, and we, his family, had no money to
give. In fact, when we left Vietnam I was really poor, and all I had to
take was salt and clothing. Unlike many of the other families, we had
no gold, no nothing." Tiger's entire family and some neighbors, more
than thirty-five people, went to see him and his Uncle Khue off at the
airport—envious, sad, but thrilled at the wonderful new life awaiting
them. And family members expected that once Khue and Tiger reached
the land of wealth and ease they would send back money to help them,
too.

Louis Nguyen

As more and more city Amerasians arranged to leave Vietnam, Amerasians in rural areas were becoming a hot commodity. The AHA required police stations throughout Vietnam to post a notice that
Amerasians could apply to leave, but for a long time many Amerasians
hesitated, fearing a police ruse. Soon Vietnamese "prospectors" for Amerasians began searching the more remote villages, and Vietnamese
families who often had a "beautiful daughter" to offer as a potential
bride for an Amerasian had begun to show up on Louis Nguyen's family
doorstep. After all, his mother had not just one but two Amerasian sons
who might be a ticket out of Vietnam for some lucky phony family. "All
the fake families were educated and wealthy," says Louis. "And all the
Amerasians were poor and on a low level. Most hadn't gone to school.
Their mothers didn't have money to pay for it. And at school they got
hit and teased every single day, so often they just quit. At least 70 percent of Amerasians can't read or write a word, even in Vietnamese.
Since most Amerasians had no education or knowledge about nothing,
and no chance for a future, when they'd hear about marrying a beautiful
rich girl it was like heaven. And the fake family often promised to give
them a motorcycle and other things."

As early as 1983, Louis and his family had applied to go to the United States, but years had passed as procedures and laws kept changing, and still they had not been approved. "We did not have money for bribes or processing fees," says Louis. As other Amerasians left after two or three years of waiting, Vietnamese officials kept moving Louis's application to the bottom of the stack. "They would wait until the last minute and then say you had to pay a bribe. The cost depended on how rich you were, and my family didn't have nothing. We were much too poor to pay the blackmail," says Louis. One day after the 1988 Amerasian Homecoming Act went into effect, a friend of sixteen-year-old Louis invited him to dinner. "His rich cousin who wanted to go to the U.S. was waiting to meet me, along with his wife and their beautiful daughter. After we all ate and talked, and the daughter was very nice to me, they said if I would go with them they would give my mom 3,000 U.S. dollars. I talk very nice to them, but say, 'No, sorry, my family don't want this.'

"A month later they invited me to a party at their house in her hometown, a six-hour bus trip away. The family paid for my ticket. They were very rich, with a beautiful house and lots of food. Again they treat me very nice, and again ask me to go to the U.S. with the daughter. But I said I didn't want to separate from my family, so they said if I went with them they would pay my way back to visit." Louis was tempted. "This girl was beautiful," he says. "But she didn't love me and I didn't love her. So still I said no." As years went by Louis kept passing up such chances.

Part of the problem was Louis's stubborn adherence to his own inner values. "In Vietnam, the fake family always treated the Amerasians very nice," says Louis. "The girl would also act loving. At that time you could only go with your wife or your parents, brothers, and sisters. Sometimes I did think about going with one of those families. My mom asked me did I want to go, but I said 'No.' My mother and grandmother and me talked, and we had the opinion, the worry, that if we did not go together we might get lost from each other. And our family love and trust each other. And besides, before this the Vietnamese people had treated me very bad, and suddenly they were turning around and treating me very nice. I didn't want to give them the chance to—to use me like that. Of course. Because of my pride, I didn't want to sell myself for money."

Louis, although half-black, must have seemed a prize because of his good reputation and good education. Striving as usual to give an honest and balanced picture, Louis says it was sometimes the "adopted"

Amerasians who acted badly. "Some would live with a fake family that would give them a car and treat them great while waiting to go to the U.S.," he says. "One Amerasian I know lived a year with a rich family, got 3,000 U.S. dollars and then said, 'If you don't let me [sleep] with your daughter too, I will go to another family.' And they let him, until they got to the U.S. Then they kicked him out. The fake families were wealthy in Vietnam, but they weren't allowed to bring money to the U.S. and had to start over again. So once they got here, they kicked the Amerasian out." No doubt most fake families had expected the Amerasians to find a rich and happy life in America, and hadn't bargained on having to continue to feed and shelter them.

As years passed, Louis sang at more and more social, political, and patriotic events, where he came to know various government officials who, he says, told those in charge of his application that his family truly had no hidden source of money. Louis's beloved grandmother, entering her nineties, realized that because of her age and poor health that she would never be able to pass the exit process, and not wanting to hurt Louis's chances she withdrew her name. Louis's married brother, fourteen years older than him and the son of a Vietnamese man who had divorced Louis's mother years earlier, would stay in Vietnam and take care of her. Finally, in 1991 Louis, his brother, and his mother were allowed to leave. While waiting for interviews for several months in Ho Chi Minh City, Louis stayed with a friend. He took singing lessons and occasionally sang at weddings and small clubs. Because so many Amerasians found ways to leave sooner for America, through bribes, false marriages, and so forth, I pressed Louis to tell me if he too had not used some similar tactic. "No, I never gave the government or anyone money or took any money to go," he said. "And it took nine years before I could finally leave. Sometimes officials would say, 'If you want your file to go to the top, pay!' But I never had the money. Listen! If I had been able to pay money, would I have waited so long? No, of course! In the end, I think officials just said, 'These people on the bottom of the stack really *don't* have money, if we keep waiting for it they will stay here forever. Let them go!'" He grows exasperated with me. "Listen," he says, "if I had had money, I would already have given it. Of course!"

Whereas Tiger didn't want to stay at the transit center because it was too regulated, Louis didn't want to stay there because "there was too much fighting and stuff there, and also the center wasn't close to the middle of the city where I needed to be for my singing career." When he went to interviews, he says, "Outside would be maybe 500 to 1,000

Amerasians. Some would be there all day, every day, watching people come and go. They had no money, they had nothing, and they looked very scary. You hid any money you had when you passed through that crowd to go to your interview, and some Amerasians in the crowd would come up afterwards and ask you a lot of questions, like what you'd been asked inside. Me and my family were interviewed four or five times, first with my brother, but then he separated from us to come later with his wife. People going to interviews were scared when they came with a fake family, but my family was real, and so was only scared some Vietnamese officials would ask us for money and we never had any. The U.S. people never asked for money. And, of course, the Vietnamese never *ask* for money—you *offer* it. They would give you some sign, like say, 'Your paperwork is very behind, and I can talk to a friend who can help move up your papers, and see what he would charge, and meet you later and tell you.' But I would just say, 'We have no money.'

"There was always lots of drama at the interview building. Outside I saw people come out crying after they were turned down. Sometimes a guy would pick his wife to go to America with him and his mom would be crying, sometimes he'd pick the mom and the wife would be crying. So I didn't hang around the center. I don't allow people to look down on me, so I don't hang around Amerasians who 'do stupid things.' Some of them would come up to me and say, 'Come with us, and if someone hits you we won't let them, we will hit them back.' And I would say, 'I won't do anything to make anyone hit me, so no one will hit me.' People who don't be nice to me, I get away from them. I don't get upset if they're mean when they don't know me. I only get upset with people who know me, good friends who 'do stupid things' to me. In my life I don't have much friends, but I have some good friends."

Louis remembers his joyous expectations on the day he was finally approved to leave for America. "We were very happy," he says. "I was nineteen. That night we all cooked food and ate, had fun, everyone together. During those months before, I was thinking that going to the U.S. would be going to paradise. I would meet my father, be given a house and car, everything! Everybody talked about their American fathers all the time. They honestly expected they would get help with money when they first got to America, and that their dads would buy them a car or a house. That's what everyone told us. That's what everyone said."

Some Amerasians first began making attempts to find their American fathers when applying for emigration. The U.S. government, saying it sought to "protect the privacy" of American fathers, prevented access to simple records that would have helped thousands more Amerasians locate their dads. But many Amerasians knew nothing about their fathers—not even their names. In fact, because most Amerasians had so little information about their fathers, the majority never sought to find them. Yet almost all created a story in their imaginations about their lost parents.

During this same period, the Vietnam War had continued to take a heavy toll on U.S. veterans. A *Geographical Magazine* article in July 1989, saying that "coping with defeat in an unpopular war has been left to those directly involved," reported that an estimated 60,000 U.S. Vietnam veterans had committed suicide since the war, more than the total of GIs who died in action.

Various U.S. religious, government, and aid groups geared up to handle the new group of immigrants. By late 1988 the Amerasians and those with them had begun to trickle into the Philippines processing center where all Vietnamese on their way to the United States were required to first spend six months studying American culture and English in the 300 classrooms used by all camp refugees. Most Amerasians were so-called free cases—emigrants without U.S. sponsors to help them make the transition to America, until ones could be found for them through churches and other sources. An updated Catholic Conference study of the Amerasians published that year compared them to other Vietnamese immigrants, saying that more than half needed extra counseling and support, a third needed more medical care, and that "developmentally, many are children, immature, inadequately socialized, and often suffering from poor schooling, poor self-image and confused personal and sexual identity. . . . [They] seem more vulnerable than other refugees, but [are] not being treated any differently by the State Department."

As with so many things the United States did with Vietnam, intentions may have been good but the performance was a tragic mess. Very few people in the U.S. governmental, church, and nonprofit agencies had a true understanding of the enormity of the problems of this new group of immigrants. No one had foreseen the massive fraud that would be involved, nor completely realized how inadequate were the resources available to deal with the tremendous complexity of this undertaking. Although no one knows how many Amerasians came with fake relatives, often leaving their real family members, including their own children, behind, most believe it was more than half, and some estimate the number as high as 80 percent.

In March 1990, with the Homecoming Act due to expire, the U.S. government noted that Amerasians and "relatives" leaving Vietnam had jumped from 400 per year to 10,000 per year, and extended the act until March 1991. The law also was changed so that Amerasians could come with both "sets" of relatives—parents and siblings as well as spouses and children. This eliminated the tragic dramas of Amerasians forced to choose. Again numbers surged, and in 1991 the act was extended again.

Approximately 30,000 Amerasians, accompanied by about 80,000 "relatives," would eventually enter the United States in the program's first five years, joined later by others. But no houses or cars would be waiting for them.

6

Following Their American Dream,
1988–93

Unfortunately, the Amerasians still in Vietnam have fewer mental, social and financial resources than those who have already come [to the United States]. . . . Meanwhile, fake Amerasians and [their] fake family members break U.S. immigration laws and consume some of the resources and privileges which are not properly theirs.

    —U.S. General Accounting Office, November 1992
    report on the Amerasian Homecoming Act,
    commenting on massive fraud by Vietnamese claiming
    to be relatives of Amerasians and paying bribes and
    expenses in order to accompany them to the United
    States

Miss Dao's nephew Anton, a young Vietnamese man who had come alone to the Philippines Refugee Processing Center (PRPC) months earlier as a boat refugee when he was eighteen, was walking along the road to his billet when just ahead of him he saw two familiar figures—his aunt, with Sara at her side, surrounded by several Amerasians who seemed to be talking with them both. "I didn't realize Sara and my aunt had even left Vietnam," he says. "I was so happy to see them that I shouted and ran up to them." Miss Dao had not told her family she was leaving because some of her relatives had objected to her devotion to the orphans, feeling they created too many problems and burdens.

"Sara was sixteen then, and just like a little kid, immature, always sticking by my aunt wherever she went," says Anton. "A lot of guys would chase after her because she was beautiful and sweet, but she would say 'No.' I think Sara loved the Philippines because even though we didn't have enough food to eat we all loved each other then. All my aunt's life she would take in any kids from the street to raise, and never sell them like some nuns did. Many nuns didn't want a black kid, or one who was handicapped, but to my aunt all people are the same. Like the day I first saw my aunt, there were always a lot of Amerasians hanging around her lodgings. They would be around her wherever she went, maybe twenty to thirty at the same time, and she would chat and laugh with them."

Miss Dao says that although she herself raised only eleven Amerasian children, in the Philippines there were hundreds of them in the processing center, many lonely and alienated from the people they had come with. Her acceptance of them drew them to her. "The Amerasians in the Philippines all really loved me and called me 'teacher,' she says. In Vietnam, teachers are considered second parents and are given the same respect. "Many Amerasians began to come to me because I tried to spread my love and attention to all of them and help them as much as I could—teaching them to sew, to make crafts, and to sell things," she says. "Amerasian kids, especially the black ones, were so often abandoned by their parents and they always feel embarrassed about themselves. I felt their loneliness because they had no families. A few people were kind and generous enough to help them, but only to a certain degree. Mostly they were left alone with no one to take care of them or have concern for them."

The U.S. Overseas Departure Program interviewers had begun interviewing Amerasians and "family members" during monthly trips to Ho Chi Minh City beginning in October 1987, and by early 1988 those who had been approved began arriving in the Philippines Refugee Processing Center. They were provided food, basic housing, and some medical treatment, and were required to attend classes and do two hours of unpaid community service work per day. The camp setting changed only slightly over the next few years. In October 1989 it was staffed by 2,100 Filipinos (almost all the teachers of ESL and American culture were Filipino, some with heavy accents) and 200 Americans, mostly supervisors and counselors.

The UN High Commissioner for Refugees (UNHCR) paid the center's operating costs, including housing, food through the World Food Progam, maintenance, sanitation, electricity, medical facilities, and administrative costs. The United States funded training for all the refugees going to America. Smaller groups were sent to France, Australia, or Canada. The State Department estimated that the per-refugee costs at PRPC in the early years were $527 for training and $100 for care and maintenance (the $100 was the U.S. donation to the UNHCR, and comprised about 30 percent of the UNHCR costs) and that Amerasians and other camp refugees received 500 hours of instruction costing 94 cents for each classroom hour. The per-capita cost to the UNHCR for the PRPC was about $333 per refugee per year, not counting the cost of staple foods from the UN's World Food Program.

The Amerasians and those accompanying them were only one of the refugee groups at PRPC. Other Vietnamese refugees included former political prisoners coming under the Humanitarian Operation program (some Vietnamese thought the program's initials, H.O., stood for "High Officials" since many in this group were former Vietnamese government officials and military who had worked with Americans during the war); boat refugees; and relatives of Vietnamese already in America who were sponsoring them under family reunification programs.

Many of these other Vietnamese continued to deride and harass the Amerasians and their mothers as they had in Vietnam. When Miss Dao attended the center's mandatory English class, Sara and other Amerasians would meet her afterward and walk back to her billet with her. Miss Dao was not recognized as a nun, because when she left Vietnam she had decided to give up her nun's saffron wrappings and shaven head, while still keeping her vows, a common practice of older religious Buddhist women. "I thought that way I would be better able to find work in the United States to support me and my orphan children," she says. But in the center, some Vietnamese would stare angrily at her and the Amerasians who surrounded her. "Who are all these Amerasians?" they would ask. And Miss Dao would answer, "These are my children." Then, she says, "Sometimes they would call me names, whore and prostitute, so I understand how it feels to have prejudice against you. I know how the mothers of Amerasians feel."

The voluntary agencies working at the center included the Catholics, the Baptist World Alliance, the Church of Latter-Day Saints (Mormons), Seventh-Day Adventists, and World Vision. They provided extra programs like classes in typing, auto repair, and carpentry and offered aid to the handicapped and elderly and some supplemental feeding programs. There were a few art, music, and computer classes, and some American religious groups offered dances, talent shows, drama and singing clubs, and sports tournaments, as well as religious services.

Several Buddhist temples staffed by monks had been built in the compound. Counseling programs run by the United States and various agencies operated in the camps, and were soon dealing daily with the many conflicts between the Amerasians and their fake relatives and spouses, as well as with the usual counseling situations. One report said as many as 20 percent of the Amerasians in the camp needed to be referred for psychological counseling.

Anton, who was able to speak some English, was hired to interpret not long after he arrived. Less than 5 percent of the Amerasians arrived in the center unaccompanied—in the early days they brought an average of three "family members," a number that later jumped much higher. Almost all the Amerasians were "free cases" without U.S. sponsors, so sponsors had to be found for them, mostly through the religious and voluntary agencies, or "volags." Each Amerasian had to promise to repay the volags the one-way airfare to America for themselves and each person accompanying them, although they could defer payment a few months until they were resettled in America. The volags charged wildly different fare prices, between $500 and $1,000 per person.

The center's rules were strict—for example, no one was allowed to change living quarters, a constant source of friction because many Amerasians were with fake relatives, or with true relatives who may never have raised them but who, like Nan's mother, appeared after years of absence to use them to go to America. There was a 9:30 P.M. curfew, although it was not well observed. People with tuberculosis and other serious conditions were held for treatment, some for much longer than six months. Fighting and drinking were common. The camp jail was often crowded, and those who committed serious offenses lost their chance to continue on to America—as did any relatives, real or false, who were accompanying them. When an Amerasian was placed on administrative or medical hold, or was sent to a Philippines jail for five years, his or her entire accompanying group was blocked from coming to the United States. Around the time Son Chau arrived in late 1989 there were fifteen to twenty Amerasians in prison, affecting about 118 Amerasians and family members.

The Amerasian Homecoming Act had not been in effect long before problems and complaints were being reported. The Vietnam Veterans of America Foundation in August 1989 called the conditions at PRPC "atrocious" with insufficient food and water, overcrowding, and "daily lives regulated by coercion and fear" by camp guards and some camp residents. The group recommended that the United States lift its refugee ceiling for Amerasians, interview all quickly, and explore departure alternatives, bypassing the camps and bringing Amerasians directly to U.S. resettlement sites. An October 1989 staff report for Congressman Tom Ridge was prepared to investigate complaints. Generally straightforward yet giving a positive spin, it said shelter in the camp was "quite acceptable by local Filipino and Vietnamese standards"; that the Filipino accents of the ESL teachers were not a major problem as some insisted; and that "there [were] opportunities to learn lessons in democracy, capitalism, leadership, and citizenship."

The food situation in the camps, conceded the report, was more problematic. There had been a "major refugee disturbance" and several petitions over the food quantity, quality, and speed of distribution. Refugees complained there wasn't enough food and there was a suspicion that some was being stolen by corrupt staff. All refugees were to get a family allocation of food from the UN's World Food Program, which was using a basic measure of 2,200 calories per day for each adult. It was not enough for male adolescents, especially some of the Amerasians who were much larger than their Vietnamese peers. In addition some families distributed food unevenly, i.e., some fake families gave less to the Amerasians.

Nan says that in the Philippines the nun who had tricked her dropped any pretense of kindness. "She divided the food unfairly," says Nan, "so Joan and I were always hungry. And she made us eat in the corner away from her own eight orphans. Joan and I both hated that nun. Joan is very hardheaded and she was very young then, so she said things to the nun that were disrespectful, and the nun and all her orphans hated Joan. As for myself, I was a little older and just gave my opinions, but I knew the nun was very cruel."

Some refugees received money from U.S. relatives or friends to supplement their rations, while others tried to grow small gardens or sold clothing or other items for extra money. (Tiger's uncle Khue brought salt to sell.) Still others stole or simply went hungry. At one point a major scandal was uncovered—a Vietnamese Catholic nun had stolen thousands of dollars from letters sent from the United States to the refugees, and had embezzled thousands more designated for camp support. Anton says he once "fought with her face-to-face" when there was not enough food in the camp and he saw her opening letters to refugees and taking out the money.

Gangs also operated in the camps, and Filipino criminals came from outside to prey on the weaker refugees, forcing the Philippine govern-

The Amerasian Tiger Hoa, age two, with his one-year-old pure Vietnamese half-sister. Photo taken in 1974, a year before the death of their mother. *Courtesy of Tiger Hoa's family.*

Joseph Love, the American veteran who developed special techniques and contacts to help track down the U.S. fathers of Amerasians. *Courtesy of Joe Love.*

The famous Buddhist nun Su Huynh Lien, (of whom Miss Dao was a follower) sometimes called the Martin Luther King of Vietnam. She was beaten and jailed during Buddhist demonstrations against the Diem regime. *Courtesy of Chi Lien.*

A group of Buddhist nuns belonging to the Minh-Dang Quang order walks to the opening of a temple in Hue in 1963. The nun Chi Lien (Miss Dao) is in the far rear. Nuns of her order walked barefoot and were allowed to eat only once a day, and then only vegetarian food donated to them during their daily walk to the market. A nurse accompanies the group.

The Amerasian Sara, eight months old, at her Buddhist orphanage in Qui Nhon, 1971. She is crying because she didn't want her picture taken. The photographer was an English or German man who offered to buy Sara for 500,000 dong, a very large sum at the time. Sara's nun Chi Lien (Miss Dao) refused. *Courtesy of Sara Phuong.*

Son Chau, left, with his mother Du, his Amerasian half-sister Linh, and a younger pure Vietnamese brother who died soon afterward. Taken about 1973 in front of the village center in Song Pha. Note the U.S. flag and the sign, which reads in Vietnamese: "Chong Cong," or "Against Communists." *Courtesy of Son Chau's family.*

Son's American father, then about twenty, helps build a small store for Son's mother Du, about 1967. *Courtesy of Son Chau's family.*

Tiger's mother at age seventeen, two years before Tiger was born, with her younger sister, about 1970. *Courtesy of Tiger Hoa's family.*

The Amerasian orphan Nan, about seven, front row third from left, praying at her Buddhist orphanage in Vietnam about 1977. Note the large number of Amerasians at the orphanage. *Courtesy of Nan Bui.*

Louis Nguyen as a teenager with his younger Amerasian half-brother, Lam, near their home near Song Be, about 1984. *Courtesy of Louis Nguyen's family.*

Tiger, right, standing near his family's altar at a funeral, about 1985. *Courtesy of Tiger Hoa's family.*

Son Chau, third from left, top row, with two teams of frankincense hunters in February 1985 at Nhi Ja village in Ninh Thuan province. Son's Aunt #9, leader of the village women, is pictured at left. Because the hunting trips were illegal, this is Son's only photo of the hunters. *Courtesy of Son Chau.*

A group of Amerasians at St. Anselm's Cross-Cultural Community Center in Little Saigon near Los Angeles, about 1992, soon after their arrival in the United States. *Courtesy of Steve Baker.*

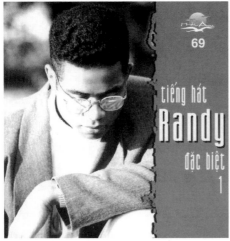

CD cover bearing a photo of the Vietnamese Amerasian singer Randy Tuan Tran, 2002. *Courtesy of Randy Tuan Tran.*

Louis Nguyen at his graduation from California State University, Fullerton. *Courtesy of Louis Nguyen's family.*

Son Chau and his Amerasian half-sister Linh, each holding their sons as they visit with Santa Claus in a store near Chicago in 1999. *Courtesy of Son Chau.*

Louis Nguyen in a photo used in a poster of himself under his stage name, Luu Quoc Viet, taken in Little Saigon in 2003. Note the extension braids, symbol of the African American half of his heritage. *Photo by Huy Khiem.*

Sara and her husband at their wedding reception in 1999 in Little Saigon. *Courtesy of Sara Phuong.*

Miss Dao, center, on a visit back to her orphanage in Qui Nhon, holding a donation. At far left, holding a baby, is My Duyen, whom Miss Dao rescued as a three-month-old orphan from her mother's arms after the mother was killed in an attack on a bomb shelter during the war. *Photo by Anthony Huynh.*

Son's Amerasian cousin Hung, about age thirty-two, standing before a Cham temple near Thap Cham in 2000. At the time he was waiting to see if his application to go to the United States would be accepted. *Photo by Anthony Huynh.*

ment to add local security personnel. Tiger remembers a mother in the Philippines camps with one Amerasian child and two Vietnamese children. "Some bad Filipinos beat them up and they lost all their papers, so they didn't have a chance to go to the U.S. and they couldn't go back to Vietnam," he says. "One night they all took poison in their dinner and killed themselves together." Serious criminal violations were handled by the Philippine government. "In the Philippines, Joan was raped by a Vietnamese man, and the rapist was sent to the camp jail," says Nan. "He would have been sent back to Vietnam if they prosecuted him, so we said 'No,' and he was sent on to America after we arrived. Also in the Philippines the evil nun tried to separate us, and Joan took some pills and tried to commit suicide. That day we were all supposed to meet and pray at the temple, and when Joan did not come, I ran back and found her. We tried to choke out the pills, tried to burn her numb feet to wake her, but we could not. The Philippines ambulance had to come. After that there was a camp counselor who gave Joan love and food and helped us stay together and away from the nun and her group."

Others were still suffering. Due to a surge of refugees throughout the world in 1989, that year the UNHCR was planning to stretch its resources through various budget cuts. It was considering reducing the food ration from 2,200 calories per person per day to 2,100, and cutting back protein. The report for Congressman Ridge noted that with more than 90 percent of the PRPC refugees scheduled to go to the United States, critics were suggesting that the United States earmark part of its UNHCR donation for the center. But some State Department officials argued that PRPC was "already better equipped than any other refugee camp in the world," and channeling all U.S. funds there would hurt poor children and families elsewhere. The UNHCR had contended that calling PRPC a UN camp was "an illusion perpetuated by the U.S.," and, said the report, earmarking funds to keep refugees "at a U.S. living standard rather than a life-sustaining standard" would only prove it. True, the United States had agreed to take in all the Amerasians and their "relatives," as well as most other Vietnamese refugees—but then, too, the United States had created them.

By far the most serious situation affecting the AHA program continued to be the seemingly endless fraud. Some interpreters in Ho Chi Minh City, supplied to U.S. Overseas Departure Program interviewers by the Vietnamese government, were accepting bribes to coach people ahead of time, move their files ahead, and translate their interview answers more favorably. Some interviewers were rejecting as many as 90 percent of the cases they interviewed, while others were rejecting far fewer. Sometimes Amerasians would be passed and fake relatives rejected. But the rejection rate as a whole had increased to 80 percent from 20 percent the previous year, partly because more and more applicants appeared questionable. For example, Steven DeBonis, in his book *Children of the Enemy*, reported that forty different Vietnamese who met with U.S. immigration interviewers in Ho Chi Minh City within a single week all blamed any lack of documents on having lost them in a well-publicized bus crash that happened a few days earlier.

Once reaching the Philippines, Amerasians often were reluctant to report fake families, fearing that they themselves might have to stay longer in the camp or that their real families in Vietnam might be hurt in some way. The Vietnamese government had agreed "in principle" to take back fake families, and U.S. visas had been revoked for fraud in some cases, but because there was no process for sending them back, they had become indefinite residents of the camp. Most, however, had gone on with their Amerasians to the United States, where disputes with fake relatives and evictions of the young Amerasians were already causing unanticipated problems for resettlement workers. The high number of pregnancies in the camps—one U.S. official estimated that one-third of female Amerasians became pregnant during their six-month camp residence—was another problem, and the rate remained high after the Amerasians arrived in the United States. In addition to the usual sexual and romantic attractions between lonely young people, and a lack of birth-control information, causes included overcrowding, a shortage of food leading to prostitution, and outright rape. Although Anton believes the Amerasians were unaware of it, one result was that each child born after an Amerasian reached America automatically became a U.S. citizen and eligible for such benefits as long-term Aid to Families with Dependent Children.

In November 1990 the law was changed to end the requirement that an Amerasian applicant choose to bring either his or her spouse and children or mother and siblings. Married Amerasians could now bring both sets, thus ending the many tearful dramas played out at the interview site as Amerasians were forced to choose one or the other. The Vietnamese cultural value of filial piety had played a powerful role in cases where Amerasians had decided to take their mothers rather than spouses or lifelong caretakers, "even if some of the Amerasians had never been raised or loved by the birth mother," writes Thanh Son Thi

Nguyen in her 1995 University of Pittsburgh dissertation, "Adjustment and Acculturation Problems of Vietnamese Amerasians in Pittsburgh: A Post-Resettlement Study." This situation arose when mothers like Nan's, who had given up the child years earlier, and whom the child hardly knew, turned up to reclaim him or her, "forcing the Amerasians to leave behind the people who had cared for them and with whom they had developed real love bonds." With the change in the law, individuals previously excluded could now be reconsidered. Stating that "ODP is aware that some Amerasians may have misrepresented their marital status at the time of ODP interviews, leaving spouses and even children in Vietnam so other family members could accompany them," the United States promised to take action on such cases brought to its attention. Anticipating a new spate of fraud, it stipulated that only cases where ODP already had a record of a marriage were eligible. Those who had claimed at their interviews to be single were not included.

"A lot of people in the Philippines were very unhappy," Anton says. "Most of the mothers had been prostitutes or bar girls, a lot of them teenagers who didn't know anything at all about birth control. They hung around with Americans to have money, and when the man left, the moms would give the kid away because they were in big trouble. Some just wanted to have fun, others needed to keep working to support themselves or their families and couldn't keep their kids with them. So some real birth mothers of Amerasians who turned up years later and got back with their Amerasian children to come with them weren't the persons who actually raised them." He estimates that 60 percent of the Amerasians came with fake families, and that a lot of their birth mothers had "showed up" when the child was grown and able to go to the United States. Another camp staffer estimated that 80 percent of the Amerasians were with false families. "Both the Amerasians and fake relatives would come in constantly with complaints against each other," says Anton, who interpreted for counselors as well as officials. "That happened a lot, almost every single day, and during the eight months I was there I handled about 2,000 cases of problems between the Amerasians and those accompanying them. Sometimes the family was bad and the Amerasian was good, but sometimes the Amerasian was the bad one. We'd send people to ask camp neighbors the real facts. During that time, for some reason I wanted everyone to be able to go to America, so often I'd change things when I translated to make them sound better. Like if the fake dad hit the Amerasian, I'd say he just shouted. Of course, if the family did something really bad, I would strongly stop them from going."

By late 1991, mostly due to increased fraud, the approval rate for "relatives" accompanying Amerasians had dropped to 52 percent, although many Amerasians were being allowed to go to the Philippines without them. Once in PRPC the Amerasians could file an "Affidavit of Relationship" asking that relatives join them in America. But there were more and more no-shows at the scheduled exit interviews, possibly because more fake relatives feared being turned down and penalized and were less willing to "invest" in what was becoming a risky venture. This meant that fewer genuine Amerasians could leave, because they seldom had resources to do so without aid from fraudulent families. Despite these obstacles, because of the continuing high numbers of Amerasians seeking to leave Vietnam, in early 1991 the Amerasian Homecoming Act was extended again into 1992.

Louis, Tiger, Nan, and Son experienced more problems in the Philippines than Sara and Miss Dao. Son arrived in 1989 with his fake wife, and then told her he wanted his paperwork back. "I said, 'OK, you have to give me the papers, we need a divorce, we are not real and I not like you at all, and I didn't take any money from your family, so I don't owe you nothing." The girl refused, says Son, "and after two days only one time I'm a little violent. When she did not give me the paperwork I said, 'You been bothering me a lot.' I just slapped her twice and she cried. She turned me in to the police. They came but they knew something was wrong." Son was required to refile, and somehow the situation was worked out, and the two separated. "Now, that marriage is no more. We came to the U.S. interview again and made everything clear, that it was not a real marriage, and that when I come to America I wanted everything clean, and to look for the lady I really wanted to marry. And they let the girl come on to America too, because she'd been OK'd already. She lived with an aunt in the U.S."

In the Philippines Son persuaded a camp official to take his family's documents directly to the U.S. Embassy in Bangkok on their next regular trip there, and "after that my family's applications moved very fast." But Son discovered that the picture of his father in his uniform with his name tag, kept so carefully for so many years, had disappeared. He thinks it was stolen. The disappearance proved to be very serious, because neither Son nor his mother remembers his father's last name, and when Du tries to pronounce his first name it sounds like no American name anyone has heard. Over and over she repeats it for American listeners. It sounds as if she's saying "Hypret." Maybe that first syllable was added by Du because she always heard people greet the American sergeant with "Hi!" Or maybe not. The search for Son's father had become much more difficult.

The camps continued to be a place of misery for many of the weaker, more helpless refugees. Self-mutilations and suicides continued, along with heavy drinking and some drug use. Tiger knew more than one Amerasian who chopped off a finger there. Tattoos in both English and Vietnamese were common, saying "Life is unjust, Hatred everlasting," or "Prison will see me again." Some of the camp guards were brutal, known for hitting and kicking the refugees.

Louis was very poor in the Philippines, but attended ESL classes and studied diligently, avoiding the camp gangbangers. "I would write my grandmother, but sometimes I didn't even have enough money for a stamp. My grandmother could read and write, even write some in Chinese, and in her letters she said she had heard some Amerasians got in trouble in the Philippines. She would write, 'Just whatever else, be good, don't do stupid things.' I loved my grandmom very much and she loved me, of course, so whatever she say to me must be good, must be true. Also the same with my mom, she loved me. Sometime you feel lonely, you feel sad, but you know they love you. And I believed that when we got in America we would have money. Everyone thought that."

Some Amerasians had substance abuse problems, fought with one another, harassed their fake families, formed gangs, and occasionally committed more serious crimes. In the heat of the Philippine nights, Son sometimes slept outside. "The Amerasians who stayed next door were wild, and one of them hung out a lot with gangs," he says. "One Amerasian who came with a fake family wanted me to join his gang, but I had too much responsibility. One night there was a party there, and there was a fight, and I saw blood." The next day one of the Amerasians was missing. "Two weeks later some little boys found a big box [in a ditch], and the body of the Amerasian was inside, cut in three pieces." Louis, who spent seven months in the camps in 1990–91, remembers "one Amerasian guy who came with a fake family, a girl and her mom, and told people the girl had promised to marry him. As soon as the three of them got to the Philippines he said he wanted to sleep with the girl, or he would tell the authorities they were fake. That guy was sleeping with the girl and her mom both, and everyone knew. Those two would cry every day. Another Amerasian asked his fake family for money all the time, but they didn't have much. They gave some, they were scared not to; but that's some reasons a lot of Amerasians got kicked out when they got to the U.S. A lot of Amerasians did a lot of 'stupid things,' like tell the camp authorities, 'That's not my real family,' so the fake family would have to stay there forever, while the Amerasian could go on to the U.S."

"That happened a lot," says Anton. "The agencies would first have to find Amerasians like that a sponsor in the United States, since most knew no one in America at all." Most of the Vietnamese were homesick, some of them worrying about pitifully poor real family members left behind. They were anxious to get to America and find a job, any job, so they could send money back quickly. "In the Philippines," says Louis, "everyone was sad because they left their family and friends behind. And there was nothing to do. Every morning you'd go get the food to eat, then go back and wait for school. So many people were unhappy — young teenagers without their families, lonely, having left everything behind. Some drank a lot. And you know when people drink, they do stupid things. Some would get sent to the monkey house, the jail, and every time somebody went, their paperwork was delayed a month. So I stayed away from them. I didn't hang around with some of the Amerasians."

Among the refugees were killers and big-time gangsters from major Vietnamese criminal groups, and some of the crimes committed were serious. There were also gangs like the one Tiger belonged to, that "just wanted to deal drugs and get money from people — and if you said 'No' they might go to your billet and get it anyway," says Anton. An early camp directive was circulated, stating euphemistically that "the [camp] administration believes it is important to make refugees aware that the U.S. is a country of laws, and that communities must have rules. In Communist countries discipline is traditionally imposed by society, so individuals do not have to develop self-discipline. In the PRPC, as in the U.S., there is a new freedom. If behavior problems are not addressed in the PRPC, they certainly will be in the U.S., where the results could be far worse."

Some of Tiger's gang homies were in the camps at the same time as he was. It was tempting for Tiger to just hang around with them, get into fights, steal, and drink. He is one of few Amerasians who says good things about the Philippines. "It was much better than in Vietnam," says Tiger. Long before he had left for the Philippines, Tiger had very high hopes about how good his life would be in America. "I thought I would have money, a job, lead a good life, and find my American father," he recalls. "And in the Philippines I was really determined to learn to read and write. I wanted to study so I could get to America." But learning to read and write English was an almost impossible task for many Amerasians. Some had never even held a pencil. Having their ignorance displayed before a classroom was excruciating. In rural Vietnam and in city street gangs, literacy wasn't so important. The skills that counted were survival skills, and most Amerasians had mastered those well.

Tiger's Uncle Khue says Tiger did go to classes in the Philippines, and that "Tiger was careful there. I tried to make sure he wouldn't get in trouble. Whenever I had extra food I would sell it to the Filipinos around the camp, and give Tiger money every day so he wouldn't be tempted to steal. Also, I had my twelve-year-old son follow Tiger wherever he went, to watch him and warn him not to get into trouble, and to stop him if he tried. Tiger did hang around with his friends. But he came home to eat, and he did go to school. He had some fights but never got arrested. Because what if he got put in jail, and they wouldn't let him go to America? And then, too, what would happen to the rest of us accompanying him, if he couldn't go?" But Tiger did get into trouble. Although he won't give details, he says a rumor went around that some Vietnamese women had been raped and beaten by some Filipinos, so he and some friends went out and hunted them down and beat them up. "Not necessarily the ones who did those things—just any Filipinos," he explains. The mysterious Raymond whom Tiger had known in Dam Sen Park was the only person Tiger knew in the camps who could speak English, and he seems to have also been involved in this incident. "But Raymond didn't speak up when the police arrested people [indiscriminately]," Tiger says, apparently still miffed, "and the police wouldn't listen. So we decided to burn down the Filipino market place. We used gasoline. It was easy." The group of vendors' stalls outside the camp was indeed burned and looted while Tiger was in the camp, although no one was seriously hurt. Anton lived next to the market, and looked out his window that night and saw the flames. He ran to his office and called UNHCR officials, but much of the market was destroyed. "The U.S. paid to rebuild it," Anton says.

Tiger says he was arrested briefly in the Philippines for drinking and fighting. "The Vietnamese boat people had money in Vietnam and we were poor, and at PRPC they wanted to have the best spots and have everything their way," says Tiger. "They said nasty things about

Amerasians and called us motherfuckers, so we cursed back and chased each other around with knives and machetes." Tiger won't reveal how he got out of trouble on that occasion, saying only: "I was smarter than them. I calculated my move, executed it, and ran off, not admitting anything." One way or another, Tiger avoided being stuck in a camp jail. Ten years later some gangsters he knew were still in jail in the Philippines. "Some Amerasians try to be good citizens, some hate their lives and are bad," says Tiger primly. Finally, in November 1991, Tiger left on the plane for America. He was nineteen years old. All his three closest Amerasian gangster buddies from Vietnam went to America around that same time, all with fake relatives. One even flew to the United States on the same plane as Tiger.

In November 1992 the U.S. General Accounting Office responded to a request from Congressmen Mrazek and Ridge, the coauthors of the AHA, to report on the program. The report referred to the increase of fraud leading to many more cases being rejected. A more serious problem for the Amerasians themselves was that some already resettled in the United States with fake families said their "strongest desire from the beginning" had been to eventually bring over their real families. They hadn't realized that, by swearing the fake family members were their true relatives, that they had disqualified themselves under U.S. law from sponsoring their real families later. "From one perspective," concluded the GAO report, "the AHA program has had a considerable degree of success . . . having generated more than 100,000 names of Amerasians and family members. More than 88,000 of these have been interviewed, with approximately 66,000 actually resettled in the U.S."

This was three times the number predicted when the act was passed. In addition, lists still being generated by the Vietnamese government contained 20,000 more names for processing. No one really knew how many true Amerasians remained in Vietnam and the report said that many Amerasians were still unaware of the program, or had not been able to apply, and that in some rural and mountainous sections of Vietnam, only about half the Amerasians had left.

The report concluded, "The AHA has given hope to a group much discriminated against in the homogeneous Vietnamese society. Unfortunately, the Amerasians still in Vietnam probably have fewer mental, social, and financial resources than those who have already come [and they] face more stringent interviews which may disqualify them. . . . Meanwhile, fake Amerasians and fake family members break U.S. immigration laws and consume some of the resources and privileges which are not properly theirs."

Finding American Fathers

As large groups of Amerasians gathered, first at the transit center in Ho Chi Minh City, then in the Philippines (and later in America), some had begun their first tentative steps to locate their American fathers. This was raising unique and serious questions for government bureaucrats and resettlement workers: How could the fathers be found? And *should* they be found? What would be the repercussions of such searches, and what were the real possibilities of finding a father? U.S. policies on such matters were being set almost entirely by men, who tended to look at things from the father's perspective. On the other hand, many American wives and girlfriends might not be anxious to welcome a child from the father's past.

The French had taken some 25,000 mixed children of French fathers, along with family members, when they left Vietnam in 1954. In August 1955 France had said all children, legitimate or illegitimate, with a French parent—including children "born in Vietnam of an unknown father and a native Vietnamese mother, who are presumed to be of French extraction or nationality and who are recognized by the tribunals as being of French nationality" were considered French citizens. Those under eighteen with a French father were deemed to have French nationality, but could choose Vietnamese citizenship when they turned eighteen. According to some reports, the French government also provided subsidies for children of mixed heritage under age eight who remained in Vietnam. But unlike the half-French Vietnamese children, the Amerasian children of U.S. fathers were never granted American citizenship, although over the years other immigrant groups to America have been given special kinds of U.S. legal status. Under the law covering the Amerasians and other children born outside the United States, a U.S. citizen father must establish a blood as well as a legal relationship to the child, which might include acknowledging paternity in writing under oath and agreeing in writing to provide financial support until the child's eighteenth birthday.

Still, many Amerasians had yearned all their lives for their American fathers. One early study done in the PRPC found that more than 60 percent hoped to find their American fathers, although only 8 percent said they knew a lot about them, 33 percent said they knew a little, and 58 percent said they knew nothing at all, not even their father's name. The dream of finding one's biological parents can continue throughout a lifetime, and knowing nothing about the father makes that desire no less strong—in fact, perhaps stronger—than knowing more. Although the search for one's biological roots is a universal human drive, Amerasians especially suffered because of certain Vietnamese cultural beliefs. They had been born outsiders (and fathered by outsiders)—"children of the enemy," as author Steven DeBonis writes—in a land where ethnic purity was a core value, and where males and fathers had the highest importance, even if they never did anything at all for their child.

Moreover, in Vietnam as in most other Asian cultures, the family is much more important than the individual, and each person's behavior reflects not only on that individual and his or her immediate family but also on his or her ancestors and *future* family members. "The burden of one's responsibility to one's family goes back in time and forward into the future," says one Vietnamese writer, "and the very presence of a fatherless biracial child [is] a trauma to the family."

Amerasians needed to be acknowledged as having a place, if not even an important place, in the lives of their birth parents. The fathers they sought were idealized figures who by accepting and loving them could heal all the misery and shame of the past. Rejection or even ambivalence on the part of the father would amount to what one psychologist labeled a "psychological death blow." And many Amerasians felt they at least deserved that acceptance, if not material restitution, from the American father and his country, since it was because of the father and his country that the child had suffered so much.

However, the United States was clearly not anxious to help them find their fathers. The State Department, "in order to comply fully with the U.S. Privacy Act," was requiring various safeguards to "protect the fathers" from their unwanted children appearing in their lives. The responses of other agencies and government bureaus to the multitude of requests by Amerasians was evasive at best. In fact, the government and most agencies were trying to duck the matter entirely. For example, a July 11, 1988, memo signed three months after the AHA went into effect by both the Office of Refugee Resettlement director and the administrator of the Family Support Administration, U.S. Department of Health and Human Services, listed these sample questions and answers intended to guide responses to queries from the public and media:

Q: "The [Amerasians] will be coming as immigrants instead of refugees. Shouldn't they really be coming as citizens?"
A: "This is, in the main, a very deprived group of people with needs quite similar to those of refugees. We are spending some $67 million nationwide this year to provide such refugee-specific services as language training, job training, and employment services to help refugees become self-sufficient. From our perspective, what is important is that these people have access to those services, regardless of their status, because that's the key to their future."
and:
Q: "Would fathers, when and if found, be expected to support the children?"
A: "Federal laws governing child support would seem to apply. However, the law is enforced differently, by State agencies, in the various States, and each State has its own case priorities. We cannot say at this point how high a priority a State would place on enforcing this type of case."

The memo noted that the average age of the Amerasians was seventeen, and called them "an extremely difficult caseload."

About the same time, the *American Council for Nationalities Services Guidelines for Assisting Amerasian Children Requesting Parent Locator Services* advised searchers to turn to the Red Cross and similar sources. Stating that "a search is less likely to be conducted for [the fathers of] Amerasians 18 or older" and that "bios [of fathers] which we send you will usually state 'no contact with father,' meaning the initial search did not have a positive outcome [and] . . . subsequent searches undertaken after arrival in the U.S. are unlikely to have different outcomes." The guidelines concluded: "It is the Red Cross's policy to permit the 'sought' person [in other words, the father] to decide about reuniting" and "to only release his address with that individual's permission." The Pearl Buck Foundation was another resource, said the memo, and its reunification procedures are "confidential and sensitive." Adding that some Amerasians "wouldn't admit their feelings of abandonment because they were so painful," and that others were unconsciously furious over the dad's "perceived desertion," the guidelines warned: "If a decision is made to contact the alleged father, it should be done is such a way as not to jeopardize his privacy or threaten his present living situation."

Peter Daniels, who directed the large Amerasian Services Program at St. Anselm's in Little Saigon near Los Angeles, says that the United States left the problem of finding fathers to individual resettlement sites once the Amerasians reached the United States. "Basically," he says, "we were lied to by the State Department when it said all Amerasians would be processed in the Philippines by the Pearl Buck Foundation and Red Cross [to find the fathers]. When we tried to contact those sources to locate the dads, those agencies would complain, in effect, that searching was so difficult, and the fathers said 'No' so often that, 'Why don't you just tell the Amerasians you couldn't find their dads?'" Tiger had his father's complete name, rank, Social Security number, and other information, but when he and his family contacted the Red Cross on several occasions they never got a reply.

A May 1989 article in *Amerasian Update*, the newsletter sent to resettlement workers during the AHA program, told about the Red Cross "family reunion and tracing program": "From 1975–79, we had a special program to assist American men who desired to establish contact with Vietnamese families. Over 400 files were established. . . . In order to make our service available to Amerasians we are now alerting our 2,800 chapters across the country about the probability that some Amerasians will eventually request assistance." If that happened, Red Cross chapters were to contact local Veterans' Service Offices, who "must give priority to the veterans' privacy."

An August 1990 *Amerasian Update* article said, "The Red Cross reports the inquiries so far number 78 since 1987, while a mere six have resulted in nine contacts of some kind between the family/individual and the fathers."

In 1990 the *Orange County Register* near Little Saigon in California quoted a spokesperson for the Pearl Buck Foundation and the Amerasian Registry ("another organization that helps unite fathers and children") who said that fewer than 500 American fathers had made formal inquiries about their Vietnamese offspring. The same year, *Boston Globe Magazine*, in an article about rape and sexual abuse of Amerasians as young children, said: "Some U.S. fathers, resentful of what they consider the invasion of their privacy, have taken legal action against relief agencies that have helped track them down." With this context, it is not surprising that few fathers were ever found, and that many of the searches ended badly. Later, father-finders like Joseph Love of St. Anselm's would develop strategies and contacts to get around bureaucratic blocks and work out approaches to the fathers that brought a much higher success rate of 75 percent. But by the end of all the years of searching, only 2 percent of all U.S. fathers were ever found, and many of them refused any contact with their Amerasian children.

There were occasional happy endings. The September 1991 *Amerasian Update* told of one sixty-five-year-old father who was waiting at the airport to bring home his sixteen-year-old half-black son and the boy's forty-five-year-old mom. But the December 1991 *Amerasian Update*, which also reported homeless Amerasians living on the streets of Chicago and Little Saigon, carried some less happy tales, along with a letter from an Amerasian girl in Chicago, who wrote: "In my mind, HE is always the most holy-beautiful imagination of my life. I had the dreams of meeting my FATHER, Mr. DAVID. All of my life I have been steadily pursued by that dream. I have dreamed of HIM a lot of times, and then awakening, there is only—the dream! Now I am in the U.S., my fatherland, a single girl aged 20, and I still keep my dream of meeting my blood FATHER. . . . I do not want to be a burden. . . . I only want to meet HIM, to call HIM FATHER, like every human being has a father. I write these words from the depth of my heart, I pray to GOD to send my thoughts to Mr. David, my beloved FATHER. May GOD bless and fill my FATHER with happiness and good fortune." She signed her name and address, perhaps hoping that somehow "Mr. DAVID" would hear of her and contact her.

The rest of that December issue told of a fifteen-year-old Amerasian boy who wrote his U.S. father and received "a swift response" from the father's brother: "Don't contact this family again, you have done enough damage to the widow! If you try, we will contact the INS to deport you!" The boy cried for a week, as did his caseworker. Another mother of an Amerasian gave the AFDC information on the father, and his daughter saw him for the first time in court, where he was ordered to pay $150 per month child support. "During the hearing, the father did not even look at her. There was no introduction, no greeting. This is truly a bitter experience. No doubt the father was also bitter." Meanwhile, most of the searches for fathers were still to come.

Even while Linas Kojelis, U.S. deputy assistant secretary for refugee admissions, was quoted as saying, "As far as the State Department is concerned, the Amerasian program is a tremendous, tremendous success . . . a major humanitarian effort by the U.S. . . . heroic in proportion and in its commitment, [and] we make no excuses for the overall program," the program was dealing with unprecedented problems. Many Amerasians say that their time in the Philippines was the low point for them during their journey from Vietnam's prejudice and poverty to America's shattered hopes. It was in the Philippines that many of them, especially the more naive ones from rural areas who had been bedazzled by the first attention and apparent caring in their lives, first realized that the fake families accompanying them were only using them. In the

Philippines they fully experienced the loss of any family, friends, and familiar things left behind, and began to understand both the difficulty and necessity of learning to speak, read, and write English. Some also began to realize that there might be no loving American father—that fantasized figure many had dreamed of for a lifetime—waiting to greet, protect, and love them as soon as their plane touched down on American soil. In the Philippines, many Amerasians were picking up their first hints of a very different America than the one they had imagined.

Yet despite all this, most Amerasians were leaving the Philippines still with high expectations of a wonderful America, where they would find their fathers, live comfortable lives with no more hunger or homelessness, earn or receive money to send back home to desperate relatives depending on them for their own survival, and, most of all, be greeted and comforted by Americans anxious to make up to them for all they had suffered because they were, after all, part American too. Those were their dreams as they boarded the planes to take them to the golden land.

7

Culture Shock in Their Fathers' Land, 1988-95

It is also important to consider the reaction of the American man, who may be very unhappy at being the focus of a search [by an Amerasian child]. Legally, if the Amerasian is a minor, there are potential grounds for child support demands. . . . It is important to . . . honor the principles of privacy and confidentiality. In some circumstances, these are not only ethical principles — they are the law.

—InterAction Resettlement Program Task Force report
explaining a decision not to set up a central registry to
help fathers and Amerasians find one another

The State Department planned to resettle the Amerasians in about fifty cluster sites across the United States, with 10 percent going to California. Tiger, Louis, Sara, and Miss Dao's group all were designated for California, arriving at different times and eventually registering at St. Anselm's Immigrant and Refugee Community Center in Garden Grove. (Its name has since been changed to St. Anselm's Cross-Cultural Community Center.) There, on the edge of Little Saigon in Orange County, California, thirty miles from Los Angeles, this new resettlement site had opened in January 1991, destined to eventually become the largest in the country. Son, sent first to Arizona, soon left for Little Saigon, where he registered for English classes at St. Anselm's. Nan and her orphanage sister Joan, along with the despised nun and the eight orphans from the nun's temple, were sent to a resettlement site in North Carolina; but a year or so later, Nan, too, migrated to California.

Americans had been responding to the arrival of the Amerasians in different ways. The resettlement program's newsletter *Amerasian Update* in late 1990 told of Amerasians given small U.S. flags when they landed in Elmira, New York, and of greeters in other cities meeting their planes with bags of used clothing and offers of hot dogs or hamburgers. Funds to resettle the Amerasians were tiny, and mostly depended on a site being able to raise additional funds from private and local government sources just to get the Amerasians into the most basic living situations.

By July 1990 almost half the Amerasians leaving Vietnam came from rural backgrounds—apparently the result of those seeking to buy them scouring the countryside. Their rural upbringing meant they were usually poorly qualified to deal with the problems of urban life and with bureaucratic paperwork. That year, to speed up resettlement, Welcome Home House (the Mohawk Valley Resource Center for Refugees) opened in Utica, New York. It was designed to resettle Amerasians and their families more speedily by bringing them directly from Vietnam without the six-month period in the Philippines. They were to be housed and fed and offered the same classes in ESL and American culture. The first seventy-four residents arrived on July 17, 1991, and the program's executive director, Rose M. Battisti, declared to the newspapers: "They are wonderful." But author Thomas Bass says in his book *Vietnamerica: The War Comes Home* that he "was surprised by the amount of fraud and sheer chicanery" in that first load of Amerasians reaching Utica. He cited phony relatives, phony marriages, patronage, nepotism, crime, post-traumatic stress disorder, illiteracy, mental health problems, domestic abuse, suicides, tuberculosis, and malaria.

Maybe, as some suggested, the Vietnamese were using the Amerasian Homecoming Act as a sort of "Mariel," the famous boat exodus from Cuba in the 1980s when the Cuban government dumped thousands of criminals, mental patients, and other "undesirables" into the United States after the United States offered to open its doors to all who wanted to leave that country. Apparently the Philippines camps had served to weed out some of the more serious problems of the Vietnamese immigrants before they reached the United States. Although a year later forty residents of the Utica center won "Best Ethnic Organization Entry" in the Independence Day Parade, marching with U.S. flags and a "Happy Birthday America" banner they had made, the problems were already out of control. By 1992 Bass was labeling Utica "a shambles."

One thing was certain—the Amerasians had much more serious problems than almost anyone had anticipated. About 80 percent needed medication for tuberculosis and were required to take it to continue receiving their temporary support payments. Yet many complained it made them nauseous and simply didn't take it. Some saved it for suicide attempts.

Many of the Amerasians felt in shock when they first arrived. Tiger's first impression of the United States was of "having a bad future ahead." He says he "looked around the airport and it was kind of scary—I saw big tall Americans, black ones and white ones, and one with a big pot belly. And they spoke to me in English. The situation was very hard because I didn't speak any English and I felt intimidated, and did not know where to go, or what to do. America was much bigger than I had realized, and I worried I would not survive. I felt hurt inside." Son says he was stunned at how different the American reality was from his dreams. "I thought for everybody life would be easy in America, so I was very disappointed when I first came here. They met me at the plane and put me in an apartment, gave me $50 and took me to Thrifty's—I felt so terrible—they gave me used clothes and five used pots. I cry and cry for several days." After a few days in Arizona ("so hot, so boring"), his survival instincts surfaced. "I let people give me money to play cards at my apartment and they gave me a ride to California. When I got to Little Saigon I found an old friend from the Philippines, and moved in with him and his friends. They showed me how to get along in the U.S. I went to ESL classes at St. Anselm's at night. There were some very crazy Amerasians there! Later I switched to Golden West College and took auto body repair classes."

Vietnamese, like many other immigrant groups to America, usually are supporting unseen others in their home countries—poor relatives and friends who depend on them for their very existence. But most Amerasians were without relatives in America, and because they usually separated quickly from their fake families, they were unable to draw on family support. Resettlement workers were soon confronted with homeless Amerasians and desperate searches for U.S. fathers. Those Amerasians arrived clutching old, creased envelopes bearing faded addresses and twenty-year-old black-and-white snapshots of their fathers, sometimes with the father's arm around a young and pretty version of the Amerasian's mother. Other Amerasians waited a long time before seeking their fathers, out of fear of what one advisory sheet on "father searches" called "a rejection [by the father] that would amount to psychological annihilation." Clearly some were afraid to give up those long-held fantasies of their fathers that had helped them survive psychologically throughout their lives.

The InterAction Amerasian Resettlement Program Task Force, pointing out that most Amerasians had little or no information about their fathers, that very few fathers had made inquiries about their children, and that "no additional funds had been allocated to enable the agencies to handle this complex reunification," decided not to set up a central registry to help fathers and Amerasian children find one another. Such a registry would only raise the Amerasians' hopes with little chance of success and, the task force added, "It is also important to consider the reaction of the American man, who may be very unhappy at being the focus of a search. Legally, if the Amerasian is a minor, there are potential grounds for child support demands. . . . Even an illegitimate relationship can be grounds for investigation that can be devastating to the individuals concerned. It is important to remember that the potential for error is always present [and] it is important to honor the principles of privacy and confidentiality. In some circumstances, these are not only ethical principles—they are the law."

Joseph Love, the American veteran who volunteered to help Amerasians find their fathers and who compiled a much better record of locating fathers and persuading them to see their Amerasian offspring, often witnessed the pain of Amerasians who failed in their searches. "Neither the Pearl Buck Foundation nor the Red Cross really tried to find the fathers," he says. "They just quoted their 2 to 3 percent 'find' figure and changed the subject. A lot more fathers could have been found." And Peter Daniels, who later directed the Amerasian Program at St. Anselm's, uses even stronger language: "Those places didn't have any interest in searching for the fathers; they lied to us about it and never looked for them at all, just dumped the problem of finding them onto the kind hearts of strangers."

Little Saigon near Los Angeles

Vietnamese had begun moving to California en masse even before the end of the Vietnam War, when some more wealthy ones, sensing the end was near, simply took commercial flights there. When the sudden collapse of South Vietnam came in April 1975, about 130,000 Vietnamese were taken from Vietnam to America by the U.S. military and housed temporarily in four domestic military bases across the United States. In California they were taken to Camp Pendleton, just below Orange County where Little Saigon is located. With almost no black population and with a large number of retired American military and defense workers, Orange County was and is quite politically conservative. Its residents welcomed these early refugees from Communism, and many retired U.S. veterans living there were willing to sponsor Vietnamese refugees, sometimes including ones they had fought beside or known during the war.

The Vietnamese immigrants fervently opposed any kind of contact between America and Vietnam as long as the Communists held power. Those South Vietnamese officials who had enjoyed the fruits of corruption during the war and left with considerable wealth settled quickly into a comfortable lifestyle. Others among the first wave of refugees were glad to take menial jobs in the mainstream American community at a time when Little Saigon was still being created. These jobs added to their contacts and knowledge of Americans and American culture. In a phenomenon called "chain migration," they began bringing other members of their extended families from Vietnam under U.S. reunification programs. These immigrants were joined in the late 1970s and 1980s by "second-wave" people, mostly ethnic Chinese businessmen and their families along with coastal fishermen and farmers all fleeing Vietnam by boat. (An estimated 30 percent of the boat people died at sea by drowning, starvation, or murder by pirates.)

About 600,000 boat people migrated to the United States after being in refugee camps, often settling in California, where they, too, were joined eventually by relatives they sponsored. Next came thousands of former political prisoners released after years in Vietnamese reeducation camps. Mostly former South Vietnamese military and government officials, along with some former civilian employees of U.S. government agencies and businesses, including a small number of Vietnamese who had worked in America's notorious Phoenix Program or in tiny secret guerilla projects, this group came under a special U.S. law called the Humanitarian Operation program. Many of the prisoners had suffered horribly, and were especially bitter and angry with the Communist government. For years they and their family members have helped fuel furious denunciations of any efforts at reconciliation.

The growing Little Saigon community included a steady stream of "secondary-migration" or "gravitation-migration" Vietnamese who had first been resettled in other areas of the country. By 1990 Little Saigon was well established and offered job opportunities where Amerasians, with their lack of both English and work skills, might find low-wage — sub-minimum wage — work. Unfortunately, many among the earlier waves of Vietnamese were disdainful of the Amerasians, unwilling to accept them or help them "join" America, although the younger generation of Vietnamese was much more open.

As early as 1989 one local newspaper noted that "Orange County has become the Vietnamese capitol of the U.S." What was in 1978 a small strip of only three Vietnamese-owned stores along Bolsa Avenue in Westminster had grown by 1989, when the first few Amerasians began to arrive, to more than 700 stores, and as years passed hundreds more spread out for miles, studded with several very large, affluent malls and countless small businesses, coffee shops, restaurants, and night clubs.

Until 1982 Vietnamese refugees of the first wave had received thirty-six months — three full years — of Refugee Cash Assistance (RCA) and Refugee Medical Assistance (RMA) from the federal government, enabling them to attend school and job training courses and become settled. In 1982, when boat people were arriving, those benefits were cut to eighteen months, still long enough to help these refugees, most of whom came from the upper or middle class, settle into America. (By 1988, the year the Amerasian Homecoming Act went into effect, the Internal Revenue Service estimated the median income of Southeast Asian refugees who had arrived in 1975 was higher than the U.S. median income.) But by the time the Amerasians — the most desperate, helpless, and unprepared refugees to come in years — began to arrive, the United States had cut refugee cash assistance and medical aid to a mere eight months. Before they could get these benefits, someone had to fill out the forms, deal with bureaucratic red tape, make sure various deadlines were set and met. If someone was ill and eligible for Refugee Medical Assistance, for example, papers still had to be filled out, symptoms translated, appointments made and transported to, and procedures explained.

St. Anselm's Immigrant and Refugee Community Center

One source of support for Amerasians in Southern California was St. Anselm's Immigrant and Refugee Community Center, which had been dealing with the problems of refugees, most from Vietnam, for fifteen years. St. Anselm's is "not faith-based, but community-based," explains its director, Marianne Blank. Founded in 1980 by the Episcopalian Church, St. Anselm's is independent of any formal religious organization. "We're nonprofit, with multiple services under one roof—resettlement, immigration, naturalization, ESL and citizenship classes, employment, social adjustment, family resources, services for the elderly, and so on," says Blank. Its Amerasian resettlement services program was especially active between 1991 and 1992, the main years of Amerasian immigration under the Homecoming Act.

Because of the pull of Little Saigon, St. Anselm's soon found itself dealing not only with the hundreds of Amerasians and "relatives" assigned to its area, but with hundreds arriving from other cities. Like other sites it received a paltry $35,000 per year in U.S. government aid, but it had the reputation and clout to be able to supplement that amount with county, city, and private donations. "We raised a lot of extra funds, but we could never get enough to compensate for all those lost years of the Amerasians," says Blank. "It was like putting a Band-Aid on a huge wound. The dads—what can I say? Some had remorse after all those years—at the time [their children were conceived during the war] they were having all those relationships, and didn't think of the consequences." Blank is a sympathetic and thoughtful woman in her sixties with ash-blond short-cropped hair, hazel eyes, and soft Southern manners that can turn quickly to toughness when necessary. But her position as director kept her preoccupied with the center's other programs as well as the Amerasian program. Later it became apparent that the Amerasian Services Program needed a much more watchful eye.

For the 1990 fiscal year, the U.S. Department of State had made agreements with twelve nonprofit mostly religion-based organizations, paying them $560 (about $185 per month) to cover costs of the first ninety days for each Amerasian and "family member" they resettled. The U.S. money was to cover only core services, listed as: (1) prearrival costs such as staff salaries and other expenses while the organizations found sponsors for the new arrivals and settled them; (2) "reception," the costs of housing, food, clothing, and so forth for "at least the first thirty days" in America; and (3) counseling and referrals "orienting" the Amerasians to healthcare, jobs, and training opportunities in America, "with the primary goal of [their] self-sufficiency at the earliest possible date." In other words, getting them off the government "dole" and on their financial own within one to eight months—or sooner. The new arrivals were eligible for food stamps and AFDC support for young children, as well as Social Security for certain aged, blind, and disabled persons on the "same [basis] as citizens." They could receive Refugee Cash Assistance and Refugee Medical Assistance for eight months, although this would be "time-limited to available funds." Translated, this meant limited to how long a state could or would pay. In "certain complicated cases," some could get RMA when they no longer could draw RCA. Those whose RCA and RMA had run out, and who couldn't get AFDC or SSI, "might be able" to get state or locally funded General Medical Assistance "if their states [had] such a program." Or they might not.

St. Anselm's is housed in a large, bare-bones building with a strip of grass and trees in front. Its furnishings are modest; people clearly worry more about money for programs than about fancy furniture or re-painted walls. The center's staff was and is mostly Vietnamese. As the Amerasians began arriving, an assortment of staffers and volunteers assembled to meet the challenge. But many of the "pure" Vietnamese staffers had prejudices against the Amerasians. "Most of my Vietnamese staff was almost speechless when I said we were going to have an Amerasian program here," says Blank. "Some of them warned us the Amerasians would all 'go bad,' and all end up in gangs, but that didn't happen, although quite a few did get on the periphery of criminal stuff." Another staffer, a Caucasian American, says that "almost our entire staff at St. Anselm's was Vietnamese and most were very prejudiced, saying the Amerasians would steal us blind and so forth." Joseph Love, the father-finder who volunteered regularly at St. Anselm's, says that whenever he approached most of the Vietnamese staffers for help for an Amerasian, "they took on a sort of manner like they were professors, barely condescending towards them. And they let the Amerasians know that they definitely were second class." This was not true of all the staff. Some older staffers like Mr. Yen Nguyen, who taught one of the ESL classes, and Blank's secretary Anne (Hahn) Nguyen, were kinder and more helpful. And many younger Vietnamese, earlier immigrants to the United States, made prodigious efforts to help the Amerasians. Because most Amerasians were teenagers or in their early twenties, with no family members in America, some staffers found themselves becoming temporary surrogate parents to some of the more desperate cases. But while some Vietnamese already settled in America did offer help to the Amerasians through jobs and in other ways, much of the larger Vietnamese exile community continued to separate itself from them. Thus an important resource usually available to other immigrant groups who could look for help from earlier arrivals was not really there for the Amerasians.

As Amerasians kept arriving, many who had arrived earlier were already homeless in cities all over America. Although some had begun to adapt to their new surroundings, others were battling alcohol and drug abuse, psychological disorders, illnesses, culture shock, and depression. And always poverty, because of the inadequacy of benefits and their difficulty in finding work. A study of 275 Amerasians in California, many of whom were on waiting lists for ESL and training classes, reported many were sitting home "watching kung fu videos, episode after episode." In March 1991 Marianne Blank put it memorably: "I think a lot of [Amerasians] are not doing terribly well. A lot of them are finding that life is not necessarily that much better here than in Vietnam. I think there is a tremendous let-down because they can't identify with anybody yet . . . it's almost as if they have been thrown away twice."

Nonetheless, Blank says, "The Amerasians are so loveable, so lively and affectionate. There's a poignancy about them. When they first came here, they had an image of America as everything good and golden. They really wanted us to like them, and to think well of them. But every one of them already had experienced a lot of rejection. They considered themselves Vietnamese, but the Vietnamese culture said to them, 'You're not pure.' The biggest stigma was the status of their mothers, whom most Vietnamese say were all bar girls and prostitutes, which isn't true.

"Then when the Amerasians came to America, their fathers' country, do you know what some of them told us? Some honestly believed their father would be waiting at the airport when they arrived, that somehow he would have heard they were coming and would be there. They had a very unreal picture of America when they first arrived. They were so childlike. Their lives had usually been so awful, and they thought people in the U.S. would be waiting to shower them with everything. Freedom has so many responsibilities, and they didn't realize it. But they do have so much resilience. Over and over again they bounced back from disappointments.

"When the earlier waves [of Vietnamese] came to America they tried to establish 'face,' or status, and a lot of them couldn't even stand some members of their own families whom they didn't consider fit their new image. Of course some of the Vietnamese were wonderful, but some were ashamed to have an Amerasian in their family in front of their neighbors. We even had one Amerasian whose fake family put him out on the freeway coming in from the airport. But I'm not condemning the Vietnamese culture for racism," she adds reflectively. "We are all evolving. I grew up in Virginia during segregation, when you couldn't even play with black children. How can I blame the Vietnamese culture because it wasn't ready for these Amerasian children?"

Mary Payne Nguyen

Much of the spadework to open an Amerasian program at St. Anselm's had been done not only by Marianne Blank but also by Mary Payne Nguyen, who became the center's first coordinator of Amerasian services. Standing well over six feet tall and weighing more than 300 pounds, Mary Nguyen was a Caucasian American married to a Vietnamese, although in the process of divorcing him. Then in her forties, Nguyen told a reporter that she had "given birth" to nine children beginning when she was seventeen, had adopted ten others, had raised thirty foster children, "and now I'm a mother to the Amerasians." Her two-bedroom household included four children of her own and several Amerasians who were "unaccompanied minors," and to whom she rented space, using the money from their benefits checks. This fact was later to become a source of controversy. Nguyen had taught ESL in Orange County schools for seventeen years, and had volunteered to help Vietnamese refugees swamping Camp Pendleton at the war's end in 1975. She spoke passable Vietnamese.

As early as February 1990, St. Anselm's began contacting government agencies to have St. Anselm's designated a services site for Amerasians, and put together a list of local Amerasians and their "relatives." When the federal funds distributed by InterAction finally came through, St. Anselm's officially opened its Amerasian program in January 1991. Piecing things together with part-time staffers and volunteers, the center signed up Amerasians and hired a job developer to help them find work. Mary Nguyen traveled to Vietnam with a group of teachers, and reported back that there were still "significant numbers" of Amerasians around Can Tho, Cuu Long, Long Xuyen, and Rach Gia. In December 1991 the Orange County Register carried a long article describing a hectic day in Nguyen's life as coordinator—teaching an ESL class to Vietnamese seniors; advising the public defender of a young Amerasian arrested for murder; searching for and finding a missing mentally disabled Amerasian reported to her by two homeless Amerasians; and visiting an Amerasian who'd been wounded in an earlier shooting that left two other Amerasians dead. But, while both creative and energetic, Mary Nguyen had a darker side. She could change instantly from being fiercely maternal and protective, and became known for her rages, when she would scream at other staffers and Amerasians alike. Some serious rumors and accusations began to fuel a growing staff rebellion against her.

As months passed, Amerasian resettlement sites all around the country, most of them far less prepared than the well-established St. Anselm's to raise extra funding or deal with cultural differences, were reporting problems with domestic violence, substance abuse, gangs, and homelessness. The paltry funding for resettlement meant placing Amerasians in slum areas and ghettos, often without enough food. Probably more than half of the Amerasians separated from their fake families within months of arriving. Young teenagers totally unprepared to deal with the American system were being left completely on their own. The government's failure to come to their rescue was blamed by U.S. officials on the Vietnamese government and on the Amerasians themselves. "Nobody envisioned that there would be fraud in this program," a Manila-based U.S. official told a reporter in February 1993. Joseph Love scoffs at such remarks. "That official apparently had never been to Vietnam," he says. "In most really poor countries, money talks and everyone listens."

Because Vietnamese were not allowed to take money out of the country, although some managed to smuggle out gold and other valuables, the fake families often supported themselves by taking all or part of the benefits designated for the Amerasians. Some would limit the Amerasians' food, or make them work in a Vietnamese restaurant or store and take their meager pay. Because of the Vietnamese emphasis on helping one's family and on respecting and obeying one's elders, "a lot of Amerasians wouldn't have found that surprising," says Love. Says Daniels: "Some of the fake families felt they more or less purchased an Amerasian when they paid for him to come to the U.S." And apparently, the six months of English classes in the Philippines had had little effect. Few Amerasians had experience with the regimen of schooling. In ESL classes they were required to sit for long periods, staring forward at a blackboard with inscrutable markings. Those used to street life were often restless, seeing no reason they couldn't move around and talk to each other. If somehow an Amerasian got hold of a car, and drove up to the front of St. Anselm's to show it off, all the students, especially the girls, would rush outside from class talking and laughing. In Vietnam, almost no one, least of all an Amerasian, had access to a car or even a motorcycle or bike. In short, St. Anselm's was a center of social life for the Amerasians, a place to meet, hang out, and learn the latest gossip, as well as to attend class or get help.

Many rural Amerasians had never developed a sense of calendar time, of geographic distances and space, or knowledge of other countries and continents, something that was not unique among immigrant groups to America. Recent waves of Hmong and Southeast Asian tribal minority immigrants, most brought to the United States because they had aided America during the war, and some indigenous groups from Mexico and Latin America also lacked this knowledge. In addition, the Vietnamese calendar is different from the American calendar, and translating "Year of the Horse" into some vague numbered year often seemed pointless to the Amerasians. "But they loved looking at maps," says Blank. "They were amazed by them. Most had never seen one. They'd have us show them Vietnam and the United States over and over."

The programs St. Anselm's established included classes in prenatal care and parenting. Under its funding agreement the center was required to arrange monthly field trips to such places as Disneyland, a college campus, and the beach, and to hold regular social functions like holiday celebrations. Later, programs were set up to deal with domestic violence and to offer drug, gambling, and alcohol abuse counseling. Job placement was always important, as was connecting the Amerasians to the network of social services offered in the United States. The center drew heavily on mental health counseling from volunteer therapists and social workers, many of whom were Vietnamese Americans.

Still, like other sites, St. Anselm's was unprepared for the enormity and complexity of problems. Over and over, the Amerasians told of surviving on their own in the streets since they were five or six years old. Says Marianne Blank, "Of course, a lot of the prejudice and problems around the Amerasians had to do with the Vietnam War."

Among those who descended on the Amerasians at St. Anselm's and other sites were numerous social science researchers. "The Amerasians were studied to bits," says Blank. One researcher said most Amerasians were functioning at five to eight years below their chronological ages, socially and emotionally. Many studies left researchers frustrated; they began using terms like "lack of or deficient need for precision and accuracy in data gathering;" "lack of or impaired need for pursuing logical evidence;" and "lack of or impaired need for precision and accuracy in communicating one's response." Blank expresses these problems in simpler terms: "The Amerasians didn't understand how it would help to do those kinds of studies, so any answer they gave was OK. And they wanted to look good."

"Six Layers of Stories"

Because of the legal necessity of claiming that fake relatives were real and false documents were true, most Amerasians were in the position of having to lie from the start. Lying and confabulating is so common among Amerasians that it is often commented on in the literature about them and may be one reason why many of the lengthy studies based on interviews with them have never been published. For example, when Amerasians coming to St. Anselm's realized, quickly, that Americans were shocked by their lack of basic education, they began to lie about it. "Apparently word got around that, to Americans, the least acceptable education they could claim was that they'd completed sixth grade," says Blank. "So they all began telling us they'd been through sixth grade. I think 95 percent of them didn't go to school at all.

"Finally we made an agreement with our staff that we would accept whatever the Amerasians told us and not press them. They would tell us so many changing stories that I began to call it their 'Six Layers of Stories.' Gradually, you would unpeel layer after layer before they told the truth, if ever. Like they'd say about the person they came with: 'She is my mom . . . actually she is my aunt . . . well, she's *like* my aunt.'" In some cases of abusive fake families, Blank sent staffers to get the Amerasian's documents and move them to another place to stay. There was an increase in emotional breakdowns by the Amerasians, who in many ways were much more helpless and vulnerable in America than they had been in Vietnam.

Joseph Love and Son Chau

Son Chau, taking night classes in English at St. Anselm's, kept watching his volunteer ESL teacher Joe Love, sizing him up. A husky, attractive Army Airborne veteran then in his fifties, Joseph Love never served in Vietnam. Broke and temporarily out of work after being laid off from a ten-year factory job, he'd been a volunteer teaching illiterate Americans to read and write when he saw a local TV news show in late 1992 about Amerasians flocking into St. Anselm's. One young Amerasian man in particular had gotten through to Love, inspiring him to volunteer there.

After Son, now twenty-three, had moved to Little Saigon in the summer of 1990, he bought a little used bike to get around, and supplemented his refugee benefits—about $350 per month for eight months—helping a Mexican man sell things at a weekend swap meet. After two months he was able to send $50 back to his mother, Du, and after that sent $50 or more per month, enough for his family to live on. Working extra hours, Son eventually was able to get a used car, passing the driver's exam on his first try.

"I never was without food in the U.S.," says Son. "Even when first here I got welfare, and still worked eight days every month on weekends, and had money extra to send to my family, because they had no other money at all." When he sent money back to Vietnam, Son sometimes included extra for his mother to "give to poor people in the neighborhood." By thus building loyalty and a promise of future rewards, and showing his own loyalty to earlier friends, Son was protecting his family from envy and mistreatment. Son's family finally joined him in California in 1992, the year he met Joe Love.

Son kept studying Love, trying to decide whether he was trustworthy, and how to approach him. Love was only a few years older than Son's American father would have been. One night during a night-class break, Son invited Love to accompany him to one of the myriad Vietnamese coffee houses in Little Saigon. Says Love, "As soon as we went in, I noticed that everybody there seemed to know Son." Son treated Love to coffee, and told him of his dream of finding his American father. He wept and asked Love if he would help him look for his father. Love said "Of course," not realizing that soon other Amerasians would begin asking his help, and that he would eventually become probably the top "father-finder" in the country. Love later realized that Son was the same young Amerasian he'd seen on TV who'd stood out in his mind, motivating him to volunteer at St. Anselm's in the first place. "The whole thing," says Love, "was something that right from the beginning was just meant to be." Love says Son is "streetwise, but with a good heart, and with complete confidence in his own abilities. But when he talks of his American dad, he goes off into a dream world."

Over the next years Love became both a close friend and a mentor to Son. Divorced, and with grown children, Love's main family included a brother and elderly mother living elsewhere. At Son's suggestion, Love rented a room for three years in the house Son and his family leased after Son brought the rest of his family from Vietnam. "When Son's mother Du first arrived in the U.S., she seemed very careworn and beaten down, not at all like she is now, with her bubbly personality," says Love. During the time Love lived with Son's family, "they included me in everything," he says. "One night Son came in yelling in Vietnamese and stomping around, and the next thing I knew everyone was yelling in Vietnamese too, and they began piling into cars to go somewhere, taking me with them, although I was still blissfully ignorant of what was going on. We all got to some house and everyone went up and began banging on the door, so then the cops came." Love says he would have been seriously worried at that point, "if I hadn't known how cross-culturally aware the police are around Little Saigon."

The problem, says Love, turned out to be that some Vietnamese acquaintances and Son had been drinking together, with Son buying most of the drinks, when somebody called him "bui doi," or "dust of life — Amerasian." After that, "Son came home and got the whole family, me included, to go back to 'get' them." Luckily, Love was able to intervene with the police as Son argued with them. "You're in the U.S. now," he told Son. "You don't argue here with the cops. When a cop says 'Go,' you go! Finally we all went home looking kind of sheepish.

"It must have been insanity over there in Vietnam," reflects Love, shaking his head. "It must have been a madhouse. Some stories I've heard — things we Americans did — Uhh! Horrible! And most of the Americans who served there had no idea of what they were leaving behind. Many of them were just kids themselves. Of course, some were married with families in the U.S., and some never even knew they had a kid, or just didn't care. But a few knew they left a child in Vietnam, and were more or less torn apart by that."

Unassuming and steady, Love has an ability to inspire trust, and was able to establish a network of contacts with various American government officials, coaxing from them fathers' addresses and phone numbers they often were forbidden by law to divulge. Love's same man-to-man but respectful manner convinced many fathers to talk to him even though their first reaction was to cut off any communication regarding pasts they had either forgotten or wished to forget. Love never hurries or pressures. He rarely expresses the anger he sometimes feels about government policies and red tape blocking his ability to find fathers. Because he refuses to charge the Amerasians for his searches, Love also either works at factory assembly work or similar jobs, or goes through a period of being broke. "I don't make money off tears," he says gruffly.

As Love looked for fathers, he could hardly believe some of the stories the Amerasians told him of surviving on their own as young as five. One grew up working for a traveling circus. Another dove for fish near a seaside restaurant. Many turned to crime or prostitution, or worked twelve hours a day as a servant for one bowl of rice per day. One told Love he had lived alone on the streets of Ho Chi Minh City since he was six, sleeping under bleachers at night. "I didn't believe him at first," says Love. "I asked him:

> 'How you survive?'
> 'I was dog.'
> 'What you mean, dog?'
> 'I go where people eating at restaurants, go "woof-woof-woof," roll over, do tricks like dog, they throw me food.'"

Love shakes his head in amazement. "All these Amerasians are natural survivors. They've had to be." But of course, many *didn't* survive.

"To grow up in a Vietnamese family without a dad is hard enough, and to also be of mixed blood is really rough," says Love. "So the Amerasians would say to themselves: 'If my dad were here, he would protect me.' Many of them had their fathers blown up so big in their minds!" As he looked for more and more fathers, Love polished his techniques. "When I first called up a dad, I'd say: 'What I have to discuss is highly personal, should I call back at another time?' So I put the dad in complete control. I'd say: 'If you tell me "No," I will never call again or give anyone this information.' I never talk to anyone but the father himself. Once he's ready to talk, I might ask: 'Do you remember Miss So-and-So from Vietnam? We have information that you may have an Amerasian child.'

"I emphasize that the kid wants nothing from the dad, not even the words 'I love you'—he just wants to have a father. These kids don't want to be a burden, they'd be more likely to gladly earn or borrow money and give it to their dad. You've got to understand the Vietnamese culture. The dad is number one. If the dad won't see the kid, then that kid knows he's everything bad anyone ever said about him in all the years he was growing up. The kids may love and respect their moms, but a mom has no status. If there's not a dad, the oldest son makes the decisions and has the responsibility. But the minute they have a real dad they have rank. They are no longer 'the dust of life.'

"When I reach the fathers, they say all kinds of things — 'Oh, my God!' or 'I don't remember anything about Vietnam, and I don't want to continue this conversation.' Or, 'You say I have a daughter? God, when can I see her?' Or 'Damn! You found my son! I've always wondered about him!' Or 'Can't you get me off the hook?' One said: 'Oh, so I've got a son? Well, if any more come in and say I'm their dad, I probably am, so send them to me too!'" Only once did Love break his own rule about talking to no one but the father. He spoke to the father of an Amerasian boy whose Vietnamese mother was dead, and who was being raised by his uncle, a former Vietnamese major who'd known the boy's father well in Vietnam. "That dad was an ex-captain," Love says. "He kept accusing me of pulling some scam, and insisted on putting his wife on the extension. Finally I got disgusted and said: 'Don't play games — I have your marriage license from Saigon with your name and photo. I have pictures of you taken in Vietnam with your arm around the boy's mother and your name on the back.' I gave that dad's phone number to the Amerasian kid's uncle — but I don't know what happened after that."

About a third of the fathers Love found said 'Yes.' Another third have died. "If I know the father is dead, I'll call up his widow or one of his grown children. I try to avoid a direct lie, just say I knew of the dad in Vietnam, and they usually assume I served with him. I ask where he's buried and then call the cemetery and get the exact location of the grave, to give the Amerasian in case he ever wants to visit." Once, Love reached the grown son of a lieutenant commander who had fathered a child in Vietnam, and learned that both the father and mother of the grown son had died. "So I asked if he would be interested in meeting a half-brother from Vietnam, but the son got real haughty. He said: 'My father was an officer and a gentleman, sir, and it would have been impossible for him to have committed adultery in Vietnam!'" Love chuckles.

One of Love's earliest cases was also the most heartbreaking. "This kid, who was half-black, came in wearing his father's dog tag around his neck. He showed it to me and said, 'You can find my dad?' I said 'Sure — just give me the tag and I'll photograph it.' He said 'No, no, I never take it off!' He hadn't taken it off for twenty-two years. His uncle had given it to him when he was a little boy, saying it was his father's and might help him find him some day. I found the guy in Texas. He'd been wounded twice in Vietnam, the second time so badly that field medics had to cut off all his clothes, including his dog tag, and leave everything in the jungle. He was shipped straight home. I told him: 'A kid has been wearing your dog tag all these years, believing you are his dad.' The guy said, 'That's impossible!' He'd been in Vietnam only a few months and got wounded twice, and never had time to 'know' any ladies there. I said, 'I hate to ask, but are you white or black?' He said, 'Snow white.' I said, 'This kid is black.' When I told the kid, he just cried. He took off the tag and left it on my desk. He never said a word. I'll never forget him—it was one of the worst things I'd ever done in my life. I still keep that dog tag in a little glass case, to remind myself I shouldn't believe everything I'm told, that there may be another story behind the first story."

The true secret of his success, Love says, is "people." Over the years he developed an elaborate network of government and military sources. "I've dealt with some people who broke the law to help the kids find their dads," he says. "There are many wonderful people out there." There were also people still carrying out a vendetta against Vietnam, blocking information that would help the Amerasians, says Love, and "others who wanted to help to atone for things they did in Vietnam." Some Amerasians never try to find their fathers "because they're angry at them because of the suffering they saw their moms go through, and say, 'I don't need him,'" Love explains. "Their moms are the real heroes. They suffered very much. Some made great personal sacrifices to keep and raise these children." But moms "are not always truthful. I make no judgments about them—I wasn't there, in their situations, at that time. Some worked in bars or as prostitutes; others were ladies in every sense of the word."

And sometimes a mother didn't know the truth. "One kid told me his dad was a spy, but I learned he was actually a member of a long-range killer team—a sniper," Love says. "The dad remembered the mom, but said a lot of guys were in and out of the little hooch where she worked, so no way could he accept that he was the father. I had to tell the kid, 'Daddy says "No." It broke his heart. But I couldn't tell him the real reason—that his mom was a hooker." Love says that many kids couldn't accept the dad's "No" as final. "One was sure there had been a misunderstanding, and brought in an uncle who spoke better English, saying maybe if he talked with me and then I talked to his dad again, he'd say 'Yes.'" Love always tried not to take a "final no" from a dad.

"I say, 'Why don't you take some time and think it over?' Then I send him a letter, with a sealed envelope. And I write, 'Inside is a photo of your child, with information about him. But don't open it if you are sure you don't want contact.' One dad called back after three weeks, said he'd kept wavering about opening the envelope. And he did say 'Yes.' '"
Meanwhile, Love continued to try to find Son's dad, but without success.

The final third of the fathers Love found refused to have contact with their children. Love was often upset by a father's adamant refusal to have anything to do with an Amerasian child who, like Son, might have spent his entire life dreaming of a reunion. "When I finally tell an Amerasian kid: 'Daddy says "No,"'" they thank me very politely and leave, but I've seen some of them go out in the hall and lean against the wall and cry their eyes out," says Love. "Those are the times I've kicked myself, wondering if we weren't just bringing more heartache to these kids. I've had to look at a kid, a great kid, sitting across my desk from me, all alert and hopeful and eager, and hear a dad on the phone saying 'No.' I just can't understand a man doing that. And now some of those fathers have Amerasian grandchildren."

Some people tried to defend the fathers, or at least to explain their positions. A refusal to see a child, they argued, might be due to the father's shame or guilt or to his fear of reliving painful memories and past losses. Some fathers were ambivalent, wanting some type of relationship but pulled away by other factors, such as a current family who might resent the Amerasian. Other fathers had never told anyone about a long-ago wartime relationship that produced a child. At the national 1989 Conference on Amerasian Resettlement, a representative of one veterans' organization told attendees: "Fathers are not the enemy. Do not put too much energy into finding fathers. There are 15,000 [actually at least five times that many] Amerasians and 3,000,000 vets, [and] most veterans do not even know if they have a child. Most people believe it was the eighteen- or nineteen-year old 'grunt' who fathered the children, but . . . it was [usually] the men in the rear—older men and civilians. Look at the fortunate side: Amerasians can now come to America with their families.

"Remember, the issue of soldiers fathering children in foreign lands is not a new situation. It did not happen just in Vietnam. Do not dishonor the Vietnam vet." At the same conference, the Pearl S. Buck Foundation, one of the organizations supposedly a resource to reunite Amerasians and their fathers, reported that during 1988 only 103

Amerasian searches were conducted, 34 initiated by fathers and 69 by Amerasian children. Out of these, 45 reunions had resulted.

Son Chau

While Son was adjusting to the United States he returned to Vietnam several times. His first visit back came two years after he arrived in America. Like other returning Vietnamese, he knew he was expected to come loaded with gifts and money, and to treat everyone to food and drink at local restaurants. Now that he was from "wealthy" America, Son estimated a trip home might cost him several thousand dollars. "Although I am Amerasian, I am very nice to everybody there, and everyone love me now," he says. "And when I go back and see poor people there, I give them $10 here, $10 there, and even more, up to $500 to special friends. The people in my town don't treat me bad now. They are all nice to me now except the Communists." Arriving in his hometown on a Friday evening, he put out the word that the next day he would treat "whoever is my friend and likes me. About twenty people showed up at the restaurant, and I paid for them all," says Son. But police officers came in to tell him he needed to report to the police station within forty-eight hours after his arrival.

"Is that so? I'm sorry, I have been in the United States and forgot the way you guys do things."

When Son did report, the head policeman warned, "Be careful from now on, whatever you're doing, whoever you see. At night here, nobody go nowhere. You got to stay in your house too, because if we see you, we'll take you."

Son laughs at this memory. His manner with the police and others was in contrast to the haughty manner some expatriate Vietnamese adopt when visiting their native country, a manner that has earned Viet Kieu, or "overseas Vietnamese," a bad reputation. "If you treat somebody no good, they treat you no good, so everything you do, you have to build the future. That's what I believe. My whole life somebody wanted to put me in jail because I sell frankincense, but I run this way and that way and they never catch me. And in my life, I try one by one to get some good friends," he says.

"I had friends who went all the way through twelfth grade, even to college, maybe were even related to Communists—smart friends, who even became police. People knew me because I grew up with them, and

I used to take them along to work with me, and give them a little money when they needed it. Most everybody need money. So when I get in trouble, I can talk to them and give them money. In the United States I could get a lawyer, but in Vietnam, no lawyers. So that's the way we do it there. In Vietnam if you got money, you can do anything you want."

A month after Son returned to California, he got a phone call from a new girlfriend, Chi, in Vietnam. She was pregnant. Twenty-five days later he returned to Vietnam. "She so nice, so sweet, that when I heard she pregnant I went back as soon as I could. We had a wedding, not big but very fun. Well, really, for me not fun at all, because I didn't want this to happen. But she so nice to me, and so we marry. I always said that whoever I got a child by, that's who I would marry. I believe I did the right thing to marry Chi. I told her: 'I only ask one thing of you, that you must go to school in Vietnam to learn English.' And I pay to send her."

Chi's parents appear honest and sensible. In the beginning they didn't believe Son would actually marry Chi. Says Chi's mother: "There was a lot of feeling that Viet Kieu would treat Vietnamese girls badly. We had to ignore the rumors and believe in the karma that one's love life is guided by spirits. We knew that Son and his mother were very poor when he was growing up, and when his mother got involved with an American she was seen as a prostitute. After 1975 his mom was oppressed a lot by the Communists, but she was brave. Son's life was terrible since he was very young. He told us he had worked hard in Vietnam but in the U.S. he had to work hard too, and didn't have money to help us at the time of the marriage. He told us, 'Let me work to bring your daughter and our baby to the U.S., and eventually we will help you.' I told him: 'Whoever my daughter loves I will respect it. Because I believe if you have a child, and she marries a foreign person, even one who is Chinese, I should respect it, because that's who they love.'"

Back in the United States, Son quit going to classes and took on more work to send back more money. "I had a plan to bring my wife and baby to America," he says. In 1993 Son's baby, a son, was born in Vietnam. "We gave him an American name — Billy," says Son.

Sara Phuong and Miss Dao

Miss Dao was shocked that so few fathers would see their Amerasian children. "In the Philippines there were many cases where the

Amerasians had addresses and all the information needed to contact their fathers," she says. "But we heard that when they got to the U.S., a friend would come to the airport to tell them, 'Your dad has a new family now and can't come here.' These are the irresponsible ones. Those Amerasian children had been through so much, and they would think then, 'What about me? Aren't I part of his family too?' These kids never had good care or love in their lives. So they were very sad.

"There are all kinds of Amerasians. Some are bad, some are nice, but they always have good hearts within themselves covered by their shyness and other masks. Because of the war that created the circumstances of the Amerasians, I wish for the American people to take care of these children. This is all about the war that created the, the—mess. As for the fathers who have died, of course they have no responsibility anymore. But for the dads still alive, when the children look for them, they should always open their arms to them. And when they know they had a child in Vietnam, they should go look for them. Because they are the father, and have a responsibility for their child."

Sara was seventeen, very pretty but also very shy when she arrived in Little Saigon with Miss Dao and the others who had accompanied them. She enrolled in ESL classes at St. Anselm's, where Bob (not his real name), Mary Payne Nguyen's son from an earlier marriage, who was a few years older than Sara, ran a tutoring group. For three years Sara attended ESL classes at St. Anselm's, where, according to one staffer, she was known as the "angel" of the Amerasians. Bob, who is tall and heavy like his mother, seemed easygoing and good-natured if not particularly energetic. He was, after all, both an American and the son of Mary Payne Nguyen, an important figure at St. Anselm's. "I liked him OK, but not love," says Sara. "During that time I felt sort of numb. I was very young and inexperienced." Soon both Mary Nguyen and Bob picked Sara as an appropriate bride for him. "When they were dating, he wouldn't let Sara go any place," says one person who worked at St. Anselm's at the time. Then Sara became pregnant.

"I moved in with Mary and Bob when I was pregnant with my first baby," says Sara. "When I first met Mary, she seemed very nice." Sara and Miss Dao, with almost no experience with Americans, may not have realized at first that Mary Nguyen's protectiveness, interspersed with angry outbursts, was not typical American behavior. "Maybe because I've been through so many things in my life I could live with her without many difficulties," says Sara, "even though she screamed and yelled a lot. Because I had lived a very poor life and suffered very much, I wanted to change my life when I came to America, and make it better." After Sara's first baby was born, her husband wasn't working enough to support his new family, and Sara says Mary Nguyen took her down to register for AFDC. "But when the baby was about one year old they cut me off because he wouldn't sign the papers they needed, and they never gave me any more money for my next two children by him," says Sara. Instead, she worked longer and harder hours in the Vietnamese sewing factory several days a week.

Once Nguyen blew up at Miss Dao as well as Sara. "The saddest day of my life," says Miss Dao, "was a time when Mary Payne Nguyen pointed a finger at me, screaming and yelling, and I didn't even understand English and had to wait until we got home so Sara could explain it to me. I felt that even though an American is talking to a foreigner in her own country, and even if that person is poor and humble and without knowledge, she had no right to treat any person that way." Miss Dao felt crushed and humiliated. Still, Sara is very circumspect when she speaks of her former mother-in-law. "I've heard about Mary taking care of Amerasians," says Sara, "but I never saw any she brought home to take care of, although several rented rooms from her. And sometimes she went home with lots of anger because of her troubles at work, and took that anger out on the people who lived with her. So after awhile we moved out because there were arguments between she and her son, as well as other problems." After the AFDC was cut off, it was Sara who brought home most of the money for the household.

Sara's children, like all children born in the United States, were born U.S. citizens, a status denied the Amerasians themselves unless they completed the years of citizenship process like any other immigrant. Sara has never bothered to try to find her American father, who, she says airily, "is probably just another black man." She points out that she has never had any way to find him, not even his name. "Why didn't he ask my mom to come to America?" she asks rhetorically, then, more hesitantly, answers herself: "It's possible he did ask her to come, but that my mother still had obligations to her parents and family in Vietnam, so she couldn't go." Her reply indicates a lot more pain than Sara admits. For many years after she came to the United States, Sara was betrayed by Americans who should have helped her but who instead abused her and even used her to support them financially.

Alan "Tiger" Hoa

After landing in California in late 1991, Tiger attended English classes for a time at St. Anselm's. A few times he even was a volunteer dance teacher there, teaching other Amerasians some of the intricate dance steps he had learned during his dancing club days in Vietnam. "During that first year, I didn't do major crimes — just petty thefts, some harassing of people," he says modestly.

But Vietnamese gangster immigrants had already been active in California for fifteen years. Among the refugees who resettled in the United States in 1975 were members of "prominent criminal organizations once active in Vietnam," writes Ahrin Mishrin in a 1993 University of Southern California thesis on Vietnamese gangs in Little Saigon. "Many were former South Vietnamese military personnel, [who] between 1975–77 attempted with varying degrees of success to re-establish [in America] the former criminal structures" of the war years in Vietnam. One prominent group headed by a former member of the CIA-trained South Vietnamese Underwater Demolition Team known as the Frogmen emerged, led by a Vietnamese man known as "the Knife" or "the Butcher." He was arrested for the attempted murder of a Chinatown publisher suspected of harboring pro-Communist sentiments — one of several political assassinations by right-wing Vietnamese in the turbulent early immigrant community where even to suggest returning to see family members in Vietnam was equated with pro-Communism and invited ostracism and perhaps violence.

After the Knife was convicted, a group of South Vietnamese veterans calling themselves the Underwater Frogmen United met to discuss how they, the 'real' Frogmen, were being given a bad name. They placed an ad in an Orange County Vietnamese-language newspaper that read: "Anyone who knows of a 'bad' Frogman, please contact [a certain person] and the problem will be taken care of." Says Mishrin: "That disquieting ad and the arrest of [the Knife] signaled the breakdown of the [fake] Frogmen as an organized criminal organization."

Many small Vietnamese youth gangs had also sprung up, much like the ones Tiger became involved with. Composed of runaways and throw-aways, they traveled around America crowded together in usually stolen cars, visiting friends and acquaintances from Vietnam or the Philippines now scattered across the United States. (Vietnamese gangs are seldom tied to neighborhoods or turf like other ethnic gangs.) They funded their trips by committing small crimes like extortions and stealing car stereos, burglarizing Vietnamese businesses and homes. Staying ten to twelve to a room and sleeping four to a bed in mid-priced motels or the homes of friends, the young gangsters spent their time in pool halls, coffee shops, and video game arcades, eating junk food; watching TV and kung fu videos; drinking; getting stoned on coke, Ecstasy, pot, and pills; playing with guns; stealing and racing cars; and showing off for girls. Their crimes usually netted just enough for the shared profits to get them through the next days and nights. These small gangs became "a family, bound by common pasts, [shared] memories of gang life on the Vietnamese streets, problems in the Philippines, and a hostile American and Vietnamese culture in the U.S.," writes Mishrin. They "created their own kind of families" and "found belonging" amid lives of emptiness and disconnection.

Tiger boasts that rather than joining a gang, "I always make my own gang." He says he started in America "when me and some friends stood up for each other and built a big reputation and others joined us. When I first came to America, I had no gang, of course, so I started fights to build my reputation. I hung around schools and showed kids what to do, and they would be impressed. People knew I fight really well and called me their leader." Sometimes Tiger makes the doubtful claim that he himself was a gang leader in District Four of Saigon, the Ton Dan area. But for a few months in America, Tiger still had not totally given over his new life to drinking, drugs, and crime. Mostly, he says, he lived on his benefits. He separated from his Uncle Khue's family within his second month in America. "I was a burden because I had no job, and when my uncle and aunt wanted to kick me out, I quietly left, so I could earn money to send back to Vietnam so my mom could have a beautiful, decent burial site," Tiger says. He doesn't mention that he also began to drink more heavily and be involved with gangs. But he continued to stay in touch with Khue and Khue's wife, who Tiger says always hated and mistreated him. One night when he had been drinking, they had a quarrel and she called police. Tiger spent a night in jail. "I had the flavor of an American jail for the first time," he says. Although he doesn't say so, Tiger must have been becoming more and more disappointed and disillusioned with how America was turning out for him. Soon his life was tumbling downward into deep trouble.

For some time he had wanted to visit some gang friends from Vietnam now living in New York, and one day, he says, he told himself "lam lieu," a Vietnamese phrase roughly translated as "I just didn't give a damn anymore." He thought, "Nobody cared about me, and I knew it was bad, but I just didn't care. I didn't feel anybody wanted me. I just wanted to take a risk. I'd either live or die. And because I felt extremely disappointed with my family and my life, I wanted to join my gang friends again. I knew it was risky, but at that point I didn't think living or dying was a big deal anymore. I just felt really tired and disappointed and wanted, needed, to get away." Tiger called three gang friends to drive with him to New York — two Amerasians and one Vietnamese who had come to America with fake families and long since separated from them. To prepare for the trip he bought a gun for $70 "in case someone attacked us." He says he never used guns in Vietnam, but learned to load and reload them "while sitting around with Communist officers who were drinking and boasting." Again, Tiger puts a lot of blame for his life at that time on Khue's wife. "Because she never listened to me and neglected me, the unhappiness in my family pushed me back to gang life again, since I had no one to turn to except my friends," he says. In Vietnamese culture, younger Vietnamese are supposed to respect and obey their elders, but at the same time the elders are often blamed if the younger ones do anything wrong. Thus, one often hears younger Vietnamese say they did something wrong because their elders advised them wrongly, or didn't meet their responsibility to advise them at all.

"Holding a knife had made me feel powerful, but with a gun I felt even more wild and powerful," says Tiger. "When I held a gun I had a feeling like a spiritual stealth power, like a ghostly monster lived within me. The power from a gun surges in you from nowhere. It made me feel like Rambo in a movie where he wins his victory." Although Tiger often seems to be shaping his stories to please his listeners — a Vietnamese cultural trait, according to scholars of Vietnamese culture — when he speaks of guns his manner changes. His voice takes on an intense emotional quality, a sort of combined yearning and threat. But the tone disappeared as he continued his tale of that trip, saying he and his friends did several home burglaries on the way to cover expenses. "We chose houses near freeway on-ramps," says Tiger, who for some reason begins to laugh a lot as he tells this account. "We had no fear, we were used to it, we'd done it before."

In New York Tiger and his friends hooked up with gang friends and at least briefly spent time with Mama J or Jacqueline, the gangstress from Vietnam who, according to Tiger, had come to America with the mysterious Raymond. "Everyone knows her. She is very famous," says Tiger, surprised that I didn't immediately recognize her name. "She was about forty-five then, with a very dark complexion — she may have been partly from the country of India — and she was pretty cool. She was a druggie, and high all the time." A madam in Vietnam, she was probably pursuing the same profession in America. But Tiger grows nervous and vague when pressed to tell more. "She took care of us when she could, and that's why we call her Mama," he says. He and his friends also stole cars and committed other crimes he doesn't name, and soon he was jailed in New York for several days, although he can't or won't explain why. Next, he says, he spent some time in a prison in Kansas, and again in a prison in Arizona, during a mysterious odyssey he went on for reasons he would not reveal. There are hints the U.S. government may have tried even that early to deport him back to Vietnam. Part of Tiger's reluctance to detail some of his activities can be blamed on the fact he usually was interviewed on the phone from prison, where all calls are routinely taped by guards.

Back in California, Tiger had been in the United States only a year when in November 1992 he had a fight with a girlfriend and drove off in her car. "She said I beat her up, but I only slapped her, and she could not prove anything else. She had a chipped front tooth, but it came when she slipped and fell against a door during our argument," says Tiger. The beating charges were dropped, but car theft charges were filed. Out on bail the day after this arrest, Tiger didn't appear in court for a hearing and a felony "failure to appear" warrant was issued. When he did show up he was jailed. Although the other charges were dismissed, the failure-to-appear felony earned him forty-five days and three years probation. When Tiger got out of jail in March 1992, something inside him had broken. He was coming apart, poised high above the beginning of a long, dizzying free fall into disaster.

Meanwhile, later that same year students at a high school in Little Saigon elected the school's first Vietnamese American homecoming queen. The school's student body had grown to 53 percent Vietnamese, most either born to the 1975 "first wave" of Vietnamese immigrants or having come as children during the Vietnamese boat exodus and family reunification programs. By early 1992 there were 600 Amerasians on St. Anselm's rolls, along with 2,000 of their family members, real and fake, who had accompanied them to America. Fraud cases continued to create problems not just at St. Anselm's but all over America. "We've had thirty Amerasians here in the last six months who were homeless," Mary Payne Nguyen told a reporter. "As they get older, frustration turns to rage, and the number of them in jail is going to go sky-high if we're not careful. It may already be too late. Too many of them may be over the hill." She had begun suggesting that Americans sponsor individual Amerasians still living in Vietnam.

That year a *Los Angeles Times* article quoted Michael Kocher, the head of InterAction, the umbrella organization disbursing federal funds to the fifty resettlement cluster sites, saying: "I think it's a shame that it took this long [to bring Amerasians to the U.S.]. . . . I think both the Vietnamese and U.S. governments have to share in the responsibility for that. The war between our two countries did not end in 1975. Without question, it's more difficult for a twenty-year-old to make adjustments than for a five-year-old." Mary Nguyen told the same reporter: "We could have done this [bringing the Amerasians from Vietnam] so well . . . But the American public just wasn't ready to deal with Vietnam."

8

Shattered Dreams

*[The Amerasians'] wonderful dreams are all gone. Unmet expecta-
tions have resulted in anger and frustration, and feelings of having
been deceived. [Unlike many other immigrant groups], the Amerasians may never be able to say from the depths of their hearts, "I
am an American."*

> —Thanh Son Thi Nguyen, in her 1994 University of
> Pittsburg dissertation "Adjustment and Acculturation
> Problems of Vietnamese Amerasians in Pittsburgh, PA:
> A Post-Resettlement Study"

By 1993, while Sara, Nan, Son, Louis, and Tiger were struggling
to deal with their new lives in America, and other Amerasians
were stranded in the Philippines or left behind in Vietnam,
thousands more Amerasians and "relatives" had continued to arrive in
the United States. Many were destined to have contact with St. Anselm's. Today St. Anselm's files, stuffed with bureaucratic forms,
memos, reports, faded letters, and clippings, and saturated with images
of loss, waste, and betrayed dreams, offer hints of the Amerasians' suf-
ferings and the problems faced by those hoping to help them during the
early years. Included, for example, is a 1990 *Los Angeles Times* article on
Loc Van Nguyen, a twenty-five-year-old Amerasian transient who said
he had been arrested "many, many times." Homeless in America as he
had been in Vietnam, he knew neither of his parents, only that his
American father was black.

As he was arrested yet again—for stealing an American flag from in front of the U.S. post office in Little Saigon — Westminster Officer Robert Trotter recited Loc's name and date of birth from memory as he wrote it down. The *Times* reported that Loc admitted stealing American flags before, saying: "I take them to throw them away. I want to [fuck] the American people. They are very stupid."

Notations from files I picked at random mention other Amerasians who passed through the center, most moving on into some unknown resolution. They report on every kind of problem — medical, psychological, domestic, criminal, and, always, economic. The list goes on and on:

- A young male Amerasian left penniless after his fake family abandoned him, who slept a few nights in the Orange County bus station and was taken by a Buddhist monk to St. Anselm's, which arranged for him to stay briefly at a temple, noting: "He is out of money and food . . . has no job and no money to pay for his room." A later note in his file from August 1994 reads: "His inappropriate behavior and threats to other students when they observed him shoplifting (third incident) have made him persona non grata here."
- A "tough-acting" Amerasian woman who dressed like a man in baggy clothes and shaved her head, explaining that "that's how she had survived in the streets of Vietnam." Part of her head was "too soft, caused by something heavy falling on it and knocking her unconscious while doing construction work . . . and receiving no treatment in Vietnam." Medical tests in America indicated "a lot of fluid between membranes, but they could do nothing."
- A female Amerasian who had left her child behind in Vietnam when her birth mother sold her to a fake family, found lying in the Little Saigon streets with her wrists cut. "Several times she hadn't eaten for days," someone jotted in her file. "She later bought a one-way ticket back to Vietnam."

"Before I came to the U.S. I heard of a wonderful, happy life in America," says one Amerasian woman. "But since coming here, life has been harder. [Most] Amerasians have no family and are so lonely. For them, coming to America was like stepping into a big, dark hole."

Amerasian Van Truong (Not His Real Name) and the Social Worker, Nhien Luong

Early on, St. Anselm's had gotten funding for a mentor program and distributed flyers seeking volunteer mentors "to provide Amerasians with emotional support and guidance as they make their precarious transition from the Vietnamese culture to the American culture." One volunteer mentor was Steve Baker, a kind, generous man then in his twenties matched with some of the most difficult cases, including the seventeen-year-old white Amerasian Van Truong. A St. Anselm's intake worker wrote: "Van's face looks terrible and full of sadness . . . he probably has had something [very bad] happen to him . . . he dresses himself completely except for tying his shoelaces . . . he is not to be trusted to cross the street alone. . . . He is not physically aggressive, he has neither a best friend nor a group of friends, [although] he does not have temper tantrums. He talks in his sleep, and cries too easily."

Like so many Amerasians, Van first came to St. Anselm's because he was being mistreated by his fake family. Younger Vietnamese who had been in America longer often made special efforts to accept and help the Amerasians. Nhien Luong, a thoughtful, attractive young Vietnamese woman who had come to the United States as a boat refugee ten years earlier, worked several months at St. Anselm's as a Vista volunteer. "I considered Van like a little brother. He called me 'Sister Nhien,'" says Luong. "He's very skinny and Caucasian looking, was homeless for a while, doing a lot of drugs and very suicidal. Of course, the way the Amerasians were treated in Vietnam wasn't just racial. It was also political." Van showed Luong a treasured photo of his American father with his mother, himself, and his younger brother. "He'd hoped it would help find his father, but it simply wasn't enough," she says. "For awhile he was doing well—he believed in the future, and Amerasians don't ever plan for the future, because if you expect and plan [for something] and don't get it, it makes more sense, and is less painful, not to expect or plan at all. And that had happened to them all so many times."

Van told Luong he'd begun drinking at age seven when his mother died, and had used drugs extensively since childhood, quitting school in the second grade. The drugs and alcohol, plus a lifetime of malnutrition, had contributed to "mental weaknesses." He also confessed he was spending some of his benefits money on marijuana. St. Anselm's arranged for a psychological evaluation, which concluded that Van had the mind of a ten-year-old. When Steve Baker became his mentor, he took Van to live with him for awhile so he wouldn't be homeless. "The Amerasians grew up without love or guidance, and with so much prejudice against them, even after they came here," says Luong. "They look very different, and most don't speak Vietnamese like other Vietnamese. They use slang and street language. . . . After Van's mom died or disappeared somehow, his grandmom raised him, but he ran away. He said it was more fun to be on the streets with his peers."

"Van was a super guy," says Baker. "He was illiterate, and grew up in the poorest segment of Vietnamese society. As a kid he swam in rivers and caught turtles and fish and sold them to restaurants, and guided people to prostitutes. He had a large burn mark on one shoulder, and when I asked him what happened, he said he'd been scalded as a baby, but didn't want to give details." Van also told Baker he'd often begged on the streets as a child, pretending to be disabled. "He laughed and showed me how he'd twist his arm and shoulder around, and sometimes pretend he was blind too," says Baker. In the United States, Van got his first tattoo. "At first," says Luong, "he wanted a tattoo of the name of a woman he liked." But in the end he chose a different tattoo, one that says "HATES LIFE" in Vietnamese.

"Randy" Tuan Tran

"One day a friend told me, 'You can sing, why not enter the karaoke contest?'" says "Randy" Tuan Tran, the black Amerasian singer who also sang on Louis Nguyen's first CD in America. The contest was at a Vietnamese club with sixty contestants, and Randy won first prize—a $500 stereo and a certificate. A famous songwriter, Thu Ho, father of the singer My Huyen, heard Randy and introduced him to a Little Saigon recording company. He signed a two-year contract in September 1992, and recorded his first CD with My Huyen, who was already well-known.

As he tells his story, Randy sits with me in a small Vietnamese cafe in Little Saigon. Expressive and open, Randy's English is good, and he is able to voice complicated perceptions and thoughts. "With my first CD, I became very popular right away," Randy says. "I made a second CD, then a video, and got famous and toured with a Vietnamese performers' show to Europe, Canada, and Australia. On one CD I sang a song I really liked about Amerasian orphans, called 'No.'"

Randy's Song "No" in English

How I lost you, dear mother!
I don't know when I'll ever see you

I never had a chance to see your image
Even if only for an instant in my dreams.
My lot is filled with darkness,
Sadness, hatred. Oh, mother!
This skinny, lonely one will always miss you —
And miss your lullaby, ever since I lay in my crib!
Life without a parent is the most sorrow thing in the world!

"It's about kids who are hungry—they want to see their mom, they don't have enough food or clothes, like my own life when I was a little kid," Randy explains. "The little boy is crying in his dreams." Randy was left as a baby at Thanh Tam orphanage in Danang, where he says the 200 orphans were mostly Amerasians. "They taught me to sing as a little kid. I was happy there," he says. When the new government closed five-year-old Randy's orphanage in 1975, a Vietnamese woman adopted him. "She wanted a boy to do the hard, heavy farm work," says Randy. "When we first got back to her village, all the neighbors came and stared at me as if they had never seen anything like me before. I was afraid and embarrassed, and got a blanket and covered myself.

"This woman, whom I called 'auntie,' treated me quite bad, horribly. People would ask her why would she raise me when I was black, but that was not my fault. She would punish and beat and torture me to the point I was almost dead, and then she was satisfied. I was very afraid of her." Once Randy was taking care of the woman's cows and accidentally let one eat a neighbor's crops. "Auntie tied me up and got a pile of pig poop and made me eat it. When I refused she shoved a stick in my mouth and forced me, with all the neighbors watching, and my pride and dignity and feelings were very crushed and I was deeply hurt emotionally." Sobbing bitterly, the little boy ran away and hid. "She found me and sweet-talked me into coming back, but afterwards she was the same," he says. Like Louis Nguyen, Randy found almost his only happy escape in music. "I always loved singing," he says. "When I was growing up in the country people would sometimes all walk around together during a full moon—there were no lights, no electricity—and sing in a group. I would memorize songs and walk down the street singing, and go to weddings and sing, and everyone said I was good. Becoming a singer was my dream. As I grew up I often stayed away from home at night and slept in abandoned places and cowsheds. We Vietnamese say: 'From the beginning of the road to the end of the market.' Until 1987 I lived very miserable."

As the laws for allowing Amerasians to go to America kept changing during the early 1980s, his "auntie" sold fourteen-year-old Randy to a Vietnamese couple for "four ounces of gold, about 1,500 U.S. dollars — very, very much. A second couple offered more, but it was too late." Randy figures that fifteen to twenty couples offered to buy him. When it looked as if families could leave with Amerasians, prices and "demand" for Amerasians would go up; when the laws shifted to make it hard or impossible to leave, prices went down, and sometimes families who had bought Amerasians would find themselves "stuck" with feeding and housing them for years. At first the couple who bought Randy treated him well. "I was so unhappy with my adopting auntie that I begged the buying couple to let me come live with them in Hoi An when I was fifteen," says Randy.

But the buying woman refused to eat at the same table with Randy, and when the law changed soon after Randy was purchased "because of some problem between Vietnam and the U.S.," she was furious. "She said she bought me to go to the U.S., not to raise me. They had to be stuck with me until we left in 1990. During those years, the buying mom became very cruel. I felt so bad, I cried and told her husband, who was kinder, that I would rather go back to my adoptive auntie." Instead, the husband found Randy a job making soy sauce. For three years, he worked marinating beans in cooking acid, then straining them, then boiling them again. It was hot, hard work, and Randy turned over all his earnings to the "buying couple," returning home only at night to sleep.

"And I tried my best," says Randy. "Then in 1990 we finally heard we could go to the U.S. after all, and the woman began to treat me well again. I had been determined to say in our exit interview that she treated me 'not well.' But when the time came I knew the family might have to stay back if I said that, and recognizing that I was hungry for love, thirsty for love, I convinced myself to lie to the interviewers."

After arriving in California, Randy, sixteen, stayed with the adoptive family only two months. "When I first got here I was eating a lot, and the mom talked mean to me and told me they were living on government subsidies, and had to divide everything by five — they had two young kids. Once I was so sick I almost died, and had to walk to the market alone to get medicine." The fake family doled out a small portion of his benefit checks to him each month. "When my money ran out I had to eat rice with soy sauce every day to live through the rest of the month," he says. Luckily, Randy was young enough to be placed in a

U.S. high school, where he made friends and moved in with them. "When I finished ninth grade my friends invited me to go play around with them," he says. "When I turned eighteen the government didn't give me aid anymore, so I quit school and worked making button holes in a Vietnamese garment factory." Then came the karaoke contest, and sudden fame and fortune.

"When my first CD got popular and I got famous, it was fun. When I toured to Vietnamese clubs in Europe and Australia people would get in a line and all try to get up on stage with me—security had to keep them from getting too close. And when I opened my mouth and sang just one line, they'd all go: 'Waaaaooooh!' The first time it happened, I got afraid! Girls kept asking me for kisses, giving me flowers. Wow! *Lots* of flowers, and money to sing one song—100, 20, 10 U.S. dollars! In Vietnam no girls ever were chasing me, and I was chasing no girls, because the girls there treated me like shit, and I had low self-esteem. But when I got famous, for awhile I had money. From childhood to growing up, I had lived my life very harsh, so now when I first got a lot of money I told myself: 'Wow, why not have fun and spend it and enjoy it? Why not just party and be happy?'" Randy also is rumored to have a serious gambling problem, something many Vietnamese share.

In 1993 Randy fell in love with a Vietnamese girl. "She had very unique features, was very likeable, so I took my feelings and loved her very much, and finally I got her love. After a year and a half there were arguments, and one day she said to me: "Older brother [honey], do you know what people tell me? They say I'm very beautiful, too beautiful to be with you, and if I'm with you it's not a match, because you are a black Amerasian.' I was very hurt and thought about all the teasing in Vietnam, and yet here in the U.S. it still happened. And worse, it came from someone I loved a lot. So I was sad and listless and depressed, and all I did was go to coffee shops and play video games and come home and watch Chinese kung fu movies every day for quite a long time." As Randy sank into a depression, he received a letter from a female fan in Australia. "She kept writing and I came to like her, and she came here to visit for three months and I was very happy," he says. In July 1997 Randy went to Australia and lived with her as his wife for eighteen months. He continued his singing career there and they had a son. "But after awhile, I don't know why, we had little fusses, and I decided to come back to America," says Randy. "Because I'm a singer, girls think I'm not faithful. My wife was jealous of girls around me all the time. In my life I've had first one good plan that turns bad, then another that turns bad, then another that turns bad," he says.

Abruptly leaving Australia and returning to Little Saigon, he arrived back in January 1998. "When I stepped back into the U.S. airport I had only $7 in my pocket, and felt I was in a world where I hardly knew where I was," says Randy. "I was very worried and confused, with no friends, no place to live, and didn't know where my life was going." Meanwhile, many new singers had become well-known. Randy claimed he was tired of singing anyway. "I get sick of it. You have to make people feel touched with your voice. And they don't pay that much—like for a wedding, $50 if you're not real popular and up to $500 if you are. But I don't want to sing at weddings, with people not paying attention and everybody eating and talking, and not clapping right. Right now I feel worthless, useless." But old and new friends offered loans and places to stay and gradually Randy began to get singing jobs again. But mostly his life was still hand-to-mouth.

Eventually, Randy got a part-time job as a deejay for a Vietnamese radio music program and met a new Vietnamese girlfriend. "But sometimes when we walk down the street holding hands and she sees another Vietnamese person coming," Randy says, "she drops her hand from mine."

Randy has a long scar up the inside of his left arm that he made when he broke up with his wife. "The scar is a mark of memory," he says. "It helps you not to do something. Like next time if I want to hurt someone, I have been hurt myself, so I can stop it. Sometimes I've been hurt from love, been hurt from life, been hurt from friends. Other times I feel guilty, so I burn myself with a cigarette to remember not to do something. I used to have a beautiful hand and now I have an ugly hand." Randy holds up his arm, turning and examining it, and laughs to himself a little. "When you're young you don't think twice, but the more you grow up, the more you understand," he says. "Vietnam is my motherland, but I don't miss it much. I like America better." He touches a silver chain around his neck from which dangles a cross with the words "God Loves You."

Kiem Do

In November 1991 St. Anselm's was drawn into a headline-making tragedy involving an Amerasian who had arrived in America only forty-eight hours earlier. On a sunny Saturday afternoon in Little Saigon, relatives and friends of eighteen-year-old Hang Thi Thay Dinh heard her screaming outside her uncle's Little Saigon home where they were celebrating the family's arrival in America. "Father, mother, help! He is killing me, he is killing me!" Rushing outside, the partygoers saw the girl staggering toward them, bleeding from stab wounds in her chest. She collapsed sobbing into the arms of the uncle, an earlier immigrant who had sponsored the family's resettlement in America. "She was saying, 'Oh my God, he stabbed me! I'm going to die! Help me, help me!'" the uncle later told a local reporter. Within minutes the girl lay dead in a pool of blood. Her killer, nineteen-year-old Amerasian Kiem Do, was nowhere in sight, and no one could imagine where he could have gone. He and the girl's ten-member all-Vietnamese family had arrived together two days earlier, and he had no relatives or friends in America. He spoke only a few words of English and knew nothing of the neighborhood or of the United States. He had no money. And having barely attended primary school, he was illiterate in Vietnamese as well as in English. In less than an hour a police detective found Do, confused and dazed, walking down a street in Little Saigon, repeatedly apologizing in broken English. "I sorry I stab her. I love her. Her don't love me. . . . I help her family go America. . . . I'm very angry. I'm very sorry. . . . Can you help me come back [to] Vietnam?" Do told the police that Dinh had promised to marry him two years earlier when he first agreed to bring her family to the United States. To Americans, it might sound like a tale of spurned love. But Amerasians and resettlement workers believed Do was one of thousands of Amerasians used by wealthier Vietnamese to get to America and then dumped. To them, the girl's family had much to answer for.

From the start, the stories told by Do and by Dinh's family showed glaring discrepancies, although at first Do himself refused to believe he had been used. "I love [Dinh's family] like my own. Dinh was the love of my life. I called her father my own dad," he told an interpreter in jail. He told the *Orange County Register* that he had no memory of stabbing Dinh, and wanted to apologize to her family and to see her coffin before she was buried. Crying, he said he would never have come to America "if she didn't promise we could be together. . . . Her mother knew that. And she had agreed to let us marry." But the girl's father, saying he was speaking for both himself and Dinh's mother, told the *Register*: "They're still children, too young for marriage. We've always treated Kiem Do well, but no promise was ever made." Do said that the night before the

stabbing the father told him he wanted his daughter to "marry well"—
"Not someone with empty hands like me, but someone with good
breeding, a steady income, who speaks fluent English." Dinh's father
claimed that all he had said was that he and his wife wanted the couple
to wait "maybe five or ten years . . . get an education first . . . then learn
English, then later work for money, a house, a car. . . . *Then* they could
think about starting a family." Such a plan, of course, made marriage
between Do and Dinh impossible. The story made major headlines in
the California media, and was much discussed throughout the Amerasian community in Little Saigon.

Do said that after Dinh's father talked to him the day after they all
reached the United States, Dinh told him "she would obey her parents'
wishes" about marrying him. Grief-stricken and panicked, realizing he
was once again rejected and abandoned, he told the *Register*: "I realized
I had no life . . . Not without her." Deciding to leave that very night
and "begin a life separate from Dinh's family," he asked her uncle for
$200 of the money due him from his Refugee Cash Assistance funds.
The uncle said it was too late to go to the bank that day, so Do decided
to wait until the next morning, Saturday. But by lunchtime—not long
before the bank would close—the family and friends were still happily
celebrating, leaving Do outside. Desperate, deciding to leave without
his money, he asked Dinh to first come outside to tell him goodbye. He
showed her a bread knife he had taken from the kitchen, saying he
would kill himself "if things don't work out after I leave." She took the
news calmly, he says, telling him: "If you want to stay, stay. If you must
go, then go." The next thing he remembers, he said, was seeing her
stabbed and bleeding, and running off as she screamed. He wandered
the unfamiliar streets of Little Saigon in a daze until he was arrested.

Dinh's family continued to tell a different story. Dinh "thought of
Do as her adopted brother, not her boyfriend," they told the *Register*,
and they "never believed Do was serious about marriage," and "Dinh
was thinking of school, not marriage." They said Do had lived with
their family in Long Khanh for ten years. But Do said he'd lived with
them less than two years, and had left his own adoptive mother and
older sister in Vietnam to come with Dinh's family, who paid all the
costs so they could accompany him. But family members kept claiming
they never realized there was any problem. "We were all frozen when
we heard her screams," a cousin told the *Register*. "We had no idea he
would do anything like this. Everyone was happy." The *Los Angeles
Times* sent a reporter and photographer to Dong Nai, Do's home village

in Vietnam, taking along Mary Payne Nguyen as interpreter. They met with the woman who'd adopted six-month-old Do from an orphanage where he was abandoned at birth. He called her "Mom" and he said that she had been kind to him, and that when he was growing up no one ever "mentioned" that he was an Amerasian—an odd assertion many Amerasians make. A country boy who worked in the fields, Do had dreamed of becoming a tailor. His adoptive mother told the *Times* that Do had hoped to someday find his American father, although he never even knew his name.

Nguyen brought back photos of Do's stunned adoptive mother and showed them to him in jail, where he buried his face in his hands and wept. A month later Do told the *Register* through Nguyen that he had come to believe Dinh's family had used him as "a one-way ticket out of Vietnam." He had called Dinh's parents from jail and told them he thought they had "set him up," but "they didn't respond. They were silent." Nguyen quoted Do as saying he wanted other Amerasians to know they would face prejudice in the United States as well as in Vietnam. "Amerasians are leftovers," he said, "something nobody wants. . . . I am speaking from my own experience and the experience of others like me." Dinh's entire family, including the uncle, moved away immediately after the murder, leaving no forwarding address. In April 1992 Do, wearing an orange jail jumpsuit and shackles, pleaded guilty to voluntary manslaughter and was sentenced to eleven years in the California Youth Authority—where, some people said, he always carried a picture of Dinh with him.

Mot (Not His Real Name)

Another Amerasian who sought help from St. Anselm's was sixteen-year-old Mot, who was brought in one day by a social worker. Partly crippled and with a diagnosis of simple schizophrenia, Mot was living in a rented trailer with his supposed "grandfather," who was spending all Mot's benefit checks. "Mot is the only Amerasian I wasn't able to find a room for, even just for a night," says Peter Daniels, who on that first day drove him to seven different Buddhist temples—mostly just converted houses that had sprung up around Little Saigon. In the past, some temples occasionally took in homeless Amerasians, although the city had begun enforcing housing codes after neighbors complained about too many homeless people there. But now all the temples turned Mot down. Daniels believes the real reason was that Mot was mentally disabled. "Mot wasn't at all crushed by so much rejection, because he didn't know he *was* being rejected. *I* was the dumb one. It didn't dawn on me until later that they weren't turning him away just because they didn't have a bed."

For awhile St. Anselm's kept moving Mot around. A couple of times, to keep Mot from becoming homeless, Steve Baker, Van's mentor who became Mot's as well, let both live with him. One day Mot began having what Daniels calls "bizarre episodes," like talking to himself in ESL class and wandering around St. Anselm's laughing for no apparent reason. Baker says Mot was never "scary crazy," but a young Vietnamese counselor called for a psych ambulance, and attendants roared up, strapped Mot down in front of everyone and took him away. Baker watched helplessly, pained at "how scared and pathetic Mot looked." The next day Mot was released, but afterward seldom came around St. Anselm's. Too many people had witnessed his humiliation. All his life, Mot once told Baker, he'd had a recurring dream in which he was reunited with his American dad.

Dat (Not His Real Name)

Several staffers and volunteers from St. Anselm's say that a black Amerasian named Dat is in many ways the most outstanding of all the Amerasians who passed through the center, not because of educational or financial success but because of his strength of character, his courage, and his uncomplaining acceptance of hardship in the face of constant bitter disappointments.

Born in a Bien Hoa hospital in October 1971 according to his probably false documents, Dat, like so many Amerasians, has a background full of unexplored mysteries and unanswered questions. He says he was given to the poor couple who adopted him by an unnamed "woman at the hospital." Described as a family friend, she was probably a relative. "My adoptive parents always loved me and were nice to me," says Dat. They were so poor they all lived in one rented room, along with an adopted daughter. After 1975 they kept Dat at home much of the time. "I was a very good boy growing up, but whenever I left my neighborhood, I got picked on," he says. "So for many years after 1975 my parents wouldn't let me go outside." When Dat was two he became very ill, and his adoptive father tried to treat him with a local folk remedy. His grandmother interrupted the treatments, and Dat believes that's why one of his legs was partially paralyzed and smaller. From early childhood he suffered from a painful limp, which, combined with the fact he is Amerasian, led to especially cruel taunts. "As I got older I would go to the market, and sometimes I had to pass areas with bullies. My parents ordered me never to fight back, but sometimes I had to," Dat says, adding, with a sudden grin, "and sometimes I won!"

When Dat was sixteen a Vietnamese couple with two children, "friends of a friend," offered to buy him. "They weren't old enough to claim to be my parents, so they decided they would tell officials that the man was my older brother," says Dat. "My family really needed the money. And we believed that in the U.S. I would have a brighter future and be able to send money back to help them." Dat moved in with the fake family, but their mask of kindness began to slip. They treated him like a servant. "They knew how much I wanted to go to America, so sometimes they'd pick on me or talk in a bad way. My real family was very sad, but told me to try to bear everything until I could get to America. We could see no other way I could have a future," he says.

In any case, the money paid for Dat was already spent, on a second-hand cyclo. "My dad started using it right away to earn money," says Dat. The day his father first pedaled up on it, the whole neighborhood turned out. "People were excited," Dat says. "But it was very difficult to drive, too hard for my dad. And in Vietnam, cyclo drivers get hurt and killed all the time. I wasn't happy seeing him doing such heavy, dangerous work." If Dat has other bad feelings about being traded for a cyclo, he never expresses them. The nearest thing to a complaint he offers is his feeling his family might have bargained better, or spent the money more wisely. "My family believed they were doing their best for me when they sent me to the U.S.," he says.

But in the Philippines Dat's fake family became openly cruel, and Dat saw people drinking heavily, knew about fights where camp residents killed each other. "Finally there came a time in the Philippines when I hated my life. I was very lonely, very miserable, angry, and homesick. I began to go places where a person could die at any time — dark and dangerous places, like bars or the visiting part of the camp jail, where there were people who would kill you at any time. But I didn't care. I was ready to give up my life." He thought of suicide, but adds, laughing a little, "I was scared." In the camps his fake family, like Dat's family when he was growing up, tried to keep him inside. "They were afraid if anything happened to me they'd be stuck in the Philippines, or even sent back to Vietnam," says Dat. After five miserable months, Dat was invited to a Vietnamese Christian church. "They were very friendly," says Dat. He began going on church outings. He made some friends, even met a girl with whom he occasionally went to church dances. At a church discussion and support group, "there came a time when I sat with them and talked openly from my heart for the first time about my feelings," he says. "And all the church people listening began crying. At that church I learned about God. And I found myself happy with God."

In March 1993 Dat, aged twenty, arrived in California. "You shouldn't be cooking. You're wasting gas," his fake stepbrother would complain nastily each morning when Dat would prepare a small bowl of breakfast noodles before leaving for English classes at St. Anselm's. Dat wouldn't reply. "I just couldn't stand being so hungry," he says. "The family took my benefits checks and food stamps, and gave me almost nothing to spend. They let me know that if I wanted to stay with them, I would have to follow all their rules. Since I had no family here, they believed I would never move out."

Dat tried to send a little money back to his family in Vietnam, but only an occasional $15 or $20. "I worried the fake family would kick me out, and I had nowhere to go. Sometimes if I had a little money I would buy a $3 tape of some local Vietnamese singers. The music was the only thing to make me feel better." Two of his favorite singers were Luu Quoc Viet and Randy.

Nhien Luong, the young Vietnamese VISTA worker who had helped Van, took Dat to doctors who said Dat's limp was caused by a polio epidemic that swept Vietnam after the war. She took him twice a week to a rehab facility to get polio braces and a cast to correct his limp. In June Dat received a letter from Church World Service reminding him that he owed them $3,085 for the one-way airfares to America for himself and his fake family. Next he got a letter that his refugee medical assistance would be cut off in October 1993, the end of his eight-month refugee assistance period. That month Luong helped Dat apply for Social Security disability because of his physical problems, including poor vision. His leg hurt a lot, and he suffered from headaches and dizzy spells. Luong managed to get him a small one-year monthly grant of post-polio financial aid. A dentist found fifteen cavities, and state-funded Dental-Cal agreed to pay to fill five.

Like most Amerasians, Dat had arrived in the Philippines as a so-called free case, one without an American sponsor required by law. Religious groups usually found sponsors for them, and the American sponsor of Dat's family was a kind, religious man unaware of the fake family's mistreatment. Dat, who had made a few friends through a local Vietnamese church, had secretly resolved to move out and had begun puzzling over ads for rented rooms. His last benefits check arrived on a day the sponsor was visiting, and the man gave it to Dat in front of the fake family. "I'm sure they felt very angry, but they couldn't dare show it," says Dat, who in October 1993 moved his few belongings into a shared rented room.

But Dat was thinking more and more of suicide. By November he was completely out of money and food. Nhien Luong, although unaware of the full extent of his problems, took him to apply for food stamps and a General Relief cash assistance loan. After waiting all day for his name to be called, he was told to come back the following day. He tried to go on a bus but got lost and called St. Anselm's, terrified he'd miss his appointment because if he did, he would have to wait three more months to reapply.

"Sometimes," says Dat, "I ran out of money for food. Once I cooked only rice for several weeks, just rice and—" Dat laughs, "sometimes, a hot dog!" He worried constantly about his family in Vietnam, who kept writing for help. "I worried all the time," he says. "I went to ESL classes at night and the rest of the time I was alone a lot. Sometimes I stayed awake studying all night. It was very, very hard, because in Vietnam I never even went to first grade."

Peter Daniels had helped Dat find a succession of temporary minimum wage jobs as assembler, printer's helper, janitor. Dat had no car and often no bus fare, and the jobs were usually far away. Someone in his church gave him an old blue bike, and with his leg aching he would pedal an hour each way to his jobs through heavy traffic. In February 1994 Social Security denied Dat's application for disability benefits, writing: "Medical evidence shows that you are able to move about and use your arms, hands, and legs in a satisfactory manner [and] medical evidence shows your polio does not prevent you from doing work that is less demanding physically." The rehab facility reported that Dat had "involuntary shaking in both arms . . . progressive weakness in his right leg . . . leg cramps, stomach aches, nervousness . . . difficulty with studying due to concentration lapses, and with writing due to involuntary shaking . . . and tires easily."

Two years after his arrival in America, the draft board sent Dat a stern warning: "Your name remains on our list of men who may be required to register but have not done so. . . . Men who refuse to register may be unable to obtain U.S. citizenship, and are not eligible for certain Federal benefits such as job training, student financial aid, and government employment. . . . If you ignore this correspondence we will send your name to the Department of Justice with a request that you be prosecuted. . . . [Refusing is] a Federal crime punishable by a fine of up to $250,000 and five years imprisonment." At work, Dat's job had become a daily torture. Mexican coworkers tormented and teased him daily. It felt like his life in Vietnam all over again. He became terrified that if he lost his job he would not be able to get another, and would become homeless. "Sometimes I felt so terrible I again thought of suicide," he says. "Finally I went to Peter Daniels and told him about my worries. He talked with me quietly and said he would help me get another job, where I could make friends." After Daniels left St. Anselm's and went to work for Catholic Charities, Dat continued to show up to talk to him every week or so. It was almost as if he thought of Daniels as his American father.

Above his bed in his small rented room, Dat had hung a large colored picture of Jesus. Dat sometimes sees his fake family on the streets of Little Saigon. "They say 'Hi,' I say 'Hi' back, but that is all. Sometimes they invite me to visit. But I do not go." When he is not at work or at church, Dat usually stays alone in his room.

Dat thinks that his dad in Vietnam has aged a great deal since he became a cyclo driver. "Someday," Dat says, his face serious yet glowing with dedication, "I want to help other people. All people. Amerasians, everyone. I don't care who or what kind of people. I want to help everyone, because I know how people feel when they are afraid and lonely."

Hieu (Not His Real Name)

Several times, I went with an interpreter to Patton State Hospital for the criminally insane to visit and interview the Amerasian Hieu. We would pass through several fences topped with rolled razor wire, and be buzzed in and out of locked gates after guards carefully checked our passes. Once inside, Hieu would trot out to meet us, as friendly and hopefully expectant as a young puppy. In his early twenties, he is tall and nice-looking with a ready smile that shows one silver-capped tooth. He has the light skin and Caucasian features of his American father. Always neat and clean, he is eager and proud to talk with the only visitors he has had in all his years inside the triple rings of high security fences. He is the only Amerasian at Patton. Yet more and more our visits and attempts to interview him ended in tension and disappointment on both sides. Over and over he changed the stories he told, and said that he could not remember even the most basic facts, such as the name of the woman who raised him in Vietnam.

Hieu says he's forgotten many things because of a head injury. Sometimes he says he fell from a wall, sometimes from a two-story building when he was fifteen, and sometimes he says he was seventeen and living in America and fell when a branch broke on a peach tree he climbed. Sometimes he says he never had any accident at all. Most people, including psychiatrists and psychologists who have interviewed him, believe he does remember more, and is suppressing or concealing whatever the truth may be. Most also believe he has some organic brain damage, although he's never been medically tested for it. It could have been caused by a fall, by some other injury, by malnutrition, by heavy drug or alcohol abuse, by beatings, or by some or all of these things.

Many details about Hieu's life in America are known; in fact, they have been extensively documented in jail and hospital records. But so far no one has been able to learn any reliable information about the missing early years in Vietnam. Once, on our fifth visit to him at Patton, Hieu suddenly asked my interpreter, a young Vietnamese social worker, if he was a police officer. Gradually it became clear that the regular interview procedures of an American journalist—inquiring about small details, going back over stories to check for accuracy—seemed to Hieu and other Vietnamese like the process Communist interrogators used. And in Vietnam, "journalists" often work for publications owned by the government or various political factions, so the distinction is not always clear.

Hieu was committed to Patton at age twenty-two. For a long time he told doctors and social workers that he was partly raised by his birth mother and his American father, and that after his birth mother died the father, who loved Hieu very much, begged Hieu to come with him to America. But Hieu, who was then aged three or four according to his own story, says he angrily refused because he believed his father had mistreated him and his mother. This would have dated the confrontation to 1978, long after the war. Next Hieu presented another version: that one evening in the tropical beach resort town of Nga Trang, a middle-aged Vietnamese nurse heard something stirring in a trash bin, and found a newborn Amerasian baby boy (Hieu). In this version, the nurse

raised Hieu lovingly until she died when he was seven, at which time
her grown daughter, Hieu's adoptive sister, took over. No matter what
else Hieu says, no matter how his story changes—and it changes constantly—at the core there is always a loving, nurturing woman, a
mother or sister, who loved him very much. He told us the adoptive
mother was good to him, although he can't remember her name or what
she looked like. He said she sang to him, cooked for him, got him medicine when he was sick, and did all the things loving mothers do. He
moved to Ho Chi Minh City with the adoptive sister when he was
seven, didn't go to school, and spent a lot of time playing in the streets.
People teased him about being Amerasian, he added. Later I learned
from a St. Anselm's staffer that Hieu once told someone that the "sister"
had been his mother's servant, who'd raised him when his "adoptive
mother" died. And just once he confessed to me that the "sister" was a
stranger who bought him on the street where he was living homeless
and alone. Later, he denied it.

Claiming at first that his "sister" was nice to him, one day Hieu
blurted out that she had actually "tortured" him, tying him to chairs
and beating him mercilessly with sharpened bamboo sticks. He showed
us scars on his wrists from the ropes. On the one or two rare occasions
when Hieu told us about the "sister's" cruelty, he trembled, his eyes
filled with tears, he had trouble speaking and hid his face. "Don't talk
about her," he begged, shaking and starting to cry. Surprised and
moved by his outburst of emotion, we changed the subject, but it took
Hieu several minutes to recover. Although the "sister" was surely cruel,
even the most abusive relationships may have a few happy moments to
cling to in memory. Perhaps there was a period when the "sister," hoping to use him, made him believe she truly cared for him. When her
mask came off, it was Hieu who felt ashamed.

Hieu ran away when he was ten. "When I first left I was afraid, and
slept in the bushes the first night. A lot of old people in houses all
around were dying of sickness, some of them paralyzed and crippled,
and many other people also were living in the streets homeless and
starving," he says. "There was a lot of hunger, and people were wearing
torn-up clothes, sleeping right on the sidewalk. Some people begged,
some died because they had nothing to eat and couldn't even get food
from a temple." Hieu formed a bond with a homeless old man about
seventy who sometimes treated him in a fatherly manner. "He was
good," says Hieu. "He was thin and short, he had a very long white
beard. He was too old to steal so I would steal food for him every day.

"One time I stole a Tet holiday cake from a house, and he and another man gobbled it like pigs. He didn't ask me to steal for him, I did it because I wanted to. When I brought him food, he would smile." But, Hieu said, the old man never thanked him. My Vietnamese interpreter said older Vietnamese usually don't thank younger ones for favors; it would go against the tradition of younger people's respect and reverence for elders.

On the streets, Hieu made a rare friend, another homeless Amerasian his age named Phuong. He remembers that Phuong's second name was also "Hieu," and thinks Phuong may be somewhere in the United States now too "because he's Amerasian." Whenever Hieu had a little money, he stayed in a flophouse—a cheap, noisy, frightening place, where several homeless people crowded into one room, some doing drugs and drinking, others trying to sell stolen property. Records show that he came to America in December 1991 with a woman, her husband, and four young children. When this is pointed out to Hieu, he says the children were the younger kids of his adoptive "nurse" mother who died, and are therefore his adoptive half-siblings. According to his surely fake birth certificate, he was seventeen years old.

Hieu says he lived in Little Saigon only two months with the "sister." He tells some people that she's moved to Alaska, and tells others that once he came home to find the house empty and the family gone. And he can't remember her name. "She was nice only when we were about to go to America," Hieu offered once, beginning to rock anxiously back and forth. "She told me I was a good person. But she started getting mean again in the Philippines." Hieu began to cry a little, twisting his hands together nervously. "When we got to the U.S. she was even meaner," he said.

Hieu says that since he came to America he has almost always been homeless. "When I had nowhere to go I slept in cars I found open, or stayed with friends. Once I slept on the roof of a church. I never begged. I was scared to do that. Sometimes I just didn't eat." In October 1992, less than a year after arriving in America, he was homeless. Records from that period show that Hieu, who denies using drugs until later in Patton, had a serious drinking problem. He was drifting into gang life and various petty criminal activities, although on a lower level than Tiger. Supposedly Hieu's gang was a "no guns" gang, but must have been into drugs, because Hieu speaks convincingly of an Amerasian friend who died of a cocaine overdose in a Little Saigon motel. In March 1993 Hieu was arrested and pleaded guilty to attempted commercial misdemeanor burglary of a Little Saigon pool hall, and was given forty-five days in jail and three years probation. In June 1993 he pleaded guilty and was given sixty days for another misdemeanor commercial burglary of an Asian grocery store.

The most serious case against Hieu came in August 1993, not long after he had served the two months for burglarizing the market. He was arrested with two other Vietnamese for stealing a Vietnamese jeweler's home safe, and was seen loading it into a car. Within hours officers tracked the burglars to an apartment. The safe, along with gold, jewelry, and $3,000 in cash were spread on the floor, and in a closet police found the jeweler's stolen gun. Hieu and one of the other burglars were arrested on the spot. An hour later, police found the third burglar, who had arrived from Vietnam only days earlier, crouching under a pile of clothing in a closet. All were charged with felony burglary, and in December 1993—two years after Hieu's arrival in the U.S.—he was sentenced to nine months in jail plus three years probation.

Two months later, in February 1994, President Clinton lifted the nineteen-year-old U.S. trade embargo against Vietnam as a first step toward normalization of relations between the two countries. That same month Hieu, who of course knew nothing about this news, was released on probation. Days later he broke into a trailer during the day and took some food and small items. Police found his fingerprints on a broken window and sliding glass door. Two weeks later when he reported to his probation officer, he refused to re-sign his probation agreement. "He said the rules were 'too strict,'" she noted dryly in her report, after arresting him for probation violation. Hieu, she wrote, told her he was "'living with friends,' [but] according to [a police investigator] . . . [Hieu] is currently under surveillance for possible involvement in several criminal activities." Back in jail, Hieu's mental condition deteriorated. Now he guesses he'd been falling apart for a year. He spent his days playing cards or watching television, especially cartoons. Some days he cried for hours. He would hit his head repeatedly, rhythmically, against his cell walls. "All I wanted to do around that time was die," says Hieu. "I couldn't speak a word of English. But I didn't try suicide. I'm so young, I don't want to die."

Hieu was seen by a psychiatrist, Dr. Paul Blair. Blair diagnosed Hieu as having major depressive psychosis, possible elements of bipolar disorder, probable organic brain damage "for reasons unknown," and serious problems with "cultural adjustment." Using the psychiatric jargon of his profession, yet with a strong undertone of outrage and empathy, Blair reported to the court: "There is no evidence of grandiose, hypersexual, or hyperreligious disorder [or] delusions or hallucinations. . . . His intelligence is dull-average [but] his fund of knowledge is totally inadequate. He is illiterate and cannot read, write, sign his own name, or do even simple arithmetic. His thought content shows a distinct poverty of thought [and] his insight and judgment were both poor at the time of the interview." Trying to learn Hieu's life history was extremely difficult, wrote Blair, since Hieu "expressed much confusion about it."

"He does not know his biological mother nor his biological father. . . . He was raised by a lady, but does not know her name. He has one brother in Vietnam"—(Hieu had probably talked about Phuong)—"and the only thing he knows about the brother is that one of his names also is Hieu."

Blair wrote that Hieu described his head injury as "having a spasm in the brain which causes me to be cuckoo. . . . The wires and veins in my head are broken." Continued Blair: "In the past he has found himself walking along the freeway for no reason at all. He admits he has been involved in self-injurious behaviors, again for no reason, such as banging his head on the trunk of a car. . . . He basically lives on the streets. . . . He states he is depressed, has headaches 'all the time,' has 'problems with thinking' and says 'I just want to break up my head. . . . In the past I have wanted to die.'" Blair summed up his findings: "Hieu's memory is exceptionally poor [and he has] enormous psychiatric and social difficulties. These are interwoven with one another and include a brain injury, probably mild mental retardation, a low-grade thought disorder with psychotic thinking, confusion, depression, and illiteracy. . . . It is likely that he has been severely psychiatrically impaired for a long time, and that this was exacerbated by his arriving in a country [at age seventeen] where he was abandoned within the first thirty days. It would be difficult enough to make the transition if Mr. Hieu were entirely psychologically and intellectually intact. Although his life appears to have been quite difficult in Vietnam . . . his life since coming to the United States has been a total disaster. It is my forensic opinion that a punitive response to this patient's difficulties would probably be both inadequate and inappropriate. The court may well want to protect this very vulnerable, weak member of our society."

Shortly after the court received Blair's report, Hieu pleaded guilty to the trailer burglary and was found, under a California statute, "guilty, but not guilty by reason of insanity." He was sentenced to Patton Hospital, which holds many of California's most dangerous prisoners. (It was, incidentally, the only hospital in the nation at that time with a full ward of erotomaniacs, or stalkers.) There was some vague talk by a few people that Patton was a "mercy placement" to save him from being thrown into prison. In June 1995 Hieu arrived at Patton, where he could be held for treatment for up to ten years (June 2005)—or until he is pronounced "cured."

Hieu's life at Patton, as recorded in daily staff notes, has been a mostly uneventful passage of years. It contains details like: "was caught giving a peer the coffee off his meal tray" and "may be selling his trays of food to peers" or "constantly clowning," or "occasional sexual preoccupation with younger female staffer" or "his snack has been cancelled because he always gives his snack to a peer" or "threw ball onto roof." One file note discussing the regular ward group sessions Hieu must attend says, "He is considered a sort of leader."

But Hieu's file also gives brief glimpses into his deeper life at Patton. At one point he seems to have fallen in love with a female staffer, an unrequited love that caused fights with other inmates and disciplinary measures from staff. He also formed a close attachment to an older white American man in his thirties, a deep connection that led to Hieu's using heroin with the man at least once and getting caught. The staff regarded the man as manipulative and more seriously ill than Hieu. The two were separated into different areas of the hospital, but once while the older man was in restraints, Hieu came to the door of the restraint room and tried to talk to him. When two female staffers Hieu had always seemed to like told him to move away, Hieu attacked them furiously, until he himself was overpowered and put into restraints. Whatever that relationship was to Hieu, it was clearly very meaningful. Looking through several years of chart notes that listed various changes of medications and resulting changes in behavior, I had the troubling thought that patients could be given a medication that made them act aggressively or "crazy," then be punished for medication-induced behavior.

Hieu's thoughts and dreams are not very different from those of Amerasians not confined in a "hospital for the criminally insane." "If I had lots of money I would get married, get a house and car, and shop all the time!" he told us one day, laughing. "And if I had any money I would consider sending it to the homeless old man with the long white beard [who once lived on the sidewalk with Hieu in Ho Chi Minh City]. He was a good person. . . . I always pitied my birth mom, although I don't know who she is. At night sometimes I see her around my bed. She's very beautiful. She loves me a lot. Her feelings towards me are really good. I also imagine that my American father is very handsome. My mother and father both love me very much and want me to live a good life. I want to go back to Vietnam to visit, but I like America better. It's been very hard in the U.S., but it's even harder in Vietnam."

Then Hieu grew serious. He looked directly at me and my interpreter, and appeared to summon all his courage as he drew himself up and stated sternly: "But by going to war in Vietnam and leaving many children behind and not bringing all the kids here, the U.S. didn't show respect. When I came to America I thought I would get money and a house from the government. I thought Americans would be nicer. I couldn't find my dad or mom here, and I got in trouble, and now I'm in prison. Nobody was ever nice to me in America." He stopped talking abruptly, his voice choking, and covered his face.

Hieu has a tattoo of five dots in a dice pattern on one wrist, a symbol of "the five Ts." He told us they stand for the Vietnamese words Tuoi Tre Thieu Tinh Thuong, meaning "Youth Lacks Love." But gang workers say the five Ts are a common tattoo meaning Tien, Tinh, Thuoc, Toi, and Tu — money, desire, drugs, sin or crime, and jail. Hieu's tattoos are nothing like some of Tiger's more elaborate tattoos. Hieu's tattoo is made of wobbly, blurry scratches, which Hieu says he made himself using a needle and soot from a burned plastic slipper. He first says he made it when he was alone, then boasts he was actually "with my gang homeboys in a Garden Grove motel, and we all did the same tattoo at the same time." He is very proud of that tattoo. It shows he once belonged to something.

While Hieu was serving his sentence in Patton, in April 1995, the twentieth anniversary of the end of the Vietnam War, a *Los Angeles Times* article was reporting that U.S. veterans of the war were also still affected. The article said that "the emotional aftershocks of the war continue to reverberate for a minority of the 3.1 million men and 7,200 women who served in the Southeast Asian war zone," and that according to a 1988 study, "tens of thousands of male Vietnam theater veterans . . . were suffering from full-blown cases of post-traumatic stress disorder, and an additional 11 percent were experiencing intrusive thoughts, nightmares, outbursts of anger, and thoughts and fantasies of traumatic experiences in Vietnam." A different report commented on the extremely high suicide rate of American Vietnam War veterans.

About the same time, a 1992–94 study of a group of Amerasians was reported in a University of Pittsburgh dissertation by Thanh Son Thi

Nguyen—"Adjustment and Acculturation Problems of Vietnamese-Amerasians in Pittsburgh, PA: A Post-Resettlement Study." Nguyen in 1992 studied thirty-two Amerasians resettled in Pittsburgh, with a 1994 follow-up. Almost a third of the Amerasians reported they had had *no* positive experiences in America. In the 1994 follow-up, they said they had not become more assimilated. The female Amerasians reported much more anxiety and depression. Seven of the eight Amerasians who were students in 1992 had dropped out of English classes, blaming pressure to work and send money back to Vietnam.

"Major personality issues related to identity and low self-esteem, [and] feelings of being a stranger or being different have never improved in the land of the Amerasians' fathers as the [Amerasians once had] so ardently hoped," wrote Nguyen. The study spoke of the Amerasians' earlier "exaggerated expectations that American society would welcome them with open arms and a guilty conscience, and thereby do anything for them to repay [them for] all the pain they had endured because of their American fathers." Instead, they had faced "a bitter and frustrating reality where they did not get much assistance [and where] survival skills they had learned previously on the streets of Vietnam were needed as much as before. Their wonderful dreams . . . are all gone. Unmet expectations have resulted in anger and frustration, and feelings of having been deceived." Although the 1994 follow-up found the subjects less worried and more confident, the reason appeared to be due to the Amerasians having "resigned themselves to the fact they would never be integrated into American society in the way they had hoped."

Adding that the Amerasians "were brought here to salve a guilty national conscience," and that they appeared to be falling into an American version of the "dust of life," Nguyen wrote: "In the subjects' hearts, the American dream is over," and that unlike many other refugee and migrant groups to the United States, "the Amerasians may never be able to say from the depth of their hearts, 'I am American.'"

Interestingly, fully a fifth of the Amerasians in the 1992 study had left Pittsburgh for California by the time of the 1994 follow-up. Doubtless many had migrated to Little Saigon, where they probably had some contact with St. Anselm's.

9

The Amerasians' Second Struggle to Survive

I used to see Amerasians come into court accused of crimes, and when I asked them about family or community ties, they always said "No," they had none. There was never anyone to come forward on their behalf . . . no parent, no sister or brother, and nobody to speak for them from the mainstream Vietnamese community here. So I was never able to tell the court that they had a chance to be rehabilitated.

—Vu Trinh, Vietnamese American attorney and former public defender in Little Saigon

In the spring of 1992, Mary Payne Nguyen wrote a report for St. Anselm's on the increasing number of Amerasians who were homeless or living in "unsafe situations." She listed a pregnant woman who had been left to wander the streets with her year-old child, and a young man whose fake family dumped him in St. Anselm's lobby, clutching his few shabby belongings. Many more, she wrote, were trying to "cling to situations" where they were subjected to regular verbal and physical abuse because they no longer had benefits coming in and couldn't find jobs.

Louis Nguyen

One night Louis got a phone call from Joseph Love.

> "I have some information for you about your father," Love said.
> "Is it good news or bad?"
> "It would be best for you to come in tomorrow so we can talk in person," said Love, "and please bring your mother too."

That night Louis couldn't sleep. He tried to prepare himself for his father's possible rejection. "I didn't think of my father that much while I was growing up, but later, when I was thinking about meeting him, I was a little worried he might not love me," says Louis. "One of my Amerasian friends found his dad, and when he called him, his dad said in this gruff voice: 'What you want from me?' I decided if my father asked me a question like that I would say: 'Nothing!' and never go see him. I just hoped to meet him, to meet his mom, his brothers and sisters, his family."

Louis had waited two years after arriving in America to look for his father, preparing himself by enrolling in college and launching his U.S. singing career in Little Saigon's Vietnamese-American pop music scene. His father would find someone in whom he could feel pride. And if his dad rejected him? "At least I knew in my heart I could handle anything," says Louis. "My grandmother had teached me how when I was growing up, when people were very mean to me because I am Amerasian."

The next morning Marianne Blank, St. Anselm's director, came with Louis and his mother into Love's small office. Although most estimates are that fewer than 2 percent of the fathers were located, Love's "find" ratio was much higher and years later he was still looking for some of them.

A psychologist who studied Amerasians at five sites, including eighty at St. Anselm's, said two-thirds had believed they would find their fathers when they reached America. But most Amerasians had very little information Love could use. "They had no idea of the size or complexity of the United States," Love says. "They said they thought Americans were so smart, with all kinds of computers, that they could find their fathers immediately. They'd tell me things like: 'My father was named Jim, he was in the service at Saigon, and his best friend was named Eddie.' Others had only a 'sound-alike' name that they can't spell in English. But some of the dads and moms had really deep love relationships. Sometimes the mom had a letter she managed to save all these years, saying things like: 'I'm in the U.S. trying very hard to get you here with me, Love you forever,' with the dad's name and return address. Or they had a photo with the dad's name on the back. If he's in uniform in the picture I can look at it and tell what part of the service he was in. And there may be insignia, or medals. I've collected all the patches that U.S. military wore on their uniforms in Vietnam and show them to the moms: 'Did it look like this?' Sometimes I ask: 'What did the dad do?' If they say, 'He don't do nothing, he just walk around—he the boss!'—then I know I'm looking for an officer or a sergeant! Sometimes, the only thing to go on is the mom's memories. She may say: 'He have bird on uniform' and I'll know he was Airborne. Or 'He have gold flower on collar' and I know he was a major." Love then uses the town and year of the parents' meeting as further clues.

But some of the fathers turned out to have served in the Military Assistance Command, Vietnam, known as MACV. If so, the government will never release any information on them. MACV partly grew out of the Air Force's secret Jungle Jim unit, when President Kennedy in 1962 expanded the role of some U.S. "advisers" in Vietnam, from training Vietnamese pilots to themselves covertly taking part in combat missions. A. J. Langguth recounts in his book *Our Vietnam* that to participate in these flights, an American "had to be a bachelor willing to sign a statement that if captured in Country 77—a code for Vietnam—he agreed that [the U.S.] government would deny any knowledge of him."

At St. Anselm's, Louis and his mother waited anxiously as Love opened a folder. "But before he told us," says Louis, "he glanced at Marianne and they exchanged a look, and when I see their eyes, I know it's something bad." As Louis translated Love's words into Vietnamese for his mother, Love said he had tracked down Louis's father. His wife and a grown daughter, Louis's older half-sister, still lived in the small Texas town where the father had been discharged. But Louis's father had died ten years earlier, and was buried in the veteran's section of the town cemetery. Then Love, following a procedure he had worked out, handed Louis an envelope colored white, to symbolize mourning. Inside was a card with the names of the wife and half-sister and the exact grave plot number where the father was buried, in case Louis should ever want to visit the grave. If the father had been alive and agreed to be contacted, the envelope would have been red, a Vietnamese symbol for a joyful occasion. "My mom and Marianne cried," Louis says, "But I controlled myself." Inside, however, his feelings churned.

Love had managed to obtain the military retirement photo taken when Louis's father left the service. It showed a stern, dignified-looking black man in his forties, wearing a master sergeant's uniform with six hash marks on his sleeve and a modest row of medals on his chest. "I always try to get a photo of the dad for his kid," Love explains. "Even if he's dead. Or even if the dad is alive and says he won't see his kid, I ask if he'll at least send a photo. The pictures are real important to the kids, proof of a real dad. They can put it on the mantel and everyone can see it. If they're Buddhists it goes on the family altar with fruit, flowers, incense, and such. With a picture on the mantel, a kid can tell any story. And some of them do." Love notes that Louis's dad had a national defense service medal, six overseas service bars, six stripes for years of service, three good conduct medals, a Republic of Vietnam cross for gallantry with palm, and had qualified as an expert with a rifle. "About the time he retired, he had some kind of temporary disability, so he must have gotten sick in the service. He joined when he was twenty-one—the U.S. military was still segregated then—and in the early 1950s got two 'Section Fours.' That's for small stuff like coming in drunk, or telling your sergeant exactly what you think of him. He might have been some kind of rascal early on. Or maybe just stood up for something. Anyway, that's about it. The file isn't special. I don't have a lot of notes like I do in some cases." Love also had news about the American father of Louis's younger half-brother. His father, too, was dead.

Alone that night Louis studied the photo of the father he had never seen. "My mother had burned almost all the pictures of my dad in 1975 because if you had a picture of an American they would put you in jail," says Louis. "In the picture Joe Love gave me, my dad is standing very straight and stiff, not smiling. But I have a feeling that even though he died I didn't really miss knowing him. Because at the moment I looked at his picture I felt I was meeting him. I even said to my mom, 'Maybe I look like him.'" Louis thinks Love may have told him that his older half-sister was studying to be a doctor. "My sister, she might be a doctor now. I would like to know her. Maybe someday I will go to see her. But I worry that she might think something bad about our dad if I did. Because I don't know if our dad told his wife and daughter about me." Love says he's "quite sure" that he himself never told the father's widow that her husband had a son in Vietnam. "A child is pretty concrete proof of infidelity," he says. "It might screw up her memories."

Although Love was used to situations where Amerasians hardly knew their fathers' first names, the hunt for Louis's father had gone fairly quickly because Louis's mother was able to give Love the name, rank, and assignment in Vietnam for Louis's father and of the father of Louis's younger Amerasian brother. Both brothers took ESL classes at St. Anselm's when they first arrived in the United States, but Louis soon enrolled in a community college with the help of a government student loan, following the difficult path he had set for himself. The handful of Amerasians who had come to America as infants or young children—i.e., on Operation Babylift—had grown up attending U.S. schools, spoke perfect English, and had long since assimilated in America. Louis, now nineteen, had only had six months of English study in the Philippines, "but I studied there very hard," he says.

Says Peter Daniels, who had tried to discourage Louis from attempting what had seemed an impossible goal: "Louis was one of the Amerasians who held themselves a little apart from the others. He wanted a better path, and didn't see many other Amerasians doing things he wanted to do, like getting an education." A close friend of Louis says: "When he first came here he was very determined to make his life better." Louis talked with his mother about how he wanted to continue his education, and she agreed to share any financial sacrifices while he tried to reach his goal. She took work in a sewing shop. "In America at first my mom and I rented one room together," he says. "We had no transportation, and everywhere I went I walked. We got benefits money for only eight months. When I got to the U.S. I started at a community college, not high school. I was too old to be allowed to do that. With the kind of government student loan I got, you have to pass every class with at least a C or they take the loan away.

"College was very difficult. Many times I couldn't understand the teachers' words in class. Some of the teachers themselves had foreign accents. A few were mean; they would say to me: 'Louis, you are in college now, not high school!' When that happened I would drop their class and look for another. But a lot of Asians can't talk back to teachers. I had a [Vietnamese American] counselor, Tina Pham, and she helped me a lot. She was wonderful to me, wonderful to every one." Louis struggled with texts and lectures that were difficult even for native English-speakers. After completing community college, he enrolled

at a good nearby four-year college, California State University at Fullerton.

He met his Vietnamese American girlfriend through the Vietnamese
Students Club. She had come to America several years earlier as a
twelve-year-old boat refugee, and settled with her family in Little Saigon. "She helped me very much," Louis says. Although herself
swamped with difficult studies for a career in science while holding
down two jobs to partially support her family, she made time to translate some of the more difficult English words for Louis and edited and
typed some of his papers.

Soon after he arrived in California in 1992, Louis had begun making
the rounds of Little Saigon's booming Vietnamese pop music scene,
known as the "Vietnamese Motown." One of the first people he went
to see was Le Ba Chu, then one of the foremost promoters and manag-
ers of Vietnamese American performers. A former South Vietnamese
navy captain who had trained with the U.S. Seventh Fleet and received
a U.S. award for bravery, Le was among 3,000 Vietnamese refugees
who had crowded onto one naval boat the day after Saigon's collapse
and escaped to a larger U.S. ship waiting offshore. In California he
spent ten years in a day job as a cook for Chicken Pie Restaurant in
Anaheim while working nights building a career as a music producer,
manager, and promoter in nascent Little Saigon. Almost every Vietnamese American pop singer at one time or another had recorded for
Le Ba Chu. Le arranged for Louis to record his debut CD. Although
Louis and Le Ba Chu eventually went separate ways, Louis recorded
other CDs, some of which he marketed himself.

A few of the dozens of recording studios in Little Saigon are quite
elaborate, with state-of-the-art equipment, but most are simply a room
or two in the producer's home. Top stars perform regularly in U.S. Vietnamese clubs—some modest, some fancy palaces seating hundreds—
and tour before refugee audiences in Europe, Australia, Canada, and
Asia, as well as other U.S. cities with sizable Vietnamese populations.
Their pirated videos and recordings have made many of them stars even
in their native country, although until at least 2002, as long as Communists ruled Vietnam's government, no exiled performer would dream of
performing there.

"When I was still living in Vietnam," says one singer, Quynh Huong,
"the Communists wanted all singers to sing Communist songs, like the
ones about Mr. Ho Chi Minh, which we don't like. They say love songs
lead us to be weak, and that when we are romantic we don't have time

to work hard." On the other hand, she says, there are Communist love songs, such as this one: "There were two lovers. He was a soldier from the North; she was a peasant from the South. Because of the [civil] war in Vietnam, they had to separate, but when the war ended he comes back to see her, and they remain on a farm, growing children and rice."

In America, political content in Vietnamese songs is common, including songs about returning to Vietnam and taking back the government. One of Louis's most popular songs is "The Communists Killed Our Love," written by his friend the late Tram Tu Thieng, a famous Vietnamese songwriter who also lived in Little Saigon. Elvis Phuong, one of Vietnam's best-known singing stars who fled Vietnam the day Saigon fell, liked the song so much that he, too, recorded it, to a Latin beat. "It's about this couple who loved each other before 1975," Louis translates. "But the man had to go to jail for his political beliefs, and the woman escaped to the U.S. Years later the man gets out of jail, and is going to the U.S. to find her, but on the way he learns she has married someone else. And he sings how the Communists killed their love." Another song written especially for Louis by Tram is "about a boy who comes to the U.S. and then 'does stupid things'—smoke, drink, not mind his parents—and so he goes to jail, and people say he had bad parents. So he regrets, and promises himself that when he gets out he will be a good person. But when he comes back, people look down on him, his girlfriend has left him, and nobody, even his family, opens their arms for him. And he realizes it's too late."

Sometimes when Louis is giving a concert or being interviewed on the radio, fans ask if he ever found his American father. He answers: "Yes. He is dead." Privately he says: "Maybe it's best. My father could have been alive and not accepted me." Unlike others who proudly show pictures of their fathers around coffeehouses, Louis keeps his dad's photo mostly private, partly because he fears it might be lost or damaged and partly because he wants to protect the privacy of his father, his father's widow, and the half-sister he has never met and may never meet—who may never even know of his existence.

While Louis, like other Amerasians, was struggling to make a new life in America, by January 1993 the U.S. Amerasian resettlement program had moved into its fifth year. Fake families continued to proliferate, and some Amerasians in Vietnam were not only selling themselves to several fake families but appearing at exit interviews repeatedly under different names. Fraud had grown so serious that the United States was planning to shut down the program. It had already lasted much longer

and cost much more than anyone had dreamed originally. The voluntary agencies that had made travel loans to Amerasians had begun sending them dunning letters. The Amerasians were terrified by the letters,
and a few brought them to St. Anselm's, where staff drafted replies in
which the Amerasians promised to pay for their own transportation but
not for that of their fake families. Some of the letters and replies:

From Episcopal Migration Ministries, with a bill for $5,257: "Ac-
cording to our records your account is seriously delinquent. We must
now remind you that this loan is your legal responsibility and you must
pay it in full, or contact us to arrange a new payment schedule. If you
do not make arrangements to pay this loan, your account may be re-
manded to the U.S. Government for future action. Please remember that
your loan payments help maintain a loan fund for other refugees waiting to come to the U.S." The reply: "Dear Sirs, I want to renegotiate
my loan. . . . The reason I am the responsible party . . . is because I am
an Amerasian [and] arrived in this country with an "adopted" family of
six others. This is not my real family, and I feel my obligation should be
only one-seventh of the loan, or $751. . . . While I do not have a job,
and know little English, I will try very hard to pay $50 per month."

From International Rescue Committee (dated April 30, 1993, the
eighteenth anniversary of the end of the Vietnam War), with a bill for
$5,125. The reply: "I was the principle party of a total of nine [adopted]
family members . . . utilizing me to come to the United States. I cannot
afford to pay for everyone but would like to contribute my fair portion,
$569.45 . . . when I have a job."

"Only a few of the Amerasians I knew were successful, mostly the
ones who were taken to small rural villages—not the NEZ areas—
where they were more sheltered from the government," says Nhien
Luong, the young former VISTA volunteer at St. Anselm's. "I'm talking
about successful by Amerasian terms, like a singer. Before Saigon fell,
some people were proud of having an Amerasian kid. Afterwards, any
affiliation with Americans was bad. It wasn't just racial; it was also political." Many Amerasians made a secondary migration after arriving in
California, moving to Iowa and states near there to work in slaughter
houses where they didn't need English and could earn good wages.
"More female than male Amerasians were sold in Vietnam, and some
left their kids behind," adds Luong. "Some were thinking they might
bring their children here later, or if things didn't work out they could
go back. But later they tended to hook up with other Amerasians or
Vietnamese here—not usually in marriages, but having kids with them.

And then the men would leave. I think all of us at St. Anselm's at first had the American mentality that a woman should control her life through getting an education, and we were trying to mold the female Amerasians into that American image. We forgot that what they needed most was for someone to love and care for them."

While some people who circled around St. Anselm's in those days had bad intentions (Blank says several American men showed up hoping to "adopt" young Vietnamese girls), other Americans and Vietnamese, including therapists and social workers, volunteered free time and help. Suzie Dong-Matsuda, a young, attractive social worker in Orange County, herself an earlier immigrant from Vietnam, helped at St. Anselm's while still completing her credentials and has worked with "quite a few" Amerasian clients over the years.

"Among the Amerasian clients I've seen," she says, "the women's issues are depression and post-traumatic stress disorder—they're usually not psychotic, although most of the suicides by Amerasians are by women. Women who married young are often in abusive relationships, and may have problems being parents themselves. The men clients are more likely to be psychotic, often disoriented as well as violent, and I also have guys with depression. Many Amerasians grew up like wild [creatures]. They do some bonding with each other, but the bonds are very fragile. There's often friction between them when they get together, because [most] never learned how to love or how to resolve conflicts. And they were robbed of respect since they were born." American rules and laws have been puzzling to many, she adds. "The Amerasians have a lot of legal problems here—" she laughs a little, "because they make 'mistakes,' do things that might not be a crime in Vietnam, like jaywalking. And many have trouble living in disciplined settings, so get a lot of tickets, and have no money to pay them and no way to fight for themselves." Amerasians who spend time in jail or prison often have psychiatric problems when they get out, she added.

"One of my white Amerasian clients was sold as a teenager in Vietnam to a family that made her into a prostitute and lived off her money. This girl has a lot of self-hate and guilt. And now the 'mother' who prostituted her has become crippled and can't walk, so this girl takes care of her. She feels that the 'mom' at least took her in when her real mom abandoned her. With medication and therapy the girl is better now, but in the past she's tried to cut herself many times. Amerasians often experience emptiness and worthlessness. I had a male Amerasian client in his twenties living at a board-and-care facility who kept hearing very abusive voices, and imagined the manager was saying to him: 'You Amerasian, you're nothing! Your mom was a whore! Your mom fucked a white guy!' and he punched the manager. That Amerasian was hospitalized and stabilized on medication. But when he's hearing voices he can't concentrate at work or follow directions, and he feels helpless.

"The Amerasians can be very childlike. They can laugh and joke and be very natural. The women cry easily, are very expressive. And they're very compassionate—they feel other people's problems more, but are very fragile. In Vietnam they could survive by many means. They could [bring things like bamboo shoots or wood] from the jungle, and sell them on the street, but not here. And here there are more barriers. I admire their coping skills, but the added barriers in the U.S. have weakened those skills. Yet somehow, so far most have survived."

Chris Duong, a young Vietnamese American policeman in Garden Grove who immigrated to America by boat, also volunteered at St. Anselm's beginning in 1992. "I noticed the Amerasians were separated from the Vietnamese refugee population, and seemed more open and outgoing, real nice and polite but very street smart," he says. "Sometimes they used slang words I didn't understand. I worked with some runaways and I saw [numerous] fake families, and how they took advantage of the Amerasians—although years later, some are still living together. I don't think most fake families were wealthy. I think the typical fake family was poor in Vietnam, and found poor Amerasians and bought them things until they got to America." Like others, he speculates some families bought Amerasians with money sent by relatives already in America.

Once in the United States, the fake families "just didn't want 'em," shrugs Duong. "Many Vietnamese are racist—and also, they look on Amerasians as a product of prostitution, and want to make their lives miserable." But why make them miserable? Duong shrugs again. "Vietnamese are afraid of blacks [and half-black Amerasians]. And plus, they took the Amerasians' [benefits] money. Eventually we began seeing more and more Amerasians committing crimes. Recently we arrested two for running a whorehouse in Westminster. They will do anything to support their families." Duong leans back, thinking, then adds: "I also had to deal with a couple of Amerasians who'd gone crazy. Just acting weird, like staring into space. There's one I arrest about every month who hangs around Bolsa, drinks a lot, and recently got hit by a car." This is a homeless Amerasian in his mid-twenties whom Tiger knew back in Vietnam and hung out with again in Little Saigon.

Duong tells his own story of coming to America. "In 1979 when I was fourteen my dad put me on a boat escaping Vietnam and told me, 'You're on your own.' When I got here I lived with an uncle in L.A. and then joined the Marines for ten years and became a sergeant. Back in Vietnam when I saw Amerasians on the street, I used to give them a dirty look too. What changed me? Ten years in the Marines and in the U.S.—that was a crash course in communications with all people. In the Marines I got treated very good by the world, with the opportunity to advance. I was put in with all kinds of people and I was treated the same by blacks and whites. We had rules in the military; I never got called bad names." Duong says his early experiences as a stranger in America are part of what prompted him to volunteer at St. Anselm's. "I feel sorry for the Amerasians," says Duong. "I'm totally in sympathy with them. What happened is not their fault. But bias has gone on in Vietnamese culture for so long I think it will take a couple of generations to iron that out. The new generation [of Vietnamese] is thinking that an Amerasian is just another kid."

Some Amerasians who came on Operation Babylift and other early placement avenues and were placed in small, ethnically homogenous towns where they stood out, have said they were discriminated against. But in more mixed locales, Amerasians don't stand out much visually from the other ethnicities that surround them. This is especially true in California, with its immigrants from all over the world. Chris Duong's views and those of many Vietnamese his age who grew up in America hold much hope for the Amerasians.

In June 1992 Mary Payne Nguyen had hired Peter Daniels as a grant writer for St. Anselm's Amerasian program. Sometimes praised for her energy and creativity, Nguyen was also being criticized for frequent temper outbursts and the mistreatment of some Amerasians. Says one staffer: "She was notorious for screaming at and belittling all staff and clients under her, including the Amerasians." Daniels, in his forties, was trained as an anthropologist. Tall and lanky, he usually seems unflappable and calm. During his first three months at St. Anselm's, Nguyen was frequently out of town and he served as acting coordinator. "A lot of Amerasians had a strange attachment to Mary because she believed in them," says Daniels. "She had a love-hate relationship with some of them. She was their champion, she fought for them, yet she also used them and would bully and intimidate them. She caused a lot of Amerasians to fail in their relationship with Americans." An Amerasian who lived for a time in Mary Nguyen's house with other Amerasians renting space there says Nguyen caused "many" Amerasians to leave California to get away from her.

In September 1992 Nguyen traveled to Vietnam, delivering medicines and developing contacts. While she was gone, a fundraising consultant turned in a highly critical report about her. "Also, the whole staff held a rebellion against Mary while she was gone, including the two or three Amerasians who had become staff members too," says another staffer at the time. "Almost immediately after Mary left for Vietnam, all of them went into Marianne Blank's office and protested against Mary." Blank called a staff meeting. Says one who attended: "Some of the most important staffers were all bonded and united, and said they were absolutely going to quit if Mary didn't leave." The day Mary Nguyen returned from Vietnam, apparently with no idea of trouble brewing, Blank, the consultant, and others were waiting in Blank's office, with Nguyen's final check already made out. Nguyen was replaced by Daniels. She eventually went to Vietnam and opened an agency arranging the adoption of Vietnamese babies by Americans. A Vietnamese newspaper reported in 2001 that she had been asked to leave the country by the Vietnamese government.

Nan Bui

When they first arrived in America, Nan and her orphanage sister Joan huddled together with other Amerasians being resettled in the home of a sponsoring family in North Carolina where they'd been placed by a religious organization. The sponsoring family was a young white church couple who at first seemed leery of the Amerasians who were frightened and disoriented. "Only me and Joan were together from the same temple," explains Nan. "At first we felt the white couple treated us badly. We were not yet used to American food and we craved noodles and rice, so we asked to take some of the food stamps assigned us to buy some, because American food was still sickening and strange to us. But they would not let us.

"Later, Joan and I were placed with a black American church couple. They were always kind to us, and took us to restaurants sometimes and other places." But Joan became involved with a Vietnamese tribal man many years older, who had been in America many years, apparently as part of an indigenous tribal group brought to America because it had been trained by the CIA and had fought for the United States during the war. Joan began living with the man, whom Nan calls "very abusive," and had the first of three children by him. Nan decided to move to California. At first she stayed in Long Beach, twenty miles from Little Saigon, with a Vietnamese couple she'd known slightly years earlier in Vietnam, and who sometimes sent money back to Nan's temple.

Many Amerasians are bisexual, and become involved with both genders during their lives. Nan is primarily a lesbian, although she has had love affairs with men. In Long Beach she had a serious love affair with a young Vietnamese woman, "but we had to be discreet because the girl's mother didn't know," she says. "Then one day the mother listened in on one of our phone conversations and became very upset. She demanded we end our relationship, and made her daughter marry. To make her mother happy, my friend agreed, although I was included in the wedding." Nan became involved for a time with a Russian security guard she met at her job in a computer assembly factory where she worked assembling computers and making good wages. Later, Nan had a new girlfriend, a white Amerasian named Terri (not her real name). Like many Vietnamese, Nan likes to gamble, but she lives frugally and several times has sent several hundred dollars back to her orphanage. Occasionally, she told me, she sends a small amount to the birth mother and half-sister whom she left behind in Vietnam.

Shopping one day at a Little Saigon supermarket, Nan saw an old acquaintance—a gangster who in Vietnam once helped her retrieve a cap that had been stolen from her. "It was a very special cap, and one day at the Ho Chi Minh market gangsters snatched it, and I let them, because I was afraid they would hurt or even kill me. A few days later I saw a different gangster take a man's wallet, but I lied to the police that I didn't remember what he looked like, because I was afraid he would kill me later. The next day the wallet gangster came to thank me, and I told him about my cap, and he got it back for me." Now living in Little Saigon, that gangster remembered Nan. "He had joined a gang here in America and said to be sure to tell him if anyone bothered me, and he would take care of it," says Nan.

Nan also ran into Tiger. "When he first came to America, I saw the gang people here take care of him when he needed food or anything," she says. "Tiger was trying to build up a gang, which stole but did not intentionally hurt people, and all the young kids when they were arrested would say that he was a gang leader. But although he has a big mouth, he would not really do anything bad, he would not really hurt

anyone," she insists. Nan says Tiger asked her to be his girlfriend, but
she declined, saying, "Let us instead be like brother and sister." One
day Tiger came to her house looking shaky and frightened. "Tiger himself knew he had done something wrong, something he shouldn't have
done, and someone had said they were going to kill him. And Tiger was
very scared of the gang the 'cap' guy belonged to. Tiger was scared even
to ever leave his house because he knew he could be killed right away."
This may have been the time another acquaintance of Tiger's mentioned—that "Tiger had been dealing cocaine for a Big Brother who
one day disappeared, so Tiger had no more cocaine [to deal]."

Nan says Tiger asked her to intervene for him with the 'cap' guy. "So
I talked to both of them together, and after that they became friends. I
also advised them to get back to normal life from gang life, and not 'do
anything stupid.' Of course, Tiger did go back to gang life, but from
then on he was always very nice to me." But Nan's relationship with
her girlfriend Terri was very difficult. Jealous and possessive, Terri
sometimes beat her. Nan ran away several times but couldn't seem to
end the relationship, although she called police on Terri more than
once. Meanwhile, Nan stayed in touch with Joan. Every year around
Tet, she sent Joan a ticket to California. One day Joan and her children
showed up unexpectedly on Nan's doorstep. They had fled by bus
across country to escape Joan's husband. Nan took them to stay at the
apartment she shared with Terri and two other women.

"But there was a lot of tension," says Nan. "Like Terri, Joan is very
hot-tempered. And Terri, especially when she was drinking, was jealous
of Joan. Also, Terri hates black Amerasians, and gets angry every time
she even hears Joan's name. People in our house were picking on Joan
when I wasn't around. I tried to ask all of them to respect my sister
Joan. Finally I even issued a warning: 'Nobody is to touch Joan—if
you do, I will not forgive you!' But one day when I was gone, Terri was
drinking beer and hit Joan and pushed her, and Joan called the police.
She told them that she was my sister." When Nan came home soon afterward she told the officers that she and Joan were actually *adoptive*
sisters. "I had to say that because our last names are different," insists
Nan. But Joan was hurt and furious. That night she wept bitterly for
hours and refused to accept Nan's attempts to explain.

"Joan kept insisting, 'There are *only two* of us! *Only two*! Why didn't
you tell the truth? Why didn't you tell the police we are *true* sisters?'"
Joan moved in with an acquaintance, and refused to speak to Nan.
"But she was wrong," Nan says tearfully, "because truly we are *not* bio-

logical sisters." She gave a mutual friend the airfare for Joan and her children to return to North Carolina, but cried whenever she thought of Joan.

Alan "Tiger" Hoa

As Tiger continued to make his way in America, he fell in love with a seventeen-year-old Amerasian orphan, Anh (not her real name), whom he met through St. Anselm's. The two planned to marry, and even sent out red-and-gold flocked invitations in Vietnamese setting a date in April 1993. "Anh was very fun," says Tiger. "I had very strong feelings for Anh." But Anh was also very troubled. In early September 1992, a high school counselor had brought her to St. Anselm's saying he was afraid she was suicidal. Having arrived in America two months earlier, with two other orphans and five nuns, all of whom claimed to have been involved in raising her, Anh had supposedly grown up in Pleiku after being found on the street as a baby. But several things about her story are amiss, and full of odd gaps and conflicting details. In any case, in California Anh ended up living with a sponsoring family that she claimed abused her.

Crying, she told Mary Payne Nguyen, who was still coordinator at the time, that she first attempted suicide a month after arriving in California by cutting her left wrist and not eating for three days, which led to her fainting in gym class. She said she'd "always been thinking about suicide." She maintained that she'd completed eight years of school in Vietnam—almost certainly a lie, but one that led to her being placed in a U.S. high school. Because she spoke almost no English, it was impossible for her to do the classwork. A few days later, Anh attempted suicide again. St. Anselm's arranged for a seventy-two-hour hold at a psychiatric hospital. The sponsoring mother said she was too old to handle Anh and wanted her to get a new foster mother, but have Anh continue to live with her—probably so she could still collect Anh's benefits, half of which she charged Anh for food and rent. Anh was diagnosed with major depression; a month later she made another half-hearted suicide attempt.

In February 1993 she was shipped off to Utah for Job Corps training, but returned a few weeks later, "apparently penniless," after having made two more suicide attempts in Utah. Now she was diagnosed with bipolar disorder, a major psychosis whose symptoms include abrupt mood swings between depression and mania. A St. Anselm's staffer noted in Anh's file that without money or family, or anyone to battle the tottering mental health system, Anh undoubtedly would "fall through the cracks." Meanwhile, Anh was writing frightened, hysterical letters to an American woman in Utah who briefly had befriended her. Addressing the woman as "Dear Mom" and signing "Your Beloved Daughter," she wrote in late April: "Last night I sat up all night and cried because I thought of the days full of your memories and favors given to me . . . you are my mom, a very beloved mother. . . . I feel very sad and alone when I'm away from you . . . and want to give you my lovely kisses." In early May, she wrote: "I very sorry I make you angry to me [for attempting suicide] . . . you know when I went to California I miss you a lot. . . . I know you always love me and look me like your daughter. . . . I never make you angry no more I sure, I want you be happy, I never hurt myself again. . . . I hope you don't forget me and you're always my mom when I'm very old, Okay?"

Inevitably, Anh and Tiger's relationship was very volatile. Tiger says he was so sad after one fight with her that he burned himself in several places and looked at her picture and drank and cried. Anh called off their wedding — partly because some advised her against it, but mainly, Tiger says, because his aunt and uncle backed out of a promise to pay $300 toward the wedding costs. When Anh broke up with him, "I went crazy and lost control of myself and cut myself. I slashed the inside and outside of my arm in several places, and was bleeding badly. People in another house called police, and they handcuffed me and took me to the psychiatric hospital." The hospital kept him for a month. Tiger's breakdown was a very serious one. America and all the things involved in his life, past and present, were overwhelming him. Perhaps he prolonged his breakdown by refusing to take his medication. "I would stand in line with the other patients to get the medicine put in our mouths," he says, "but after I went back to bed I would spit it out. I was very afraid the medicine would make me crazy." Whenever he was forced to swallow it, he would try to vomit it out. He was terrified of the other patients, who "bit on things like bedposts." But he was even more frightened by his own *am anh* — mental visions, flashbacks, and obsessive, haunting memories of things he had done wrong, of people he had harmed, and of harm he himself had suffered — visions and memories so frightening that he still won't talk about them. "With *am anh* you feel trapped in the past, you are bad, sorry, and scared, and sometimes it is both ways and you also have feelings and memories about bad things done to you," a Vietnamese doctor once explained to me.

As for Anh, "I had very strong feelings for her," says Tiger bitterly, "but now I hate her. I think she called off our wedding because she learned I had no money. I know she smokes grass, and I think she now works in a whorehouse. If you want to find Anh now, go to the Asian coffeehouses [actually whorehouses] around Atlantic Avenue in Long Beach, where girls wear skinny clothing. She might be out in front."

The year 1993 continued to be a bad one for Tiger. He was collapsing under the loss of his dreams and the challenges of an America he was totally unprepared to deal with. "After I returned to California [from Kansas and Arizona] my old friends came around and of course I started to drink, and we decided to go steal and so forth—and it started all over again," says Tiger. "I thought of quitting gang life, but my gang friends told me, 'How can you walk away from us? You were a leader before.' And they pumped me up and told me I was 'already on the tiger's back' [into gang life] and I could not get off, and if I did the 'tiger' would eat me anyway, so I might as well stay involved." Tiger says he was drinking very heavily then, and getting into fights. "If you want to build your reputation as a gang leader, you have to fight. That's why I am a crazy fighter. Sometimes when I fight it is a stupid fight, like if someone looks at my girl and I jump him. But the fighting when I am drinking or when I am feeling crazy is different. At those times I don't even know what's happening. I just fight with whatever is in my hand, a bottle, a knife, whatever. It don't matter to you when you fight like that whether or not you get hurt too. Afterwards you think, 'Oh my God, I got hurt!' But at the time you don't even know it. And in those days, living or dying was not a big deal to me anymore."

The same month the Amerasian program was shut down, Garden Grove police stopped Tiger at 2:30 A.M. driving a stolen van with its lights off. Inside were two other Amerasians and a Vietnamese man, along with $200 in cash and a karaoke machine taken earlier that night from a Little Saigon coffeehouse. "I was drinking a lot at that time," says Tiger. "After I was arrested I was very upset with myself. The whole thing was not even worth it. That first long time in jail here in America I was really afraid. I was afraid of going hungry, and also afraid of the dark. I cried a lot, too. I was always hungry because I didn't like American food, so I had to discipline myself to tolerate the hunger." Tiger often speaks of his powerful fear of going hungry again as he did so often in Vietnam.

During the preliminary hearing on his case, Tiger's court-appointed public defender, alarmed at Tiger's deteriorating behavior, told the judge: "I'm going to declare doubt concerning my client's current mental condition. I have received some confirmation information that gives some substance to believe we need to have him examined before we proceed." The judge agreed. "They sent me to the jail psych ward—I was there quite long," says Tiger. "For a month they kept me in a solitary glass room, with three glass walls, where they could watch me." It was a suicide watch. "There was no one there to talk Vietnamese to me," Tiger says, "so I mostly talked by hand signs, but some English. A doctor there treated me really nice. Everyone was very kind." After a month he was sent back to the main jail. "Of course they let me go back, because they saw there was nothing wrong with me," asserts Tiger, who shares the Vietnamese view that admitting any kind of emotional problem is a huge shame. "Yes, I did have a breakdown, but I told them to release me because I told them: 'I'm perfectly fine, I'm not crazy! Let me go, I don't have any mental problems, why are you keeping me here?' And of course they realized I was perfectly fine, and not crazy at all, and sent me back." But much of his confusion, rage, and grief continued, and he was kept on medication.

He pleaded guilty to car theft and burglary, and was given 120 days in jail—most already served—and three years probation with the condition that he was to "cooperate in a plan for psychological, psychiatric, drug, and alcohol treatment or counseling" and "to reside in a psychiatric recovery home or residential treatment home." Within weeks of his release, on March 23, 1994, Tiger was arrested again. Probably drunk, he had gone to the home of the Vietnamese man who had agreed to sponsor Tiger's family to the United States, waved a gun, and fired several times through the door. Apparently neighbors were circulating a petition asking that Tiger move out of the neighborhood where he sometimes stayed with his uncle. No one was hurt, but at least one neighbor testified that he saw Tiger walking away afterward, looking very angry and "firing a final shot." Tiger's probation officer revoked his probation, saying: "Probationer Alan Tiger Hoa has reported to me on four separate occasions, and has indicated much confusion and many problems in his life." Tiger pleaded guilty to "discharging a firearm with gross negligence" and was sentenced to three years in Chuckawalla Prison. This was his first "strike," and under California law, people accumulating three strikes must spend the rest of their lives in prison.

The year 1993 was also a bad year for the resettlement program. So far 22,000 Amerasians and 60,000 "family members" had been settled at a cost to the federal government of $500 million. During that same time 61,000 Vietnamese refugees and 161,000 Vietnamese immigrants seeking family reunification had come to the United States following the first immigration wave of 150,000 Vietnamese refugees at the end of the war in 1975. St. Anselm's monthly Amerasian Services Report called September 1993 "a tragic month," during which two Amerasians attempted suicide—a woman who swallowed tuberculosis medicine and fainted on the street, and a man who took amitrylimine and tried to hack off one of his fingers. Both survived, and St. Anselm's arranged for them to receive counseling. The same report reccommended that one or two staffers get suicide prevention training, and added: "[Often] through conversations a few Amerasians mention the idea of taking their own lives or of taking revenge on the fraudulent families who have taken advantage of them. Mental depression is the Number One problem with the Amerasians. None can escape that stage."

In October 1993 *Amerasian Update* carried the headline: "Michael Kocher Bids Farewell to the Amerasian Resettlement Program." The former head of InterAction, which oversaw the program for the federal government, Kocher had taken a new job with the International Rescue Commission in Croatia helping Bosnian refugees. The last issue of the newsletter was December 1993; the resettlement part of the Amerasian Homecoming Act was closing down. Only two sites, one of which was St. Anselm's, were left open for 1994, each receiving only $17,500.

"St. Anselm's was the only thing those kids had," says Joe Love. "They came there with all their troubles, all their tears, all their problems like letters from the phone company up to serious medical problems. A lot of them would never have found a job if it hadn't been for St. Anselm's. We also got them into the social service agencies and filled out the papers for them."

Although most Amerasians were unaware of it, in February 1994 President Clinton had lifted the nineteen-year-old U.S. trade embargo against Vietnam. "Taking a historic step to close the wounds of a divisive war," the *Los Angeles Times* reported, "President Clinton ordered an immediate end to the embargo. . . . This step, still short of normalizing relations, culminates years of anguished public deliberation over a conflict that has continued to sow bitterness and division nearly two decades after its conclusion." But the bitterness in America over the war was not "ended." Added the *Times*, "Although many U.S. Vietnam veterans had pushed for a lifting of the embargo, major veterans' groups were quick to condemn the move by a commander in chief [Clinton] who avoided military service." Another 1994 news report, commenting on the closure of the U.S. Amerasian resettlement efforts, quoted Marianne Blank: "No more fraudulent families are being accepted along with Amerasians, and that means the Amerasians will have no chance to migrate here," as so few could afford the bribes and fees.

Blank and Daniels divided the remaining funds earmarked for the Amerasians—about $4,000—and distributed it among those needing it most. Otherwise the Amerasians were now on their own, forced to once again draw on their hard-learned survival skills. Some began the traditional path of immigrants to assimilation in America; others saw only crime or suicide as a solution. Meanwhile, some of the pressure within the Vietnamese exile community that for years had prevented Vietnamese from returning to visit their native country was decreasing, and tens of thousands returned for a visit in 1995. But, having established full diplomatic relations with Vietnam in July 1995, the United States was still blocking bilateral economic assistance to the country, although since 1991 USAID had been giving small grants to private U.S. voluntary organizations such as CHEER for Vietnam and the Vietnam Veterans of America to provide prosthetics and rehabilitation services to "civilian" war victims and to help children and orphans.

In the mid-1990s Amerasians were still arriving in America. With resettlement programs closed, many were drifting on their own. The Philippines camps also were closing down. A new problem situation had begun developing there a few years earlier, and in July 1994 a newspaper reported that more than 500 Amerasians and "family members" who had left Vietnam as legal emigrants bound for America were being held in the Philippines. They had been found to have counterfeit documents, and were kept trapped as years passed, with the United States, Vietnam, and the Philippines all unwilling to take or keep them.

U.S. veterans of Vietnam also continued to experience the residual effects of the war. In April 1995, in an article about the twentieth anniversary of the end of the Vietnam War, the *Los Angeles Times* quoted the head of a national counseling service for veterans on the continuing phenomenon of post-traumatic stress disorder (PTSD) in U.S. Vietnam veterans: "The onset can come years later, and once you have it, it tends to have long-term effects," he said. "It's not as easy to get rid of as we once thought." Veterans of other conflicts also were coming to vet centers for counseling, but in the previous year, out of 91,972 clients, 68 percent were Vietnam veterans, and 60 percent of those had a PTSD diagnosis. Said one vet, referring to how a crisis in his life had triggered memories of Vietnam: "I started feeling guilt—survivor's guilt, guilt I had killed people who were innocent, guilt that I didn't stay over there, and guilt for just everything I did. I felt I was being punished for Vietnam." He'd gone for counseling three years earlier, saying "I wasn't even aware of the impact Vietnam had on my life" until a day he broke down crying on hearing a helicopter near his California home. That year, the average age of Vietnam veterans seeking counseling for PTSD was forty-seven. "Midlife makes them particularly vulnerable," commented the *Times*.

In late 1995, after eight months in Chuckawalla, Tiger was released on probation. Somewhere along the line, in and out of prisons and jails, he had been adding more self-mutilating cuts and burns to his body. Explains Tiger: "In my life there have been so many ups and downs I cannot count them anymore, and therefore I cannot count all my scars anymore. They are all over both of my arms, and sometimes I look at them and cry, or sometimes when I hurt myself I cry because it hurts so much. In every person it is different how they want to scar themself. Some have more scars than I. Some have lived even worse situations than I, but have less scars, because they were not brave enough to make them." Tiger also had added a few new tattoos. Although he is clearly proud of the splendor of his fancier tattoos and the tough bravery of his self-mutilations—that also serve as a warning to fellow prisoners—the tattoos he has chosen "show he feels shame and anguish, and as if he is a big failure," several Vietnamese told me. And Tiger's mother's spirit was again appearing to him.

After getting out of Chuckawalla, Tiger went back to Little Saigon and worked sporadically for a few months at a Korean-owned business doing welding. Like most prisoners at the time of their release, he planned to go straight and make a new life start. But soon he was back into gang life. In early 1996 he was living off and on with a Vietnamese woman who became pregnant with his child around the time he was arrested for stealing a 1985 Toyota Camry. Two close gang friends from Vietnam, Duong and Ha—Ha had come to California with a fake family on the same flight as Tiger—were arrested with him. Tiger's probation was revoked and he was sent to Chino State Prison for three years, getting out in October 1997 after sixteen months. His daughter Jennifer was born in December 1996, but he did not stay in contact with her or her mother. Tiger was sent to live for ninety days in a Little Saigon

halfway house with thirty other inmates, including only one other Vietnamese. Again, there was counseling about drugs and alcohol and Tiger
did occasional work for the iron company. He also went back to stealing, and formed a common-law marriage with a Vietnamese woman
named Tammy (not her real name), with whom he had begun to corre-
spond while in prison. Tammy was the sister of a black Amerasian boy
and drew AFDC for her two young children. Says Tiger: "My relationship with her was a very serious one."

"During those months after I got out of prison I thought I had a good
life," Tiger says. "I had a job building bars on windows at the iron
working place, making good money—$5.50 per hour—and a wife."
Tiger grew close to Tammy's mother and her younger Amerasian
brother. He ignored Tammy's little girl, but took her little boy, who
was four, everywhere. "Whenever Tammy wanted a gold chain or gold
bracelet, I tried to get it for her," he says. He stole small objects like car
radios. Another friend of Tiger's says Tammy "always wanted money,
she would gamble it away." Tiger was also dealing drugs. And he was
drinking. "I would come home and see Tammy's little boy dirty, and
she would be gone, and I became upset and depressed and then became
mean," says Tiger. He and the little boy would sit and watch cartoons
together for hours. "The boy said he loved me like a father, and that
made me happy. Sometimes I prayed and sat and thought about things
to stay calm. I knew I had a hot temper so I drank lots of beer to make
myself calm down." On January 21, 1998, just days after Tiger's three-
month term at the halfway house ended, Tiger was arrested again. He
was visiting two Amerasian friends and drinking away the afternoon
when the group decided to steal and sell a TV set from the owners of
the house where one of the friends rented a room. Two children saw
them loading the TV into a car and identified Tiger from his Amerasian
appearance and his many tattoos and scars. Within hours, he was back
in jail along with his two friends, his parole revoked. Because he sold
the TV to his girlfriend Tammy's mother, the mother was also arrested
and jailed briefly, and Tammy's family was furious. Tammy, several
months pregnant with Tiger's daughter, refused to speak to him and
vowed to give the baby up for adoption to break any and all ties to him.

Tiger sometimes claims he was a very important gang leader in both
Vietnam and America. He says his arrest for stealing the TV involved
swooping police helicopters and a phalanx of screeching squad cars, but
Garden Grove police officer Peter Vi, who arrested Tiger, says Tiger
"barely had a place to stay. He was sleeping on the sofa. He's not a big

shot at all." Vi, a young Vietnamese American who came to the United States in 1975, says, "I first met Tiger after he'd just gotten out of jail for something else, at a pool hall in Garden Grove when we were doing patrol. Lots of gang members hung out there. And I'd see him on and off at domestic violence incidents, but he wasn't involved in them, just standing around. When I came to arrest him over the TV set, he was on parole. I don't think the burglary was gang related—I think it was just people who needed some food or beer, not a big gang thing. Tiger stands out in my mind because he has so many scars. He had slashed his arm pretty good, I remember. Of his many scars he told me, 'This is my sorrow.'"

Vi says it took only six or seven hours to solve the burglary. Vi saw the missing TV at Tammy's mother's house, "and she finally told us, 'I've been lying to you, I bought the stuff from an Amerasian for $100.'" Many Vietnamese who were in gangs in Vietnam are now in gangs in America, says Vi, "only now they're in their thirties, have become Big Brothers, wearing suits and driving expensive cars. Some may even be running some kind of business." Vi doesn't see many black Amerasians involved in gangs. "Here in America, lots of Vietnamese are still ex-pressing their prejudice against the Amerasians. The white Amerasians progress much more quickly here. They blend in easily with the whites and [pure] Vietnamese." Still, says Vi, most Amerasians in America "are financially not very well off. They're not sleeping in boxes, and they might stay with friends a few days or whatever—they know what to do. But there's prejudice against them. No, I don't think Tiger is a big leader. But with his scars and all, he's very unique."

Vu Trinh, then a young ponytailed Vietnamese American public defender, spotted Tiger and his two Vietnamese-speaking codefendants in court not long after their January 1998 arrest. The three were hand-cuffed together, wearing bright orange jail jumpsuits, and struggling to talk through an interpreter. Impulsively, Trinh, who was there to file a motion for a new Caucasian client, swapped clients with the men's Caucasian public defender. Some three years later, Trinh meets me in a restaurant in Little Saigon to talk about Tiger. The ponytail is gone; Trinh has left the public defender's office and joined a prestigious Little Saigon law firm. He is the first Vietnamese American criminal lawyer in California and one of only 300 criminal attorneys in the state to have passed the difficult tests to become board-certified.

Trinh states what Tiger has repeatedly denied—that this latest felony was Tiger's second strike. (The first was when he shot up his sponsor's house.) Under California's "three strikes and you're out" law, if Tiger ever receives a third felony conviction he could be sent to prison for the rest of his life. Although Tiger says he has been in prisons and jails in several other states, Trinh says he looked at Tiger's rap sheet for out-of-state prior felony convictions, something he does routinely for "strikers," and found none that could be strikes. This doesn't mean Tiger isn't telling the truth, because only felonies would show up, and, "of course," says Trinh, "if he used different names something might never show up." As did Officer Vi, Trinh dismisses Tiger's claim of being a serious gang leader. "If he had been a top gang guy," says Trinh, "the gang unit would have prosecuted him, but this wasn't flagged as a gang case, nor was Tiger flagged as a gang guy.

"Tiger's other two [codefendants] were pressuring Tiger to plead guilty. I see that kind of pressuring go on all the time when more than one person gets charged together. I told Tiger that if he gave in and pleaded guilty, he could eventually become a third striker, and that sometimes you have to look out for yourself. I would have torn apart those two child witnesses [who said they saw him take the TV] on the witness stand. But he pleaded guilty." Trinh says Tiger knew if he didn't take the plea bargain his two friends couldn't have gotten short sentences like they did. "Under that plea bargain," says Trinh, "the judge gave Tiger five years, and since it was his second strike, he had to serve 80 percent of that sentence—about four years. Otherwise he would have served only two-and-a-half years. The other guys got out right away.

"You know," Trinh muses, "until you told me some things about Amerasians recently, I didn't know anything about what happened to them. I used to see Amerasians come into court accused of crimes and they never had any education, never had any family or community connections to speak for them. I always wondered, 'Where's the family?' But when I asked them about family or community ties for bail purposes, they always said 'No,' they had none. There was never anyone to come forward on their behalf, so I was never able to tell the court about how they had a chance to be rehabilitated. They'd have no parent, no sister or brother, and nobody to speak for them from the mainstream Vietnamese community. I was never able to present any of that kind of thing in court to help them."

Occasionally, says Trinh, he runs into a prosecutor or judge who served overseas in the U.S. military. "Those people have seen how sad it is that [mixed] children of war are always abandoned after the war's over. The guy who prosecuted Tiger had served in Korea, and he was basically agreeing with me that the children of GIs and Korean mothers are treated worse than dogs." Trinh said he'd been doing felony arraignments in a major court [in Orange County] for the past year and a half, "so I've seen every case coming through—about 5,000 cases. But I haven't seen any Amerasians in all that time. I don't know where they are now. Maybe all are in prison."

Because Amerasians "have no education," added Trinh, "they just commit crimes. A lot of them have been stealing all their lives—it's all they can do to survive. And then we punish them. And also, they got deserted here in America. They should have had more help assimilating." In a hurry to make his next appointment, still Trinh lingers a bit. "Some Vietnamese joke about the Amerasians," he said. "They call them 'Frenchies,' because many of them claim to be half French instead of half American. The Vietnamese believe all the mothers of Amerasians must have been prostitutes or they wouldn't have been involved with GIs in the first place. I have friends who wouldn't socialize with an Amerasian, because they're not truly Vietnamese. It's a bit racist, I guess. But now a lot of Vietnamese are marrying out of their race, mostly to whites, so things are a lot better. In America, families teach their kids not to be racist, but that's not true of Vietnamese families. I learned my own feelings not from my family but from going to school in America." Trinh looks thoughtful. "You know," he says, "I've never seen anyone scarred up as bad as Tiger."

Certainly America is no paradise for racial relations. Its shame runs deep. But there are gradations of racism, and Americans themselves have undergone (and are still undergoing) changes in consciousness over the past thirty-five years. A young Vietnamese graduate student who came to America by boat in 1988 tells about a close sixty-year-old friend of her father, who, like her father, came to the United States twenty years earlier. "I've known him since I was a little girl, and I call him 'Great-Uncle,'" she says. "His nephew, who was born in Vietnam but raised here, married an Amerasian who looks white, but has some black blood—the American father must have been very light. The nephew and his wife have two children who look very black, with very curly hair and dark skin. My great-uncle said to my father, 'It's a disgrace to have those black grandchildren around me.' He said his nephew feels bad too, and 'is so embarrassed to walk with her and their children now.' And my dad agreed, 'I know, that's such a disgrace.' But my older brother and I said nothing. Because it seems so weird to us to think that way in America, living in such a multicultural world. And my father and great-uncle and my own family all have yellow skin, and some people might want to get away from that. But my father and great-uncle still think they're above black people and Amerasians."

Westminster police officer Nick Tran, in his mid-thirties, husky and muscular, works on cases involving Vietnamese and other Asian gangs, but hasn't heard of Tiger. Like many other younger Vietnamese Americans, he has undergone changes in his views on race since coming to America as a boat refugee in 1979 at age twelve with his fourteen-year-old brother soon after their mother died. As a teen, he was befriended by a Caucasian American family. "The son was my best friend, and the family sort of adopted me," says Tran. "The dad was a police sergeant, and that's how I got the idea to be a cop. As a police officer, I make it my responsibility to get to know newcomer Vietnamese families to America."

One sometimes suspects an inability of Vietnamese Americans in law enforcement to resist a certain pride at the cleverness of Vietnamese criminals. Says Tran: "I'm not saying that criminals and gangs of other races are dumb, but, well . . . the really big Asian gang leaders are like executives of big corporations now. They follow the Big Brother system, they help the younger gang members. The older gang guys who have graduated from street crime, now in their thirties or even forties, are probably all doing white-collar crime now. And Asian gangs don't have territories—they don't care about 'turf.' They can kill someone here and end up tomorrow in New York. We don't see many home invasions by Vietnamese now because the Vietnamese in the U.S. don't keep much money at home anymore and Vietnamese criminals are learning they can make more money doing fraud, with less prison time. Other ethnic groups are moving into home invasions now." After a moment, Tran adds: "With home invasions, Vietnamese victims may pretend in their heads that it never happened.

"As for Amerasians, there's a lot of them in prison, although I haven't run into many Amerasian gang members. The Amerasians weren't treated well in Vietnam and are not treated well by the Vietnamese here, either, especially the black Amerasians. I think it's just due to ignorance. I don't feel that way in America."

Prison populations tend to group along ethnic lines, and Tiger is less optimistic about any changes in racial attitudes. He is left somewhere in limbo because, while Vietnamese, he looks black. "The reason for discrimination against black Amerasians is we look ugly, we seem dirty," says Tiger. "If the same crime is done by a black Amerasian and a white Amerasian, the punishment is worse for the black one. That's everywhere. When Latino or white inmates are sitting in groups and are approached by a black inmate, they scatter, because that's the rule of discrimination. Even here in prison in this tiny little world where there are so few Vietnamese, the Vietnamese prisoners don't want to hang out with me because I am Amerasian. When I have something they want like Vietnamese food they come to me, but behind my back they say unkind things about me and my skin."

10

Left Behind—Amerasians Still Living in Vietnam

My life in Vietnam is very terrible. I have no true friends. I hope the Americans can help me find my father. If anyone reading what you write could help in any way, I hope Americans will please think of Amerasians, and remember those still in Vietnam.

—Amerasian Hung Nguyen, 1999

In December 1999 the remains of eleven U.S. servicemen missing since the Vietnam War—eight killed in 1966, one in 1969, two in 1972—were returned, leaving 2,032 U.S. troops still counted as missing in Southeast Asia. Three hundred thousand Vietnamese also were still missing. In the late 1990s, as Gerald Nicosia noted in his powerful book, *Home to War*, hepatitis C "suddenly loomed as one of the most critical health issues for [U.S. veterans of the war]. . . . Tens of thousands had been exposed to this virulent liver disease in Vietnam, but because of the long latency period (up to thirty years) only now were significant numbers starting to manifest the symptoms." The Vietnam War also dragged on through spiteful actions of the U.S. government. The fall 1999 issue of *Indochina Interchange* reported that Vietnam owed the United States $146 million, "a relatively small amount [yet] a bitter pill Vietnam has been forced to swallow as the price of 'normalization' with the U.S." When South Vietnam fell in 1975, its government had owed the United States $76 million. The United States had continued to assess interest on the loan until 1997, when the "new" gov-

222

ernment of Vietnam agreed to repay this debt as part of the price of reconciliation with the United States. By then the loan had swollen to $146 million.

By 1999, since the war's official end twenty-five years earlier, approximately 750,000 Vietnamese had permanently resettled in the United States, including 40,000 veterans of the South Vietnamese Army who were living in Orange County and Little Saigon. One hundred ten thousand U.S. Vietnam-era veterans, of whom 37,000 had actually served in Vietnam, also lived in Orange County. During 1999 the 3 million Vietnamese living in the United States and other countries sent $1.2 billion back to family members. The influx of outside funds was a powerful force in improving living conditions in Vietnam.

In November 1999 a survey throughout the United States by *USA Today* of 500 American students aged twelve to seventeen found that only one-third said they had learned anything about the war in school, and half said the United States had won. But, wrote Fredrik Logevall, author of *Choosing War: The Lost Chance for Peace and the Escalation of War in Vietnam*, in an April 2000 article in the *Los Angeles Times*: "Beginning in the late 1970s, examination of the Vietnam experience became something of a national U.S. obsession. . . . At various points . . . commentators have come forth to announce that 'the war after the War' was over, and that Americans had at last put Vietnam behind them. But they hadn't. . . . Vietnam still divides America." And in a *Times* opinion piece the same month, author William Prochnau wrote that twenty-five years after the war's end, "[Americans] have spent our time in a perverse national passion for endless and disputatious post-mortems that have left us seeing our way no more clearly than when we entered the Vietnam War in 1961."

The older Vietnamese immigrant community in Little Saigon also continued to be obsessed by the war. After Vietnamese immigrant Truong Van Tran posted a picture of Ho Chi Minh in his Little Saigon video store in 1999, his action prompted weeks of riotous protests in the Vietnamese community. After fifty-three days of demonstrations, police arrested Tran and charged him with illegally duplicating and selling videos. He was fined $200, sentenced to ninety days in jail and three years probation. Police destroyed his tapes and gave his VCRs to charities. It had cost the city $700,000 to deal with the protesters, who now quickly faded away.

To the bewilderment of many Vietnamese immigrants, the demonstrations caused a backlash against their community. In April 1999, as the twenty-fifth anniversary of the war's official end approached, *Nguoi Viet* reported on City Council hearings in Westminster over whether South Vietnamese flags could be flown on the same level as U.S. flags. One World War II vet argued: "There seems to be a feeling [among the immigrants] that they've got to bring Vietnam to the States and carve out a section in Westminster. That's not, in my estimation, practicing good citizenship. What they don't understand is that they're not still Vietnamese now. They're Americans." But in 2004 the city councils in Westminster and Garden Grove, two adjacent cities where Little Saigon is located, passed resolutions banning North Vietnamese Communist officials from visiting there.

While Son and the other Amerasians were moving on with their lives in America, Vietnam and America had continued tentative steps toward "normalization." In late 1999 U.S. Secretary of State Madeleine Albright dedicated a new $3.3 million U.S. consulate building in Ho Chi Minh City, a few steps from the site of the former U.S. Embassy, from whose rooftop the Americans had made their final departure in helicopters twenty-four years earlier. The embassy itself, vacant twenty years, had been torn down. At the consulate dedication ceremony, Albright, saying "the U.S. and Vietnam will forever be linked in history," expressed a desire that the two countries could "add to our shared history bright new chapters of hope and mutual prosperity." However, Albright, who proudly admits that she sees the world through a 1950s cold war lens rather than a Vietnam War lens, asked Vietnam's Secretary General Le Kha Phieu a bizarre question — "when he thought Vietnam was going to abandon Communism."

Some months earlier I had traveled to Vietnam with an interpreter, flying on the same plane with Miss Dao. I planned to spend most of my trip meeting friends and relatives of the Amerasians I had been interviewing. All but Louis, who had recently had a stressful interaction with relatives over funds he had been sending for his grandmother, helped arrange these meetings. I also hoped to learn how many Amerasians still remained in Vietnam. But the answer appears to be that no one really knows, other than that it is several thousand. Many are scattered throughout rural and hard-to-reach mountain regions in Central Vietnam. Others, now in their thirties and forties, live in miserable conditions in Ho Chi Minh City, like those interviewed by the *Wall Street Journal* in March 2002. The Amerasian Homecoming Act is officially still in effect, I learned, and perhaps sixty to seventy Amerasians each year have left under it for the United States, but emigrating under the

Act is almost impossible now. And many Amerasians are now so damaged and unprepared to deal with life in America that the United States doesn't want them. With no more fake relatives to pay their way, and no more U.S. government funds to resettle those who might reach America, most Amerasians cannot afford to leave. The Philippines camps have long been closed, leaving a few hundred Amerasians and fake relatives drifting there in limbo, caught with false papers or having gotten into trouble while in the camp. Among Amerasians still trying to leave Vietnam are some turned down long ago, but reapplying, like the two mentioned earlier who approached Genh Rang orphanage in Qui Nhon. A handful has chosen to stay in Vietnam for various reasons. But clearly the United States is discouraging the immigration of any more Vietnamese Amerasians. Letters replying to applications from Amerasians omit any signatures, and an American official interviewed by the *Journal* did so only on the condition that his name would not be used.

So I was forced to rely on anecdotal bits of information. A young Vietnamese spokeswoman who answered a call to the Vietnamese Embassy public information department in Washington, D.C., told me: "Nowadays Amerasians who stayed are treated the same as anyone else. I see very few when I go to Vietnam, although some I see with children of their own, still showing the mixed blood. But there is no prejudice against them now."

An elderly Vietnamese woman who directs a small well-respected government social services agency in Hanoi, asked if she had information or statistics on Amerasians, said she was not familiar with the English word "Amerasians." Prompted by the Vietnamese phrase, "My lai" (mixed-American), she is at first puzzled, then exclaims: "Oh, yes! . . . But . . . aren't they all in the South?"

A Vietnamese man in Ho Chi Minh City tells how, twenty-five years after the war's end, he often sees a black Amerasian woman selling things in the market. "She is very poor, apparently of very low education and status, and has a little son about seven, apparently not in school, who goes around the city with her, helping her sell fruit. Does she seem sad? Well—I can only say that she seems as if she has accepted her fate."

And a Vietnamese cyclo driver told me: "There is a white Amerasian boy, about twenty-seven, I see in Ho Chi Minh City working as a laborer. He has only one eye; he lost the other, I'm not sure how. I have heard he applied to leave Vietnam seven years ago. The man who claimed to be his adopted father was very stupid. He was actually a Communist soldier, so of course they were turned down."

Another Vietnamese man, a middle-aged former schoolteacher, struggles to find the right English words to express what he wants to say. "You understand," he says at last. "I am a man. And so about 1986 I used a black Amerasian prostitute in Saigon. She was about seventeen and very poor. I paid her very little—about 10,000 dong [less than $1 U.S.]. I only saw her once."

"Some Amerasians say they just don't want to leave Vietnam," says Louis Nguyen. "In the town where I grew up, there is one Amerasian left. He is a white Amerasian I have only said 'Hi' to—I don't know him, really. He has a very quiet personality. He was adopted by a rich family that wanted to go to America with him. He used to work in their fields for pay, and take care of their cows. But they failed the exit interview." Louis thinks the Amerasian and family still live together.

Son Chau says he knows of one black Amerasian living near Song Pha. "That man says, 'I love my grandma, I won't leave her.'" Sara and Miss Dao say that many Amerasians still live in the mountainous Central Highlands region.

Son Chau's Amerasian cousin Hung, whom we also met on our trip, ventured the opinion that there were probably "very few" Amerasians left in Vietnam, and that he knew of only two, adding, however, that he seldom traveled outside the remote area where he had lived since childhood. It was dominated by government soldiers who "might even try to kill an Amerasian to stop him from leaving the country," he told us. He'd slightly known a homeless white Amerasian who died near there about 1996, Hung said. The man was trying to survive by living in the jungle, but died of what Hung believed to have been "a voodoo curse."

"Maybe he tried to steal food from some tribal people, because he got so hungry," speculated Hung. "And he probably stole some vegetables from one of their gardens. Then they must have tried to kill him in a mystic way, maybe with effigies. Probably they put a voodoo curse on him, [or somehow got him to drink a potion] called bua ngai, because his body turned yellow, and two days later he died."

On this trip I also visited the orphanage of Miss Dao on the outskirts of Qui Nhon in Central Vietnam. Since she emigrated to America, Miss Dao has returned several times, lugging heavy suitcases of used clothing and other gifts. Whenever she returns, nuns and now-grown orphans come from several cities to see her. Qui Nhon seems a bit like some "heartland" town in America. A port city, it seems sleepier than other cities we visited. People seem friendlier and less complicated, like midwesterners in Kansas or Oklahoma.

This orphanage is not the one where Sara was left so long ago by her mother and from which, more than twenty-five years earlier, she and other terrified orphans fled the approaching North Vietnamese troops. That orphanage, confiscated by the new government soon after the war, is now an elementary school. Miss Dao warns us that it's best not to go there or try to photograph it; the government might not like that. There could be trouble.

The newer orphanage is small, but just inside its gates is a large, cheaply made but beautiful sculpture of intertwined grey dragons. A large statue of the Goddess of Mercy, one of the female Buddhas, rises above them. Miss Dao and a small band of nuns and orphans gather to greet us. There are only eleven orphans here now, some fully grown. The youngest is a one-year-old boy left a few months earlier. He is carried everywhere by a smiling ten-year-old orphan girl, whose half-shaved head indicates that she will become a nun herself someday. When she reaches sixteen and takes her final vows, her hair will be shaved off entirely.

My Duyen, the first orphan Miss Dao took in, who survived in the arms of her dead mother when bombs leveled a shelter during the war, is there too. Still with a piece of shrapnel embedded near her ear, My Duyen carries her own plump, smiling baby girl. Ninh, who was brought to the orphanage as an infant during the war by the soldier who tearfully begged Miss Dao to save baby Ninh's life, is in his twenties. He lives with his wife and their four-year-old son in a one-room house built on a tiny adjoining patch of land given him by the orphanage. Ninh and his wife, with one hired helper, built the house by weaving grasses together and covering them with mud. Ninh works as a servant and fixes bicycles on the side to make a marginal living. His health, he says, is "normal to weak," because one of his lungs was damaged by the wound to his throat when Miss Dao first took him in. Often, he says, he thinks of the soldier who left him. Miss Dao told Ninh while he was growing up that the man said he would come back for Ninh someday. "But I think he must have died in the war," Ninh says tentatively. The soldier who once cared about him has great importance in Ninh's thoughts, like the phantom American fathers in the minds of so many Amerasians.

Only one of the six disabled orphans who once lived at the orphanage is here this day. Named Le, he is in his late twenties, and cheerful and alert. He gets around in a wheeled cart, or sometimes by walking on his hands. Recently he released several birds he was raising to sell after Miss Dao told him that he "couldn't keep the poor birds," using the Buddhist phrase "phong sanh" for releasing imprisoned animals.

With the war long over, Vietnam no longer has the big population of orphans it once had. A nun explains, "If a child is brought here now occasionally, and we don't have the ability to raise and feed it, we give it for adoption or send it to another orphanage." A Vietnamese man accompanying us whispers a further explanation: "The people who support this temple are very, very poor, so sometimes the nuns here don't even have enough food for themselves. So that is when they have to send a new orphan away." In the front yard, near the Goddess of Mercy statue, the nuns and orphans have planted a small, sickly vegetable garden. Everyone helps gather and chop wood from the forest to sell for money to buy rice, and helps grind wood fragments into dust, mixing it with a bit of glue from a scented fruit they gather, and rolling it into incense sticks to sell.

One of the Amerasians who comes to see Miss Dao during this return visit is Tung, a thirty-two-year-old white Amerasian. Handsome, mustached, dressed each day in a sparkling-clean white shirt, he looks like an American movie star from the 1930s. And yet, the touch of Vietnamese features is also there. He brings a copy of a recent unsigned form letter to him from the U.S. Orderly Departure Program, rejecting his application to go to America. His mother, he says, is now a U.S. citizen. Aged eighteen when he was born, she turned him over to his grandmother to raise soon after his birth in 1968, and returned to her work as a prostitute. Three years later she went to America with a different American. She never told that man that she had left a child behind.

Apparently perceiving me as powerful and probably wealthy, the way Americans are often imagined to be in poor countries, Tung is hoping I can help him get to America. "When I was five, my grandmother couldn't feed me anymore so she put me in a Buddhist orphanage and also sent away some of her own children to work as servants for food and shelter," he says. "She told me that times were very hard, but promised that someday she would come back for me.

"At the orphanage I was very lonely and very sad." He pauses a moment, as painful memories overwhelm him. "But I understood her difficult situation, and I kept telling myself that someday she would come back. And after two years, my grandmother *did* come and take me home with her, and I felt very happy. She is seventy-one now, and she is a good woman, very kind." His eyes fill with tears.

Tung grew up working "just for food to eat" as a laborer or servant. "I was loved by my family but menaced by Communist police," he says. "When I was twelve they said they wanted to tear out my eyes." In 1996 his mother came from the United States to visit, bringing color photos of her new family in America, three plump, prosperous-looking daughters. He shows me the photos; his mother's face appears hard.

"She told me my father was a soldier killed in battles at Bong Son, and that just before he left to fight he told my mom, who was pregnant with me, that afterwards he would take her to the U.S. But later she learned he had been killed." Tung asked her to sponsor him to the United States, "but she said she couldn't. I'm not sure why. I felt a bit of anger towards her, and thinking over my life I saw it wasn't a lucky life. I realized that it is my karma to suffer, and that I had to get used to it."

In 1991 a Vietnamese man offered to pay Tung's way to America but they couldn't pass the exit exam. When Tung applied again in 1998, he received the form letter dated May 1999, which he showed me. It stated that he was being rejected because:

> *"On the basis of the information provided by you . . . and on the basis of the results of a personal interview of you by the consular officer, it has been determined that you do not meet the requirements for consideration of an Amerasian visa. Specifically, you do not have the physical appearance that is characteristic of Amerasians, you do not possess documentation that would support a claim of Amerasian status, and you are not able to provide a personal account that would support a finding of Amerasian status. . . . We regret that this decision could not have been favorable."*

The letter was unsigned.

Although Tung believes I can help him, I have no official role, no connections, no more than modest resources, and no way to explain the exotic (to him) role of an American journalist independently gathering information to write a book. He has trouble believing I cannot somehow override all the barriers he faces. I try to explain how a book can raise consciousness and perhaps even bring change within an American system, but it makes no sense to him and sounds phony even to my own ears, although I do believe what I am saying. Defeated and dejected, he gives up. "I am an unlucky one," he murmurs as he leaves.

Son, living outside Chicago at the time, had arranged for us to talk with another Amerasian, Thuy, at the home of Son's father-in-law near Song Pha. Thuy is very pretty—rather Irish-looking, with slightly freckled light pink skin and curly light brown hair. But she is so shy, so seemingly frightened of us, she can hardly speak. Despite much coaxing, in the end she tells only tantalizing bits of her life story. Speaking painfully in a whisper, she gives one-word answers. Her mother died when Thuy was six, after a long illness. She never told Thuy anything about the girl's American father. People called Thuy's mother a prostitute because she had an Amerasian child. After her death, an aunt took in Thuy, who quit school after the first grade. When Thuy was a young teenager, the aunt sold her to a Vietnamese family, and she worked as their servant while they put together fake papers. In 1991 they were approved, and even had their plane tickets. But the fake family was cruel to her. "They didn't treat me like their other children," Thuy whispers. For two years she was a virtual prisoner whom they seldom let out of their sight. If anything happened to her, their escape to America was gone too.

But one day Thuy ran into a young Vietnamese man she had known as a child and they fell in love. Afraid but desperate, they plotted her escape. "He helped me get out of the house secretly," she says. They ran away and hid. "The Vietnamese family was very angry, and tried to find me." Without Thuy, they couldn't go to America, and are still in Vietnam, although she has never seen them since her escape. Thuy and her husband applied to go to the United States after they had their first child, but were turned down. Their life in Vietnam is very hard, says Thuy, and she and her husband continue to dream of living in America someday.

The Family of Alan "Tiger" Hoa: Vietnam, the Present

Tiger arranged for me and an interpreter to meet his family on our trip, as long as we promised not to tell them that he is in prison. "Just say I am very busy working and going to school," he urged. His Uncle Khue, who knows Tiger's prison record all too well, has long since sworn never to reveal Tiger's secret to the rest of the family. "It is very sad, because they have never understood why Tiger doesn't help them," Khue had told me. "In Vietnam he made many promises to send them back money. I have lied to them, I have always told them Tiger is working, but truthfully since he came to America he has almost always been in jail."

My interpreter and I go with two of Tiger's uncles on the long trek from their town of Hoc Mon to the grave of Tiger's mother, a trip they have not taken in many years. Nowadays the drive to Bu Dop on the Cambodian border is very different from how it was in the early years after 1975. Now the road passes through several small towns with ragged but lively market places, where used, tattered goods and jungle plants and fruits are spread out on the ground. Small, dirty cafes offer home cooking served at tiny outdoor tables of broken plastic. And in almost every town one or two thin, medium-sized brown hounds—a kind of dog one can see throughout Vietnam—wander about. People seem poor, yet mostly energetic.

The two uncles, Lam and Binh, stare out the window of the taxi hired to drive us on the three-hour trip. They talk little; they are lost in memories. Binh, who has not taken this trip in more than twenty years, occasionally wipes tears from his face. Lam, who suffered through the hard years in the Bu Dop jungle with Tiger and Tiger's mother and other relatives, visited the grave seven years ago, but he too occasionally has tears on his cheeks. Even Tiger's Uncle Khue, toughened by a long, hard life, had wept when he sat with us in his living room back in Little Saigon and recalled to us that terrible time and the death of his fragile younger sister. As the road draws closer to Bu Dop it passes over more and more rough patches; at one point it is only ragged gray stones piled atop one another, tearing at the taxi's tires. On either side of this road are long rows of perfectly tended rubber trees. Some farms are government-run, some privately owned. Frequently the road passes attractive new homes freshly painted blue, peach, or rose. It's hard to gauge the wealth of a Vietnamese homeowner from a house, I'm told, because some have been built with the shared wealth of an entire family, and others with money sent by relatives in the United States.

It's been so long, and the setting has changed so much, that at first even Lam has trouble finding the exact spot where the road turns off toward the grave. The untouched jungle where Lam's family and Tiger once struggled to survive has been pushed far back from the main road, and an area cleared for rubber trees and thriving coffee plants. To reach the small cemetery of eleven graves requires walking a half-mile up a mud road, with the still-untouched jungle ahead. There on the left, near the center of a small coffee farm, lie the graves. When the jungle was cleared and coffee planted, the graveyard was preserved, its center marked with a heavy, dark stone. At the grave, Lam and Binh silently arrange the things they have brought for the Buddhist ritual—paper clothing and artificial money to burn, incense, a small altar, rice wine, cookies, and eggs. A tribal family, workers on the coffee farm, can be heard shouting across the fields, and someone goes to invite them to the ceremony. The family arrives—a young mother carrying a baby, along with a teenaged boy, and two men, all in ragged Western clothing, looking a bit like American hillbillies. Tiger's two uncles squat near the grave. Incense is lit, prayers said, the paper money burned, the rice wine sprinkled over the grave. Afterward, Lam and Binh share the rest of the wine with the tribal men; the baby is given the cookies, and is soon happily covered in crumbs. The tribal family agrees to watch over Tiger's mother's grave, and in exchange the uncles agree to send back malaria medicine from the city. All the tribal family has malaria, as probably does every person in the area.

It's time to start back. The uncles glance back at the thick jungle where the shack Lam patched together years ago has long since fallen apart. A strange, large, hideous caterpillar, multicolored and moving quickly on a hundred hooked claws, skitters across our path. Silently, we begin walking up the mud path toward the main road and waiting taxi.

Back in Hoc Mon, Tiger's aunt and four uncles gather to meet us in the family house. We meet Tiger's now grown half-brother and half-sister and the family's assorted children, but only the aunt and uncles are allowed into the family discussion. Keeping my promise to Tiger to tell his family nothing of his years in prison, I have said only that I am gathering information to write about Tiger and Amerasians in general. They ask few questions of me, probably because Khue, in phone calls from America, has assured them as the oldest brother that it is alright to meet with me. The family home is quite nice. An altar, with photos and ashes of deceased family members, stands at the rear center of the open court serving as the living room. It is April 30, the anniversary of the North Vietnamese victory and the fall of Saigon, and from a nearby house come the sounds of a happy, drunken celebration—no doubt a group of North Vietnamese veterans celebrating the long-ago but still proud victory.

On one side of the courtyard is a karaoke machine. Two of Tiger's uncles manage a small hotel in the daytime and in the evenings operate a neighborhood coffeehouse here with the karaoke, the craze of all Vietnam, to earn extra money. Other family members, including Tiger's crippled uncle, sew piecework at home to bring in income. But most of the improvements—the wheelchair for the crippled uncle, the house repairs and expansions, even the karaoke machine—have been paid for by money sent by Khue. Part of this evening's entertainment is a lengthy video sent by Khue of his daughter's recent graduation from a Little Saigon high school.

Because Khue now lives in the United States, Lam, as the second oldest brother, has become the family spokesperson in Vietnam. The rest of the family forms a solemn semicircle around a festive meal for the American guests. They seldom interrupt, and usually venture an opinion only when asked directly. They listen intently, polite and hospitable but cautious, not really certain why I have come. I feel guilty and duplicitous because of my pledge to Tiger. Lam in particular is hurt and angry at Tiger because Tiger has so seldom contacted the family, and never sent back anything to help them. Perhaps imagining Tiger living the rich American life, these feelings color some of Lam's remarks when he maintains that, "Tiger never had low self-esteem or lacked confidence," and that, "Tiger never had anything to worry about, he just lived his life." Because it was Lam and his wife who raised Tiger until he was eight, it is natural for Lam to be defensive when anyone speaks of Tiger's childhood problems, and he insists with rising emotion that is apparent even before his words are translated into English that, "Tiger was like my son. And we raised all the family children as family members and never treated them different if one is black and one is not. And Tiger *knows* we all love him, and that he shouldn't feel bad about himself!" But some of the family does concede that there was a great deal of prejudice against Tiger outside his family. And as for Tiger's feelings as a child, as a Vietnamese man once told me, "When parents work from 6 A.M. in the morning til late at night, all they have time to show they care is to ask, 'Have you eaten?' It doesn't make sense to ask, 'Are you happy?'"

"Ten years have gone by since Tiger left for America," Lam says bitterly, "and except for one early letter, in all that time our family has heard from Tiger only once. He never even called to ask us for our help. No, only one phone call—and he spent the whole call crying." The hour-long call came in 1995, apparently when Tiger was between prisons. Another uncle of Tiger's speaks up: "Tiger has never sent back money from America even once." Sharing possessions and money is the way of Vietnamese families, and Vietnamese relatives in Vietnam, usually mired in poverty, expect to receive aid from family members who have managed to arrive in rich America. Their expectations are often quite unrealistic because they don't understand what it takes to get by in America. At the same time, Vietnamese who have gone to America expect to send back money and do, with few exceptions.

"Tiger's one phone call came five years ago," says Nho, the youngest uncle. "I asked how he was doing in America and he said he was doing very well, so I asked him to send me $100. He said he'd do it right away, and gave me his American phone number. When the $100 didn't come, I called the number, and the phone was disconnected." Tiger's family has no way of knowing that Tiger has been in and out of prisons, jails, and psychiatric hospitals—sometimes following suicide attempts—almost continuously since he first arrived in the United States at nineteen. There is another thing Tiger's family does not know: that the U.S. Immigration and Naturalization Service wants to send Tiger, as well as other Amerasians and Vietnamese who have committed felonies in the United States, back to Vietnam. Because Vietnam refuses to take them back, they often languish for many months in a U.S. holding facility after their prison time has been served. In 2000 the U.S. Supreme Court ruled this unconstitutional, but as of 2003 at least, the INS still held former prisoners for months. Perhaps as diplomatic relations between America and Vietnam continue to improve, Tiger will become eligible for legal deportation.

Knowing nothing about Tiger's miserable life in America and believing he is living out some golden dream and is only selfish, his relatives' comments, while carefully phrased, are puzzled and hurt. They contrast Tiger with Khue. "When we returned from the NEZ, we were all very poor, but now we have this house and everything is good, thanks to the support of Khue," says Binh. Becoming more and more upset as he talks, Lam tells us: "Since the day Tiger left, not even one piece of cake or candy was sent back to us as a gift. Absolutely nothing at all. And he made only that one phone call to our family. Of course, if I knew what kind of job Tiger has, or any idea how much money he has, I could ask him to help the family, because I am his uncle and Tiger is my nephew, and that is the right thing to do. I spoke on the phone with Khue in America several times and asked how Tiger was doing, and Khue just said, 'He's doing OK.' But I didn't hear anything about Tiger bothering to ask about his family's needs, or even to say 'Hi.'"

Tiger's Three Messages

Tiger had asked me to take three messages back to Vietnam on my trip. The first was to his sister, born a year after Tiger to a Vietnamese man.

Now in her twenties, Tiger's sister looks very much like her mother at the same age, and has a baby of her own. Shy and wistful, she replies with a sweet "Oh" of disappointment and understanding to Tiger's message—that he is sorry he has not been able to help her, mainly because he has been so busy working and going to school at the same time, and that in about two years he will be able to send her money. The second message of apology was to Nga, the woman who paid Tiger to take her to America with him, who gave him spending money, clothes, and gifts and sometimes let him stay in her home before he left without her. He wanted to apologize for never sending back the money he had promised. But he insisted she mustn't know he is in prison. Tiger said she lived near the Song Be jail where he'd once been interred, now a somewhat dilapidated building with a rusted chain-link fence surrounding its small dirt courtyard. If this is truly where Nga lived, no one can say what has become of her. Eleven years after Tiger last saw her, even the postman says he has never heard of her.

The third message was added only the night before I left for Vietnam. Hesitantly, Tiger confessed he had left a son behind in Ho Chi Minh City, a boy named Phong. Phong was the child of Thom, the prostitute Tiger also once had promised to bring to America along with their son, then also had left behind. When he knew Thom, said Tiger, she was working near the Tu Thiem floating restaurant in Saigon and in bars on Nguyen Trai Street, along with her sister, Chien #9, also called Crippled Chien. Tiger's message was simple: "Tell Thom and Phong that in the year 2003 I will go back to Vietnam and take care of them. Apologize that I can't do that now—say I am working and going to school at the same time. Just tell them I'm sorry." Tiger must have chosen the year 2003 because that was the year he was to be released from prison.

A Ho Chi Minh City cyclo driver who spoke a bit of English thought he had heard of Crippled Chien. He led me through crowded back alleys in search of anyone who could tell us anything about Chien or Thom or Phong. Some eleven years had passed since Tiger last saw them, but after following confused and contradictory directions and suggestions, a tiny one-room lodging was found where, neighbors said, Thom once lived with little Phong along with Chien, Chien's boyfriend, and his family. But the few neighbors who claimed to remember said it had been too crowded, and Thom was asked to leave. One old woman seemed to know the most, and as neighbors swarmed into the narrow alley to argue the facts, she said Thom had gone to America with an American "husband." Others said she had gone away with a German.

But as for Phong, no one seemed to know what had happened to the little boy.

After some difficulty, a former boyfriend or perhaps pimp of Chien's was sent for, and he arrived on an expensive motorcycle—husky, large, tough-looking, chain-smoking, wearing a rich leather jacket, and seemingly in a hurry. He had no information to add and, impatient, soon roared off again. So the fate or whereabouts of Tiger's son Phong remained a mystery. Tiger says, and his relatives confirm, that Tiger stole a motorcycle just before he left Vietnam. He says he sold it and gave Thom and Phong $20. Phong was two when Tiger last saw him. "Next time I see him, he'll probably have a girlfriend of his own," Tiger jokes ruefully. But it is unlikely that Tiger will ever see Phong again, even if Phong is alive.

Son'ɗ Frienɗɗ: Song Pha, Vietnam, the Preɗent

When we met Son's friends Hai, Tieng, and Kim in the Song Pha area, our group included not only my interpreter and myself but also our van driver and the cyclo driver we had befriended in Ho Chi Minh City, who spoke some English. Son's friend Hai operated a tiny store in a tribal village near Song Pha, where Son's former frankincense-hunting friends talked with us in the part of the store that is Hai's home. With its miniscule refrigerated cooler holding a few bottles of beer and soft drinks, its almost-bare shelves carrying soap and a few other necessities, and the ever-present karaoke machine in the corner, the store represents the closest thing to "bright lights" the village has to offer. Outside, it is mostly deserted in the afternoon heat. Most of the villagers have gone to work on the rubber trees in the surrounding jungle. Hai's wife quietly tends their new baby, listening to the men's reminiscences. Everyone enjoys Kim's story of how once, climbing a mountain alone, he came face to face with a giant, open-jawed python. "Its eyes stuck out as big as toes," he says. "It leapt on me and I screamed!" Kim also told of a time he and Son stumbled onto a tribal settlement where the villagers had gone to collect rubber sap. Inside one of the rattan huts they spotted an R-16 rifle leaning against a wall. Frightened, they hurried away.

"Every person who went into the jungle to look for frankincense was afraid of dying," says Hai. "And I have many dark, tragic memories from that time. But because of the desperate economic situation then, we had no choice." It was, he says, their only hope of staying alive. Kim echoes those words: "Of course everyone was afraid of dying in the jungles, but in the situation then, bravery came to us, because of our strong desire to stay alive."

As they grew more experienced, Son and Kim had noticed an area near Bac Ai heavily guarded by government soldiers. "We figured it had lots of good frankincense there, probably untouched because it was so hard to get in," says Kim. They walked three days to reach the river they needed to cross. The area was inhabited by tribes that worked gathering rubber sap, but that returned to their village every day at 3 P.M. "After we reached the river, we hid until they returned, then swam across floating our cooking pot and supplies," says Kim. "Then we started into the jungle about 6 P.M., because once we crossed we had to go forward no matter how dark it had become, or we might be seen. We never put up a hut, but would find a cave and go deep inside to do our cooking—always at night, so our fire and smoke wouldn't be seen. One day on that trip we saw three tribal men crawling along the jungle floor, also hunting for frankincense. They were from Phu Khanh, wearing regular clothes, unlike the members of another nearby tribe who usually wore no clothes at all. We were so frightened we ran away to our cave."

"During the hard years," says Hai, "everything depended on money. Our goal was mainly to make enough just to get through each day." He pauses a moment. "We also had greater dreams," he adds, "dreams that only money could satisfy, so we had to try our luck in the jungle. What did we want? Well, things like motorcycles." He laughs. "Men can face all kinds of danger to be able to see different places."

Did they ever get the cycles?

"No," says Hai.

"No," says Kim.

"No," says Tieng. After a moment of silence he adds: "But the goal was mainly to survive."

"After all these years," Kim laughs ruefully at himself, "I still couldn't get a motorcycle!"

Hai believes that discrimination against Amerasians no longer exists in Vietnam. "That was in the past," he says. "People go on with their lives now. Even the soldiers who worked for the American government and went to reeducation camp are treated OK now." Why is it, I asked

Hai, that many Vietnamese say there's no prejudice, but the Amerasians say that there is? He tries to explain: "There were cases when Amerasians broke the law and made trouble, when some would do bad things. In those cases people treat you badly, but if you obey rules and work, there is no prejudice. And usually Amerasians did end up as troublemakers or gangsters. Because when they were born they already lacked family and love and discipline, and when a person misses those things they have a wild side and don't care. They can fall into bad paths, the same as with any other people." Some people were even afraid of Son, says Hai.

Kim wanted to be sure that we talked to Son Chau's thirty-year-old Amerasian cousin Hung, who had come to meet us after a long bus trip from the remote area where he lived. Hung worked making mud tiles, Son had told us, adding that "Hung's hands and whole body are all covered with scars from the hard work he has had to do all his life. He is very, very poor." In Song Pha, government authorities still worry about activity by FULRO (the French acronym for the United Front for the Struggle of the Oppressed Races), the armed tribal guerrilla groups. Some even were active as recently as 2002, probably with the support of militant South Vietnamese exile groups in America as well as tribal groups given residence in the Carolinas following the war. Overnight visitors to Song Pha must register with the police. Kim had bravely offered to let us spend the night in his tiny, sparkling-clean house with him, his wife, and baby, saying he would go with us to the police station to register. But we decided instead to spend the night in a tourist town nearby. Hung, who came with us, usually walked a little apart and seldom spoke.

Late that night after dinner at our hotel, our group sat outdoors on our patio on the edge of the beach. Across from us, dark palm trees were outlined against the moon's silvery glint on the sea. An occasional stranger passed by, one or two leaning on the patio wall to listen quietly; Vietnamese sometimes include themselves this way, always staying very silent and still. Kim, talkative and energetic, announced politely that it was now Hung's "turn" to talk to us, but despite attempts to draw him out, Hung said very little at first.

When Hung did speak, his murmured answers were humble and brief. Only for one moment did he show a flicker of hopeful emotion when Kim urged him to try to remember anything at all about his American dad. But Hung had almost no information, and said he believed it was too late to find his father. His mother had told him that his dad came back and forth to her house, then left for the United States. He thinks his father came to Vietnam in 1966, and that he, Hung, was born about 1968, but definitely before his dad left Vietnam. He knows that his father was building roads—Kim says Hung's father was "cong binh," doing construction maybe as a civilian on what used to be Highway 20. Hung thinks his father left for America in 1972, but all these dates were only approximations.

After a wretched life growing up, Hung at twenty-three was approached by a Vietnamese family who wanted to use him to get to America. "They took me to Bien Hoa to live with them for a year and a half so I would be able to answer on the exit exam," explained Hung. "There was a woman and two kids. The dad was North Vietnamese and hated Americans, and didn't want to go to the United States. When I thought I was going to America I was happy, but we did not pass the exam." Standing outside the interview building immediately after the failed exam, the family ordered Hung not to return home with them. "I had no money, and they told me to walk back to my own village. I was too sad, but I did not blame them about the money. If they don't give it, they don't," said Hung. He began walking back, sleeping wherever he could, eating if he found anything to eat. After he'd walked several days, hungry and heartbroken, some people in a temple gathered a few coins for him to take a bus the rest of the way. He never saw the fake family again.

Kim kept encouraging Hung to talk to us. Hung had been homeless for many years, said Kim, sometimes sleeping in the yard outside his aunt's house. He often went hungry. "But I have given up hunting for my dad," said Hung. "It's difficult to find one's father. It's too far for him to come here to find me." Finally Hung said maybe his father's name was CooRah—those of us able to speak English experimented with saying it several ways—could it be Quentin? Caroll? Conrad? Pressed further, Hung finally admitted: "I do think about my dad, but I do not know his last name. I think he may someday come to look for me. But it might not be possible for me to leave with him." Hung shifted in his chair and continued, straining to communicate a complicated thought he wanted to get across: "As for Amerasians, if you mix with white it's better than if you mix with black, because if you are mixed with black, people tease you and make fun of you more. If you are a black Amerasian, you feel bad about yourself and sad for yourself." Hung added another insight that perhaps explained why he often gave away money when he himself was so poor. "When you have no money it's like you are invisible—people just ignore you. If you have money, people treat you better. Life for Amerasians here got better when there was the law they could go to the U.S. People valued them more. Now life is just OK, but not as bad as when we were small."

Kim, realizing Hung's difficulty in talking, finally spoke on his behalf. "I have known Hung for very, very long, but he's not good at expressing himself," said Kim. "I hope Americans will help him find his dad, but what he needs most is economic help because he works as a laborer and doesn't have enough money." Hung did tell us though, when we asked, that during recent years he "almost always" had food. Then Hung grew quiet again, like someone who has often been taunted and disdained, but has achieved a lonely dignity and pride. Kim explained to him that I was writing something that would be read by Americans, and urged him to try to send a message through me. Finally Hung, forcing the words, sent this message: "My life in Vietnam is very terrible. I have no true friends. I hope the Americans can help me find my father. If anyone reading what you write could help in any way, I hope Americans will please think of Amerasians, and remember those still in Vietnam."

II

The Amerasians Today

"We are still accepting applications [to emigrate to America] from Vietnamese Amerasians, but new processing of them was ended in January 2003. There are new concerns post 9/11 . . . and also there are different realities now. The Vietnamese Amerasians aren't little kids anymore. They are adults aged from their late twenties to their mid-forties."

— Pamela Lewis, Congressional Liaison for the Bureau of
Population, Refugees, and Migration with the U.S.
State Department

In November 2000 President Bill Clinton became the first U.S. president to visit Vietnam since the war ended, and the first ever to visit Hanoi. Arriving around midnight, Clinton was greeted by thousands and thousands of people lining the streets on the long ride into town from the airport. Some had been waiting for eight hours or more. The *Los Angeles Times* designated it "a trip designed to bring formal closure to one of the most painful chapters in American history." It quoted Vietnam War historian Stanley Karnow: "It's a curious thing. A lot of American kids don't know about Vietnam, [but] ever since, when the U.S. has become involved in a conflict, the big question is whether it will become another Vietnam. This trip helps exorcise that ghost."

In America, Clinton's trip sparked some bitter reactions. "He has a lot of nerve after he dodged the draft [for Vietnam]," retired Adm. Thomas H. Moorer, chair of the U.S. Joint Chiefs of Staff from 1970–

74, said. "I wrote to the mothers of the men who were killed and I know how they feel. I don't see how he has the nerve to go." Retired Army Gen. Frederick Kroesen, who did two tours of duty in Vietnam, called himself "one of a few million who look with disdain and disgust" at the trip because of Clinton's decision not to serve in the military during the war. At the time of Clinton's trip, 1,498 Americans were still listed as missing in action in Vietnam. The United States and Vietnam were conducting a joint program looking for bits of their corpses.

St. Anselm's

The halls of St. Anselm's are much emptier and quieter now, unlike the years they were filled with the clatter of young Amerasians, resettlement workers, volunteers, reporters, and researchers come to study the new crop of immigrants. By 2003 the center had "run out of" refugees, at least temporarily, except for a few Bosnians and a dwindling trickle of former Vietnamese political prisoners. But St. Anselm's had grants to help Vietnamese immigrants integrate into the community and for TB prevention. "We're becoming involved with the human trafficking issue, too," says Marianne Blank, the center's director, referring to the latest "hot" problem in social welfare circles at the time.

Although the Amerasian program formally closed down in 1994, for years a few Amerasians continued to come by, to borrow bus money, find help looking for a job, or to seek referral to a social service agency. Blank herself continues to play a minor role in the lives of some as an expert witness. Immigration activists and defense attorneys in Texas, Arizona, California, and Colorado have sought her "testimony" through a carefully worded form letter in which Blank explains to judges and other authorities why they should show mercy to Amerasians arrested for crimes, and why Amerasians should not be sentenced to eventually be extradited back to Vietnam. At the time this was written in early 2004, Vietnam still refused to take back convicted Vietnamese, including Amerasians, and they were being held in immigration detention centers after their prison sentences were served. But Vietnam and the United States were actively negotiating the issue, and it was expected to be only a matter of time before Vietnam would accept them back— including Tiger.

"The stigma and shame borne by the [Amerasian] children . . . produced a group that had little chance of success in this country," Blank writes in her letter. "Here in the U.S. our [nation's Amerasian] program was very well-intended, but really unable to address the deficits the Amerasians brought with them. A certain number were so high risk for social problems that very severe problems were inevitable. The United States never did anything for these children, and they were expected to somehow adapt here as adults, even though they were taught to be ashamed of their existence." She adds that black Amerasians "are in double jeopardy and experience the worst treatment," and that deporting them back to Vietnam would be "like locking the door and throwing away the key."

I ask her if she thinks the United States did the right thing in bringing the Amerasians here. "Yes," she says without hesitation, "because they wanted to come, and for a lot of them it's better here. Some have demonstrated that you can get into college, you can get a job, and that nobody cares what race you are or if you are mixed race. And some have become citizens. But this country did too little, too late. The Amerasians paid a terrible price. We neglected them for many years, and by the time we did anything for them they had grown up with enormous stigmas that it was impossible to overcome."

According to an Asian psychiatrist in Little Saigon, numerous Amerasians are losing their children to the foster care system. Growing up with little parenting themselves, and usually with no extended family, many have no idea how to raise their offspring, so the courts take these part-American grandchildren away. Suzie Dong-Matsuda, the social worker, had predicted at a time most Amerasians had been in the United States ten years or less that things for them might get worse instead of better. "But the Amerasians work hard," she had added, "and as time passes, some will get acculturated, although I don't think many will pursue an education. The women are often in abusive relationships. And some Amerasians have died here from gangs and substance abuse." While praising the Amerasians' survival skills, Dong-Matsuda added that the many barriers they had been forced to face in the United States had "weakened those skills. We just haven't given them enough support here. They were set up with such high hopes and expectations for America. Between Vietnam and the U.S., they've had double abuse. All they've known in their lives is pain. They have been betrayed so many times. Although some of them 'make it,' many of them don't. I would expect their lives to be short."

Most of the staff and volunteers who worked at St. Anselm's during its "Amerasian years" have moved on. Peter Daniels works at Catholic

Charities overseeing job placements and welfare-to-work programs for immigrants. By late 1997, he says, many Amerasians were coming through the social service system as welfare cases. "Their spoken English is good, but they can't read or write," he said. Like Marianne Blank, he has not been able to forget the Amerasians. In late 2001 he sought a grant for funds to address their continuing mental and emotional problems. "All the Amerasians go through periodic depressions," he says. The grant proposal was turned down.

Son Chau

Son, his wife Chi, their son Billy, and new baby, Celine Tran Chau (born in America in 2001 and named after the singer Celine Dion), stayed with Son's mother Du in Little Saigon in 2003 while Chi studied for her nail work license. In 1997 Son had received his own nail license and opened his first small salon. He sold it and bought a bigger one on Chicago's outskirts a month before Chi and Billy came to the United States, so that Chi could go to work right away and earn money to send to her family. (Because so many Vietnamese enter manicuring work, in 2001 California began offering the exam in Vietnamese.)

Son had held several other kinds of jobs in America—factory and slaughterhouse work, car body repair. "I like to work hard, use my head—not sit around home watching the TV and talking. I keep confidence in myself," Son says.

Chi is smart, calm, and centered. She and Son appear quite close. "When Chi started work in my nail salon, she was supposed to go to nail school first—" Son slides over this situation, continuing quickly, "but so anyway, it worked out OK for her to work these last two and a half years first. Sometimes [the government] said she had to have a license, but I have other permissions, other paperworks, to make them feel OK. My son Billy, the way he looks and acts, is very much the same as me. He's very 'activitive,' he never sits down like some little boys. And now my daughter, I want her to be more like my wife. We kind of try to invest whatever we get now and give our kids a little better future. I want my daughter to work in an office, do more gentle things. I hope when she grow up she can spend several years in college, have a totally different life."

A year earlier Son bought land and built a house in Press near Dalat and gave it to Chi's parents. They raise and sell bonsai trees at a roadside stand in front. "I designed my house all by myself," Son says. "That's my money, my house, so I want it how I like. That's a good spot to do business, too; people who go between Saigon and Dalat have to pass by. Someday I want to open a restaurant there."

In 1998 Son brought proof he'd paid $4,000 in U.S. taxes to show U.S. Embassy authorities in Hanoi that he would be able to support his wife and son in America. "I wanted to keep the relationship with my wife," he said. "My wife is very active, very good, not a slow one to sit at home. She have very good responsibility for her family. That's one thing I think that my American father, he did the right thing. That's why I went back to Vietnam to get a girl like that."

That year, Son became a U.S. citizen. He took out papers for Du, who'd been half-blind since she was nine, and Joseph Love completed the complicated forms. Du receives $650 per month Social Security Insurance, which Son points out "is not like welfare or food stamps." He says of his mother, "I believe my mom is a good woman. Whatever she did, you know, life make her. Most all people in the world, they want money, and not many people you know will help you, especially in this country. With Vietnamese families, your money is their money. Our family all try to make the money and bring it home. One person is not strong like one family." Son sent Joe Love a ticket to fly from the Midwest to join a family celebration. Says Son: "The last time we both lived in Little Saigon, Joe know I have a body shop in my yard with damaged cars, and his car had tires very old and worn out and he didn't have money to buy more. He ask me if I can give him some used tires, but I didn't have time to find just the right ones, so you know what? I give him a lot of money and say, 'Go find the tires you want.'"

Joe Love says: "I think I've become the father figure. But I'm still looking for Son's real dad. It appears he was a sergeant in charge of Vietnamese civilians working in food services at Thap Cham air base." Love laughs about a recent phone call from Son. "He told me, 'Mr. Joe, you are old. You probably will not live very long. You need someone to watch you.'" Love, then sixty-four, says he was very touched, "although it made me feel I might keel over at any minute."

Soberly, Son says: "I know Joe Love have concern for me. Maybe someday soon I buy a house, put money down, and take him back to live with our family. It good for him and good for me too, because he's American, he know more than I do. And I know he old and have no relationship, no children, no wife, no family—he unlucky, you see. And he feel lonely, you know. Joe is older, like my real American dad is older now. So anything I give Joe, I think it's like I give it to my dad. I don't need help from my dad, I just want to know who is he. So when I give to Joe, that's one way I am still looking for my dad."

When the California Medfly Program where he worked was phased down in early 1996, Love had been laid off. He lived off unemployment another six months while continuing his volunteer father-finder work, but then, he says only half-joking, "I was two months from living under an overpass and had started looking at shopping carts." Talking to an old girlfriend in another state, he mentioned his plight and she drove 1,500 miles to California to bring him back to stay with her in her trailer. Within two weeks he found a job in a large assembly plant in an area where many Amerasians had migrated to work in slaughterhouses. Love arranged to continue his volunteer work at the local Catholic Charities office.

"I never quit. Never quit," Love emphasizes. He attributes his tenacity to his paratrooper training just before the Korean War ended. "I'm still Airborne all the way," he says proudly. "They had me believing as an eighteen-year-old that I could whip any ten men if I just never quit. So I'm still looking for one dad whose daughter had only a "sound-alike" name for him—shoot, boot, foot, something like that. I found a guy named Foltz who fit the profile perfectly—same unit, same job, same year. But when I got his photo, the mom said, 'That's not him.' So now I'm looking for this Foltz because I figure he must have known the real dad. I find lots of dads through guys who served with them."

Love guesses that at least 10 percent of his cases "had some kind of fraud involved," although usually the Amerasians didn't know that. "Once, an Amerasian brought in his dad's papers. I found the dad and he said he'd left a son in Southeast Asia and always wondered what happened to him. He had no other children, so he flew down to bring the boy home. This dad had built up a nice little business and planned to bring the boy into it eventually. And since the kid would inherit all he had, he first wanted to pay the $900 for a DNA test. It showed there was no way in hell this kid could have been his son. I called up the kid's so-called uncle and said, 'I don't care what you had to do to get into this country—you're here now—but I want you to tell me the truth.' You have to back the fake ones into a corner, not let them smile and back out." The Amerasian was very upset with Love for telling the father he wasn't his real son. The father, too, was sad, and told Love he planned to go back to Vietnam to look for his real son.

Love says sadly: "The Amerasians are life's losers. I don't want to say that, but . . ." After a long pause he adds with anger and resignation: "And now we've left thousands of Amerasians still in Vietnam, and they'll never get here because nobody's interested in them anymore. They're no longer big-eyed orphans on TV—they're grown men and women, thirty-five and forty years old, many with kids of their own. Grandchildren of Americans."

In June 2000, a few months before Clinton made his reconciliation trip to Vietnam, Son Chau received news from Vietnam that his thirty-year-old cousin Hung had committed suicide by drinking a Vietnamese rat or insect poison called Thuoc Chuot or Thuoc Tru Sau. "When I heard about it, I cry and cry," says Son in a long-distance call. "He was so poor! He was homeless and staying with his mom and aunt. He still lived in the mountains in an NEZ area, making bricks from mud just to earn food whenever he could get work. He had scars all over his hands and legs from hard, dangerous work. He used to have a girlfriend, but something happened. And when he died he still had no girlfriend, no children.

"He had wanted to come to America, and when he talked with you he still had a little hope, but after that no hope," says Son. I had gone to great lengths to explain to Hung why it was pretty impossible he would ever be able to leave Vietnam for the United States, and why he could never find his American father if he did. In my American way I believed it was best to know and face the truth, then move on with knowledge of that reality. In fact, I'd been rather proud of my explanation of the situation. But when I told Vietnamese friends how I had explained everything to Hung, they were aghast. In Vietnamese culture, one tries to cushion the pain of reality, I was told, and often Vietnamese just give the answer they believe the questioner wants to hear. Thinking back on how I had tried to convince him he would never find his American father, I realized it was not just a cultural mistake I had made, but one much worse. I had never really grasped what it meant to Hung to keep alive his belief that he might have a better life someday, and thus I had killed much of the hope that kept him able to go on. And, as it later turned out, factually I was completely wrong.

Son continued his story of Hung's suicide: "My half-sister went to visit and gave him $100, and within an hour he had given it all away to other poor people. Whenever he got money he would give it away. That night he had a big meal and drank a lot, and sometimes when he did that, he lost control. No, no, not lost his temper! He never did that!" In the context of being so desperately poor himself, Hung's "losing control" meant giving away the money he needed so much himself. "When he came home that night his mom and aunt yelled and yelled at him, saying 'Money is not easy to make, and yet you give it away!' And in the morning they found him dead of the poison. Then his mother had a heart attack and fainted, and they had to take her to the hospital." Money that Son sent for her to buy food was spent instead on a doctor.

I go to Little Saigon to see Son's mother, Du. I am very upset, believing I am partly to blame for Hung's suicide. We sit in Du's apartment, drinking tea; as Du speaks, her older sister, Aunt #9, another of Hung's aunts, listens, weeping. Aunt #9 says, "Since the day Hung died, his mother has been very depressed. Months later, she has never recovered." Du says: "Hung would have loved to go to the U.S., he was dying to go." Once Hung went to live with a girlfriend in Ban Me Thuot, says Du, "and Hung's mom didn't hear from him for so long that she thought he was dead. She dreamed he was in water struggling to get out, and kept saying 'My son is dead.' But I could read the future and I told her, 'He is alive.' And a few years later, he came back."

The suicide story is retold. After Hung gave away all his money and returned home, says Du, his nephew, the grandson of Aunt #9, said to him: 'You are so stupid! You could have gone to America like Son, if you were as good, as smart, as Son. You are such a loser!' And Hung felt even his nephew didn't respect him, so he went out and got more drunk, and drank the poison and came home and died."

A few days after Hung committed suicide, papers arrived for him at his mother's house in Vietnam from the U.S. Embassy, saying he was eligible for another interview under which he might be able to go to America. The letter carried no signature. The envelope, bearing the return address of THE UNITED STATES OF AMERICA, U.S. CONSULATE GENERAL, 4 LE DUAN BLVD., DISTRICT 1, HCMC, is marked OFFICIAL BUSINESS, and under the address is printed by hand "RRS," [Refugee Resettlement Services]. It is addressed to Tran Van Hung, Unit I, Village II, Ninh Phuoc, Ninh Thuan, File Number AC 99–0285.

Translation of the letter, dated July 13, 2000:

> "*We request the following persons:* Tran Van Hung, Tran Van Thu, Tran
> Van Hoang, Tran Van Tri, Dinh Thi Mai Nam *to come to the U.S. Consulate
> General at 4 Le Duan, District 1, Ho Chi Minh City on 22 August 2000 at 8*

a.m. in order to work further on your interview file if you have already obtained passports or the Introduction Letter to an Interview.

Note: Make sure you have with you: Originals and copies of personal identifications (Identification card, family registration, marriage license, birth certificate, death certificate, passport, etc.); Letters [and] pictures. [AFTER THIS ABOUT FOUR INCHES HAD BEEN CROSSED OUT WITH HEAVY BLACK INK]; The letter continues: *Please inform the Refugee Resettlement Service (RRS), U.S. Consulate General in HCMC, at 822.9433 if you have not obtained passports, Introduction Letter to Interview, or LOI.*

At the bottom of the letter is no signature, only:

"Refugee Resettlement Service (RRS)"

So I had been totally wrong when I told Hung that his dreams of going to America had no realistic chance. The letter showed that he definitely *did* have a chance.

A few months after Hung's suicide, his mother, Dinh Tran, still had not recovered. In the meantime Son sent her more food money. "When people are hungry you give a little and they are appreciative, that's the way I do," he says. "Anyway, they are old, so if you don't give them, how do they live?" Dinh Tran's home was 100 feet from that of another of her elderly sisters, and the two visited every day. One day Dinh Tran gathered up the small amount of money and valued things in her home and walked very, very slowly to her sister's. It was hard for her to breathe. "But there was a very, very poor woman who lived with my aunt, and this woman helped my aunt walk there," says Son.

Dinh Tran's sister kept a picture of Hung along with other family photographs on the Buddhist altar in her home, and Dinh Tran sat down beside it. "She called all the family to come sit around her," says Son, "and told them, 'I will die today.' And she divided up all the money and other things. When she finished, she said, 'Everybody get away from me, because I am going to die now.' And they all went away except her oldest son, and she drew long deep breaths, and in ten minutes she died. And they buried her next to Hung."

Sara Phuong and Miss Dao

After Sara made a final break with her children's father, she married another Caucasian American, a deputy sheriff. They lived with her husband's brother and Sara's children in an ethnically mixed apartment complex on the edge of Little Saigon. In their living room is an entertainment center with a large TV set and a karaoke where Sara practices singing. To celebrate their Buddhist wedding, the couple worked months to save for a lavish reception in a Little Saigon restaurant and a long American-style honeymoon. Sara began studying for a nail licensing examination, although she still worked at sewing six days a week. She also began pursuing her long-held dream of becoming a singer, mostly singing at weddings. At her own wedding reception she sang two songs—"Cha Yeu," about a young girl planning her wedding and lovingly remembering her father who died a few years earlier, and a song about mothers, which Sara dedicated to Miss Dao.

Weeks before Tet, Miss Dao begins making special vegetarian foods that she sells in Little Saigon, at a booth operated by the Minh-Dang Quang pagoda, named after the monk who founded Miss Dao's order in Vietnam. Years ago, when first arriving in the United States, Miss Dao applied for food stamps and for disability because of arthritis and heart trouble, but was turned down. Her health still is not very good, but in 2002, aged sixty-five, she began receiving Social Security—$750 per month. Asked whether life is better now for Amerasians in America or Vietnam, Miss Dao answers quickly and decisively: "In the U.S. it is much better. Because even though the Amerasians have to work and struggle in America, they have enough to eat, and the basic necessities. In America they have a chance for an education, and through that they can fulfill their lives. For Amerasians still in Vietnam, it is also better than before. But in America their self-confidence [*su tu tin*, self-esteem or self-confidence] is much better."

She adds that she would like to go to government leaders in the United States to try to get the Amerasians still in Vietnam brought to the United States. It is courageous but characteristic of Miss Dao to speak out on behalf of the Amerasians, in a world where much of her own community still looks down on them, and in a country where she may still be unsure of the consequences of speaking out so freely. But she is now studying for her U.S. citizenship exam, and says she "loves the U.S., a country that cares about human rights, and rights for women."

Still, Miss Dao stresses that even in the United States, "the Amerasians still have many emotional problems, and I want the American people to realize that the Amerasians were very mistreated, so all have inferiority complexes. They always were unwanted, so their emotional life is still difficult, and in their hearts they are very unhappy. As for Amerasians in Vietnam, I myself know of dozens left behind, barely getting by, living hand to mouth, day by day. The most heartbreaking thing for me is to see the Amerasians left in Vietnam, who are so poor and who have no one to care about them."

Every year in her home in Little Saigon on Vietnamese Remembrance Day, or Day of the Dead (*cung co hon*, the seventh day of the seventh month of the lunar calendar), Miss Dao marks prayers and offerings for the souls of the tiny abandoned babies she once cared for long ago and who died as infants during a terrible war. Probably no one else in the world remembers them.

Back in Vietnam, more than a quarter century after the departure of U.S. troops and the end of bombing raids and battles, the war continues. Exploding leftover ordnance and toxic chemicals are still reaping injuries and death. In the final two months of 2001, for example, Reuters news agency reported that at least twenty-six people, twenty of them children aged three to twelve, were killed in five central and southern provinces of Vietnam by explosions of U.S. grenades or cluster bombs left over from the war. Added Reuters: "[Such] explosions . . . kill and maim dozens of people each year, many of them children." In March 2002, thanks to an initiative by the Vietnam Veterans of America, government scientists from both countries met in Hanoi with world experts to consider the effects of the millions of gallons of Agent Orange and other chemical defoliants the U.S. sprayed on Vietnam between 1962 and 1971. (Spraying was ended in 1971 because of a high rate of cancer in laboratory rats exposed to the chemicals.) One expert on Agent Orange said recent, new tests on people living in a heavily sprayed part of Vietnam around the former U.S. air base at Bien Hoa had found "startlingly high" levels of dioxin, up to 206 times higher than average.

In 1995, as part of "normalization," Vietnam had dropped claims against the United States for war compensation and reparations, which would have included aid for Agent Orange victims. But thousands of U.S. veterans also had been exposed to the chemicals. Since the war they, too, had reported serious repercussions from their exposure, including an abnormally high number of cancers and of birth defects in their children. Although the United States has insisted for decades that there was "still no solid scientific proof" that the chemicals had caused the continuing catastrophe, if such proof *were* established, then U.S. veterans, at least, would have a better claim for compensation from the U.S. government and from Agent Orange's makers, Dow Chemical Co.

and the Monsanto Co. After much wrangling, the two countries signed a "memorandum of understanding" in 2002 to carry out joint research, despite a plea by the chairman of Vietnam's Red Cross, who said Agent Orange victims "need U.S. help now, and cannot wait years for more research."

He added: "The conscience of the U.S., I am sure, will never rest until that country has fulfilled its responsibility."

Sara Phuong

In 2002 Sara planned her first visit back to Vietnam. At that time, Miss Dao gave her the letter which Sara's birth mother had placed in Sara's basket so many years ago. Sara had believed the letter was lost forever. But actually, Miss Dao had found it among ransacked papers scattered on the orphanage floor after she and the orphans returned from their escape to Cam Ranh at the end of the war. "I put it away, and kept it all this time," Miss Dao says. "But now that Sara is grown and planning to go back, I decided to give it to her. Because I want her to find and have the love of her birth mother, the mother from the blood and the bone." The letter is sad, Miss Dao said, because the mother was a student, "and with a baby, she could not go back to her family."

At 7 P.M. each night in Vietnam, where most of the 300,000 Vietnamese missing at the end of the war have never been found, a list is read on television of people looking for lost loved ones. Sara could read the letter, or part of it, on TV during her planned trip back to Vietnam. But she is not sure if she will show it to anyone. "It is very sad," she says quietly, looking away when I ask her about it. A few weeks later, I ask Sara again about the letter. At first she evades my question, saying the letter is brief, that she read it only once. Finally she blurts out that she recently talked to a Vietnamese psychic about it. "That psychic was a very, very good psychic. She cost $30," Sara says. The psychic told Sara that her mother came from a family that had some kind of special powers, perhaps did voodoo kinds of things—"not voodoo exactly"— Sara couldn't really explain, it was a Vietnamese practice hard to translate—and they even could turn people into something like zombies. The family had forced Sara's mother to give her up.

"The psychic told me that my mom thinks of me and cries every day of her life, and that even though she has other children, it is me she wants and needs." Sara pauses a moment, then adds passionately: "And

I know how she feels, because it is *her* I want, too. And I love her, because the psychic says my mother has never been able to forgive herself for giving me up. And I forgive her for giving me up, because I know her family made her, and that she always thinks of me and loves me." I ask Sara about going to Vietnam and reading the letter on television, and she says she's not ready yet to go back and that her husband doesn't want her to go this year. In the end Sara postponed her trip. I wonder to myself if a fantasy mom may sometimes be better than a real mom.

Louis Nguyen

Louis is one of very, very few Amerasians arriving in America as teens or young adults under the Amerasian Homecoming Act who were able to even enroll in college in America, much less graduate as he did. He lives with his mother, Luc, in a large modern Little Saigon gated apartment complex whose sunny courtyard surrounds a turquoise swimming pool. Several Latino and Asian children—some Korean, others Vietnamese—giggle and play together among palms and flowering bushes.

Louis's mom has an engaging smile, and often teases her son with witty Vietnamese one-liners. When Louis translates her Vietnamese into English, he turns short questions into long streams of rapid Vietnamese and then answers for his mother before she has a chance. When she's asked, "Do you think your son is a good singer?" he cries out excitedly before she can reply, "Of course! Of course she does!" And when she's asked why she didn't sell her son to some wealthy Vietnamese fake family, he cries out again, "Because she loved me!"

Yet studies of the mothers of Amerasians in the United States have concluded that most are more lost and depressed than their children, and not long ago Luc suffered a serious depression, with many physical symptoms. For hours she would listen to CDs of Buddhist chants, and talked often of her fear of coming death. His mother's illness was one of several crises that attacked Louis's life about the time he graduated from college. He and the longtime Vietnamese girlfriend who had helped him through college had broken up. Not long afterward he went to Vietnam to see his ninety-eight-year-old grandmother (who as one friend points out "was his life") and soon after returning to the United States he received news she had died.

"Every month my mom and I had sent back about $50–100 for her, because even though we were very poor, we knew later on we would want to send her something but she'd be gone," Louis once told me. Sometimes he would watch videos of his grandmother that his mother brought back from a visit to Vietnam and tears would run down his cheeks. Says a friend: "He cried double tears, happy to see her and re- member their time together, but sad knowing she was old and sick and would not live long." Louis says he sometimes talked long distance to his grandmother on the phone. "I could hear her, but she was deaf, so someone had to tell her what I said. And she would cry." Unable to return to Vietnam immediately after her death, Louis managed to send back $1,000 for a lavish village funeral in her honor.

Vietnamese have a very high rate of becoming U.S. citizens. In 1997 Louis had passed his citizenship exam. A few years later, he was asked to volunteer his singing at a campaign event for a candidate for county sheriff, organized by a committee of Vietnamese Americans and at- tended by hundreds of them. America's political parties and candidates had begun to notice and court the Vietnamese Americans. Usually con- sidered solidly Republican, by the year 2000 an increasing number of mostly younger Vietnamese Americans were joining the Democratic Party. Louis personally chose the expensive material he had fashioned into the "star" suit he wore — white, with silver glitter threads sparkling through it. He sang a song he told me was "famous all over the world." One of hundreds about missing the lost Vietnamese homeland, it is called "Dem Nho Ve Saigon":

> *At night I remember Saigon . . .*
> *I remember friends . . .*
> *Now my friends are scattered all over the world . . .*

The candidate spoke and prominent community leaders were intro- duced, along with a former Miss America. She posed for photos for $5 campaign donations and performed a finger-snapping, hip-swinging version of a song in Vietnamese, her effort enthusiastically applauded. The emcee announced that this Miss America had once sung the "Star- Spangled Banner" seventeen times in twenty-four hours. Tonight she sang it again, as the audience stood and proudly joined in. Most of the Vietnamese at the gathering seemed to know the words better than a native-born American crowd as they sang along with the former Miss America:

> *"Oh, say can you see, by the dawn's early light,*
> *what so proudly we hailed at the twilight's last gleaming? . . .*

And the rockets' red glare, the bombs bursting in air,
gave proof through the night that our flag
was still there.
Oh! say does that star-spangled banner yet wave
o'er the land of the free
and the home of the brave?"

The audience members seemed oblivious to the irony that some of the words might have carried for this crowd—the references to rockets and bombs, the final question in the song about whether the star-spangled American flag yet waved, in light of America's ignominious departure from Vietnam. They only seemed proud to be taking part in this very American type of gathering, and to be celebrating their new country.

"Up until the mid-1980s there was this outlandish wish of some Vietnamese that the Americans would come back," a graduate student from Ho Chi Minh City who was studying in America told me. Her wealthy family had owned two eight-unit apartment buildings rented to U.S. soldiers during the war. "After 1975 the new government took them, saying, 'You are capitalist, you are landlords, you consorted with Americans, and so on,'" she said. "They filled one of the buildings with police singers," hired to sing songs praising the police at various events. "One of my neighbors was a South Vietnamese army vet," she continued. "He lost both legs and one eye in the war. At night, all the neighborhood kids would gather around him and he would tell us ghost stories, and also say that the Americans were going to come back and rescue us some day. He missed the Americans. Now he is living in the United States."

I told a Vietnamese friend who immigrated to America years ago that I had felt uncomfortable hearing Vietnamese sing some of the words to the anthem. "But all national anthems grow out of some kind of military moment," he said. "Even the Vietnamese national anthem was written by a North Vietnamese before the country was divided. It's about liberation, exchanging your blood and bones for your country's pride and its freedom. When I hear the American national anthem I don't think of those war images in it; I think of the ideal of America, that people were created equal, that you have equal rights, freedom, and democracy, and while you don't always achieve those ideals, you are striving for them. We can all disagree among ourselves, but America still is a government of the people, and of people bonded to the *idea* of it.

"Because there is no America. America was just a name. It's really a strange country, 200 years old, yet we own it. There were the Indians, then it was divided between French, English, and Spanish—then others kept coming, like the Chinese building the railroads, and all the other groups kept coming and just built this country America. We are all from someplace else. America was never perfect, it always had corruption and injustice and racism if you study American history. But there is always that ideal of America, and you are always striving for it. All of us are bonded to that ideal. In another country it's very rare for a poor person to 'make it,' or be respected, because, in Vietnam for example, your family name can be traced back for centuries. The Vietnamese really wanted to come to the U.S., and the ideals of democracy and liberty are so valid to them. People always sing the American national anthem at Vietnamese public functions. But for me it's about more than the time or the place, it's about the ideal."

Meanwhile, Louis was looking for an African American singing teacher, because he thinks a teacher like his father could best understand his singing style.

Louis's photo was on the cover of the October 2000 issue of *Nang Mai*, Little Saigon's major Vietnamese-language magazine. The article said: "Despite having people talk behind his back and look on him as a black Amerasian, with all the bad stereotypes such as wild, violent, careless of the future, and careless in relationships, Luu Quoc Viet tries his best to quietly step over the wall of that opinion. He is obedient with his mom, sincere with his friends, respectful of elders, and has a great way of getting along with other people." The article quoted Louis saying, "I am trying to raise myself up from all the bad stereotypes and prejudice despite what people think." The debut of his new CD at Little Saigon's ritzy Majestic Club drew an enthusiastic crowd of 650 people.

I ask Louis how he ever managed to graduate from college despite overwhelming obstacles. He tells me: "Sometimes I myself wonder, 'How did I get through some of the terrible times in my life?' Even now when I think of those five years of college I don't know how I got through it. No one can believe I did it, even myself. Actually, my former girlfriend is the one who helped me. She studied biology and chemistry and I studied business, totally different fields, but she would help correct my writing. Because of her I would go to class even when I was very tired, because I wanted to make her happy. I knew that to stay with her I would have to keep going to college. So she is the main reason I was able to do that.

"Also, I had a rule for myself—that no matter what, I had to push myself to go to school and study. My rule is to not 'do stupid things.' Like when I was a kid, I wouldn't play with kids who said stupid words. Other singers can go every week to sing, to tour, and build fame, but I often must say, 'I am sorry, I cannot go because I have to study.' Do you know how that hurts me? I feel so bad, of course! Because music helps me; when I am sad and go on the stage, I forget everything. Now I am studying to become a financial adviser. I have my business degree and my real estate license, and I am studying about mutual funds and bonds." On a brochure advertising his real estate work, Louis calls himself the "Singing Realtor." One of his closest friends says that now Louis's "confidence is higher, but he still treats everyone the way he thinks they should be treated. Money can change people, but Louis always will stay the same person."

Louis believes things are better now in Vietnam for Amerasians, if not perfect. "Growing up some people wouldn't let me play with their children," he says. "Many things bothered me a lot then, but now I don't care anymore. A lot of people were mean to me, and it hurt me, it hurt my stomach. I been hurt too much already, but now when I go back to Vietnam, I'm not Amerasian now. I am an American! I have money! People want to talk with me nice now. And also now I have God in my life, and when you have God in your life you don't feel bad anymore. In the U.S. everything is 1,000 times better than in Vietnam. People here don't have the chance to look down on you. You have enough money, you have food to eat. Older Vietnamese people here are more prejudiced, but younger Vietnamese people don't care. As for me, I still am not a successful person. But I am not a hopeless person."

When he dreamed of coming to the United States so many years ago, thinking there would be a car, a house, and he would find his father, "those were happy dreams," Louis once told me as we talked in his apartment. "But in the U.S. everything turned out different." He stopped talking abruptly, then shrugged and picked up a newspaper, holding it in front of his face to read it, thereby ending our conversation as he muttered half to himself: "But it's still better here anyway."

Louis seldom mentions his American father now. "Of course I feel a little sorry for myself because I didn't meet my dad. But he is still alive in my heart. And in 1997 when my mom and I became U.S. citizens, and I took my new American name, I used my dad's name as my middle one. I will someday go to my dad's grave. Maybe bring him a flower. I am not sure, but someday I even might write a letter to my half-sister. Or maybe someday just go to her house . . . up to her door."

Nan Bui

Twenty-five years after the end of the war, the *Long Beach Press-Telegram* reported on a return of many survivors of Operation Babylift to the crash site in Vietnam, where 144 people, including 78 infants, being airlifted out of the country in the final days of the war were killed in the crash of the C-5A Galaxy cargo plane. The paper reported how four Operation Babylift survivors clasped hands and prayed at the site, having "traveled halfway around the world . . . to pay an emotional tribute to the victims. The returnees were joined by twelve others who had been evacuated as children during the airlift, and who were visiting Vietnam with their [adoptive American] families for the first time since leaving."

The visitors sang Christian hymns. The Catholic nun who organized the reunion said she hoped the trip "would help the adoptees come to terms with a past often shrouded in mystery." The returnees were taken to the nurseries and orphanages where some lived before going to the United States. All had grown up in America speaking English, and said they knew little about Vietnam or the war. They had led very different lives from those of Nan and Amerasians like her who had been left behind for at least another thirteen years. Nan, one of the children at the orphanage from which many other orphans were chosen for evacuation, still wonders about her father, and says, "I really want to find and meet my American dad some day. Even if he ends up to be a homeless person, I will still call him my dad."

Nan's former partner Terri stays with her only occasionally now. For a time, Terri had a boyfriend, and then had a baby, a little boy. But Nan and her orphanage sister Joan are back on good terms. "We always make up," says Nan. "Once I dreamed me and Joan would stay together always, but . . ." Nan looks away and shrugs. Soon after that Nan moved, and I was unable to reach her at her former beeper, phone, post office box, or former apartment. As of this writing, I don't know where she is.

Alan "Tiger" Hoa

Looking exhausted, Tiger's Uncle Khue sits in his living room in the rent-subsidized apartment in Little Saigon where he lives with his wife and their five children, two of whom were born in America. When Tiger's family in Vietnam had the showdown long ago over who would go with Tiger to America—a conflict they mostly now play down and laugh off, but which once was bitter—Khue was the apparent "winner." But that victory sometimes seems hollow now, for it is Khue who slaves to send money back constantly to his family. Thanks to his help, they have lived in better and better circumstances—maybe even materially better than Khue.

"I am very tired now, old and tired," he says, "but there is a responsibility I have. One must try one's best to do one's duty to help one's family. If Tiger's Uncle Lam, who mostly raised Tiger, had come to America with his poor eyesight, he could not have handled this big responsibility. And I take care not only of my own family, but I must also take care of ten members of my wife's family in Vietnam. If someone says they don't have enough money to buy rice, I send them $25-$30. Life in Vietnam was so much simpler. You had a house, you didn't have to pay rent or your family end up on the street. If you had no electricity it didn't matter. Here I have to work very hard, but I can never get my mind free to sleep at night because everything is such a big responsibility. The only good thing here is getting out from the Communist system.

"As for Tiger, every month he calls me from jail and asks me to send him $40 or $50. I thought America would be a good opportunity for Tiger to rebuild his life, but if I had known all the trouble he would get into here I wouldn't have done it. When we came to the U.S., we told Tiger he had to get a job and stay out of trouble. But Tiger didn't listen. And it makes me very sad, because he never understood that we were worried about him. Tiger's life in the U.S. has been hard because he doesn't want to work, he just wants to party. I don't know anything about any breakdowns or suicide attempts by Tiger. And if he does have mental problems, it's even harder for me to understand him. But those guys in prison like Tiger are really slick. As soon as they get out, they get a wife right away. Well, maybe this time when he gets out he will be a better person. Still, I think that if he had stayed in Vietnam his life would have turned out the same. It's just the personality he was born with."

Tiger counts down the days until he will be released. Basically good-natured, he can be quite witty. He claims he has not only been in jail in California, New York, Kansas, and Arizona, but also spent time for "drinking and fighting over girls" in both Canada (where he picked up the tattoo "Tiger Canada") and Mexico. "I got wild when I was in Tijuana. I got into fights with Mexican guys," he says. As a connoisseur of life behind bars in several countries, he complains that Mexican jails are "very bad." He adds, still half-joking: "I saw that American prisons were nice and comfortable, much better than in Vietnam, with a nice bed to sleep in, TV and movies to watch, and programs to teach you English and other things." As a matter of fact, Tiger reads and writes English fairly well now, partly thanks to years of prison classes. And although he still has some trouble speaking English, he continues to improve. In prison he has earned a certificate in landscape gardening and another for passing academic classes. When Tiger gets out this time, he swears he will "go straight," get a job, and live an upright, law-abiding life. He knows if he is arrested again it could be his third strike, and he could go to prison for life. Also, if relations continue to improve between America and Vietnam, the United States soon may be able to contract with Vietnam to take back deported felons like Tiger. And he doesn't want to go.

After Tiger pleaded guilty and was sentenced for the theft of the TV in January 1998 (his second strike), he was sent to Wasco State Prison for a thorough evaluation, including a psychiatric one. His scars alone gave prison workers reason to check him out. "At Wasco, they gave me sleeping pills because I couldn't eat or sleep," Tiger says. "I felt very sad and I regretted all the things I did in the past." His obsessive memories, *am anh*, kept coming back "bothering me all night," he says. Because of his heavy drinking and possible drug use, Tiger was sentenced first to the California Rehabilitation Center for treatment, although he still denies he has ever had a drug or drinking problem. In Vietnam, drinking by men is regarded as more natural, less serious. He becomes somewhat agitated if a connection between his drinking and his problems is pointed out.

When Tiger was arrested, his wife Tammy was expecting their baby in a few months. Tammy, who has two older children, said she was going to give Tiger's baby up for adoption. Tiger seemed genuinely sad about losing Tammy from his life. He says it was a "very serious relationship." But he also accuses her of having a gambling addiction, of neglecting her other children, of having affairs with various friends of his whose names he keeps changing, and of having become a prostitute in another state.

While some blamed Tammy's greed and gambling habit for Tiger's continued involvement in crime ("he would steal a car stereo and sell it for her whenever she wanted something," says one) others think Tammy was the victim. Tammy's sister, for instance, whom Tiger reached by accident when trying to phone Tammy on a call I put through for him from prison, launched into a serious scolding that reduced Tiger to tears. When he tried to assert that he had changed since going back to prison this time, she responded sarcastically that she'd "already heard that so many times," and added, "when you first got out of jail before, you said that then, too. . . . How many times did Tammy give you another chance? Why did she have to give away your child when she can raise her other two children? Because she hates you, and wants to wake you up so next time you'll think clearly." Tiger tried to interrupt several times, interjecting "my fault, my fault," but finally began to cry quietly. "I have grown up now, and anyway, I'm sorry, alright?" he said. But the sister reminded him of "how you used to talk to me, like you were the leader of some really powerful gang" and how he and people he sent to her store had threatened her. "You think you're 'all that'?" she demanded. "You think I'm scared of you? Open your eyes and see who survived! I just laugh! Think about why you wanted to come to America, and what you've achieved so far. Nothing, except spending almost your whole life in jail! If I were you, I'd rather have stayed in Vietnam!"

Although Tammy's family swore they didn't know where Tammy was, or who had adopted the baby, Tiger heard through friends that his little girl was being raised by one of Tammy's relatives. Meanwhile the mother of his older daughter, born in 1996, filed in 2000 for back child support of $18,000 while Tiger was in prison. The filing was the bureaucratic step required before she could receive AFDC, but Tiger was angry and upset. Eventually, Tiger was transferred to Avenal Prison. He is a talented artist, and draws wonderful pictures for friends and fellow prisoners—cards with Mickey and Minnie Mouse and other cartoon characters, and sometimes more complex pictures of automobiles, prisoners behind bars, weeping big-eyed children, and tigers. Even after many years of prison he hasn't grown used to American food, and certainly not to prison baloney sandwiches and burritos. He longs for Vietnamese foods that seem strange to most non–Asian Americans— dried baby crabs, fish jerky, durian melon-flavored candy, dace (a kind of fish), and the legs and eyes of shrimp, sent occasionally from outside prison by a friend.

Tiger tells a confusing story that may or may not have happened: Mary Payne Nguyen or someone else at St. Anselm's—not Joe Love—arranged for him to talk on the phone with his American dad soon after he arrived in America. Tiger says he still spoke very little English at the time and that the one phone call he received from the man was unclear, and ended abruptly. The man never called again, and Tiger doubts it was his real father. And now after years in prison Tiger has some hesitation about hunting for his dad. "I have never had any hateful feelings towards my American dad," Tiger says. "What I have done with my life is my responsibility. But I have visualized that when my life is straightened up I will go looking for him and see him at least once. Just see how he is doing. I think we may look alike. Because of my skin color I know he was black, although when I was a little boy I thought the tribal man was my father because he had dark skin. I want to get rid of my [visible] tattoos first. I'm not sure whether my dad would want to see me if he knows what I've done. But if I find him, I will be a good person from then forward. I don't want to cause him pain. And anyway, I think my bad behaviors didn't come from my dad." Tiger begins to joke a little: "I think my bad behaviors come from my mother's side. Maybe from my youngest uncle Truong." Truong, a few years older than Tiger, sometimes hung out with him and his gang friends.

Over and over, Tiger says that the elderly dark-skinned tribal man in the NEZ is the one person he loves most in his heart. "He was very kind to me, and when I wanted something, he gave it to me with all his heart. I don't know if he is alive—I haven't seen him since I left the NEZ when I was seven years old. But if I ever have money, I will travel back to Vietnam, visit him, and help him as much as possible to thank him for his kindness when I was in hard times."

Tiger's voice takes on an uncharacteristically emotional, sincere tone. Although he has admitted that his Uncle Khue does love him and has helped him steadily and repeatedly, he says most of the rest of his family "did not love me like I was one of their own. They disrespected me and looked down on me. I received scorn and criticism and was sometimes beaten and told to get out. My family is not always telling the truth about what happened. They covered up a lot when they were asked to tell my life story. They don't really know me much, so anything they say is automatically wrong. Only *I* know what I did and how I feel inside. I loved my family a lot, but no one understood. I lived in a very poor life, and everything was very difficult for me. In all the world, money matters very much, and even in prison people beat each other over a small bag of noodles."

During Tiger's regular collect calls to me from prison, he began telling me about a new Amerasian recently sent to Avenal, a gay man about twenty-eight sentenced to five years for slashing his homosexual lover with a broken beer bottle during a drinking bout in an Orange County bar. U.S. officials had allowed the Amerasian to come to the United States alone in 1997, after holding back the fake family who had applied with him, and he had spent only one day in Bangkok on the way. The Philippines transit camps had long been shut down, but in late 2003 Pamela Lewis, Congressional Liaison for the Bureau of Population, Refugees and Migration with the U.S. State Department, told me that the AHA itself has never been shut down.

"We are still accepting applications from Vietnamese Amerasians, but new processing [of them] was ended in January 2003," Lewis says. "There are new concerns post 9/11 . . . and also, there are different realities now. The Vietnamese Amerasians aren't little kids anymore. They are adults aged from their late twenties to their mid-forties." She estimated that "sixty to seventy Vietnamese Amerasians, accompanied by relatives, are still being admitted every year." Apparently, Tiger's new friend was one of that handful accepted. "He was very sad when he got to prison," Tiger said. "People their first time in prison are always sad. He knows nothing about being in jail so he cries and worries. He's weaker than other people, and the guards treat weaker people worse. He had one friend outside, but lost the friend's phone number and address." Tiger befriended this new prisoner, and, seeing that he spoke almost no English, gave him his Vietnamese picture dictionary and was teaching him a few words of English. "He told me he dreams about guys instead of about women, and when I showed him pictures of some of my girl friends he wasn't interested. But when he saw a picture of one of my homies, he liked *him*," Tiger giggled.

But one day the man tried to approach another prisoner as his lover, "and the man said, 'I not love you, I have a wife and children,' and the Amerasian felt no one ever would love him. So he tried to kill himself." The man slashed one of his arms with a razor blade. "Blood was everywhere, and the man fell unconscious, so the other prisoners ran to get the guard." The man was rushed to the prison hospital, where "they tried to find out if he had a mental problem." Only a few Vietnamese inmates were at Avenal and no other Amerasians except Tiger, who says the man was taunted and "picked on" by pure Vietnamese inmates "because he is gay, and he is weak—and because he is Amerasian. They don't pick on me because I am a gang leader. But everyone picked on him, so he wanted to kill himself."

Over the next few weeks, Tiger reports that the man had gotten out of the hospital; that he had stabbed another prisoner in the neck with a pencil for teasing him; that he had then been sent back to the Orange County jail to be sentenced for that assault and given an additional year in prison, and that while in that jail had tried to attack another prisoner. He was finally returned to Avenal, where he again attacked a fellow prisoner who was tormenting him. The Amerasian was put into a sixty-day lockup, then transferred to a Level Three prison, designed to hold more violent prisoners than Level Two Avenal. After that, Tiger lost touch with him.

Reflecting on that Amerasian friend, Tiger says: "Nowadays, I think less of suicide. Nowadays when I am upset I would rather go beat someone up. But I think there are many Amerasians who *will* attempt suicide. If you carry two bloods it's already a bad thing. If you mix with black like me, it's especially bad." This half-casual, half-shamed reference to the "evil" of carrying "two bloods," as the Vietnamese phrase it, is often tossed off by Amerasians in passing, while they are discussing something else. They say it as if it is a given fact that "mixed" blood is "bad" and that anyone with mixed blood is intrinsically bad or infe-rior—a fact with which, they seem sure, everyone agrees.

"Some days now I feel happy, and some days I feel really bad," Tiger says. "I question myself, 'Where did it go wrong? Why did I become a gangster? Why did I live a bruised life? How did I end up a bad person instead of a good person?' Sometimes I did very well—I am a welder, I earned decent money, $5 per hour when I got out of prison the first time—and I wanted to be a good person. But I lived in an environment full of temptation, and there was always some kind of mysterious, irre-sistible *force* that drove me back to a gang life. And also everything in my life was driving me crazy. When I finally realized what I was doing, it was too late." Although he often talks of leading a new life when he is released from prison, Tiger also told me several times that getting out of a gang is not possible, "unless you are dead, or beaten until you are heavily injured, even paralyzed. And I'd rather be dead. I cannot go further into this speaking on the phone from prison.

"Now in prison sometimes at night I lay on my bed and think of what I did in the past, and feel very sorry and ask *on tren* to forgive me." *On tren* is a general Vietnamese term meaning a higher power or a heavenly blessing, which only comes to one who is a good person. "I didn't mean to do those bad things, but it just happened in my life," Tiger continues. "I believe that everyone's life is set up a certain way, and that's how mine was set up." Tiger believes in the Buddhist concept of karma, that in a past life people did things whose consequences they now reap in their current lives, and that what they do in this life will determine what happens in their next one.

I ask Tiger what he thinks is the future for Amerasians both in the United States and in Vietnam. He thinks America has been better for Amerasians, but he believes the future for female Amerasians in America is a dark one. "I believe 85 percent who came here have become prostitutes, because most don't speak English and don't have any friends or family to help them," he says with the authority of someone who himself has been involved with running a few prostitutes in America and who himself has been a male prostitute. "There are many brothels in Little Saigon. [Prostitution is] wasteful of human life, but"—he strikes a brighter note, finds a silver lining—"it's an easy way to earn money."

All the Amerasians Tiger knew in Vietnam, including his three closest Amerasian gang friends, are now in the United States. Some are in prison now too, including Ha who flew to the United States on the same plane as Tiger. "The lot of Amerasians has improved quite a lot since coming to the U.S.," says Tiger. "It's better because they can be educated, and because nobody can pick on them. There is also some welfare here to help you survive. But quite a few turn to crime. Generally those who still suffer in America were bought by rich families who were using them and abandoned them.

"As for me," Tiger continues, "what went wrong here in America is my fault. I thought I would find my father and that America would give me everything: money, a car, a job. But basically America itself does not disappoint me."

Epilogue
When Does a War End?

How long is it going to last? When does it go away? Something hap-
pened to me [in Vietnam], something was lost. . . . I've stopped the
drugs. I've stopped the alcohol. When do you stop paying penance,
and move on?

> —25th Infantry Division veteran of Vietnam who earned
> both a Purple Heart and Bronze Star for valor, quoted
> in a *Los Angeles Times* article on veterans still suffering
> from post-traumatic stress disorder more than twenty-
> five years after the war's end

Sara invites me to join her at a Little Saigon restaurant where two
Amerasian friends of hers are hosting a small dinner party. She
stresses that both are "very, very nice Amerasians." I arrive
early. So far, only the two Amerasian hosts, Danny and Tommy, are
there. Both are dressed in dazzling white suits of different styles.
Danny, the main host, is much taller than most Vietnamese, and handsome, with carefully trimmed sideburns. The omnipresent karaoke ma-
chines of Little Saigon are going out of style, replaced by an emcee and
live backup musicians—in this case, a guitarist and keyboard player.

Tommy sits across from me. Shouting our conversation in English
over loud Vietnamese pop music, many words are lost or imperfectly
understood. Tommy is smaller than Danny, and somehow seems more
vulnerable. He wears the wire-framed spectacles that have become a
cool accessory for some Vietnamese. One of his jobs is as a security
guard at a nearby military base. Like Danny, he also is a security guard
at one of the many large Vietnamese malls of Little Saigon, and
recently added a third job, at the Medfly Project. Tommy tells me he
came to the United States in 1993 toward the end of the Amerasian

267

Homecoming Act program, and after one year was so miserable that he applied to return to Vietnam. "No job, no money, no friends," he explains. A young Vietnamese staffer at St. Anselm's helped him meet other Amerasians and got him a job with the Medfly Project. Tommy decided to stay in America.

Later I learn Tommy was abandoned or lost during a bombing raid when he was seven, and joined a roving gang of eight young Amerasian boys led by a teenaged Amerasian "Big Brother." Tommy's new gang managed to stay alive by stealing and foraging food from the jungle at the edges of small villages, traveling from town to town after the war, moving on when they got into trouble or when a town came under the control of the new Communist regime that was gradually taking charge in remote areas. One day a soldier shot one of Tommy's fellow gang members. Perhaps the boy was stealing, or perhaps the soldier just felt hatred for him. Tommy saw his friend fall to the ground with a large chest wound gushing blood. Terrified, he and the other boys ran stumbling into the jungle, crashing in every direction, getting lost from one another. After that Tommy wandered mostly alone for several years, eventually coming to the United States.

Sara arrives a bit late, looking very pretty in a tight, short red silk dress she made herself. Her black hair seems reddish, and I think she's added blonde streaks. She, too, is wearing a pair of gold wire-rimmed spectacles. Three other Vietnamese women, including Danny's sister, join our group, along with a Vietnamese man. Sara has brought me a tiny black-and-white photo of herself as an eight-month-old in her orphanage. In the photo she is crying. She tells me she remembers nothing about the photo except that she was wearing a special pink dress. The photo is creased and damaged; I tell her I will get it copied and repaired. As Sara hands it to me, she reminds me it is the only picture she has of herself as a child. "Only one picture," says Tommy, smiling. "Every Amerasian has only one picture!" He volunteers to copy it on his computer and repair it.

The first of several Vietnamese dishes ordered for us by Danny arrives, a soup sizzling over a flame. In the darkened restaurant, Danny stands and begins ladling the soup with flourishing gestures. Everyone seems to have gadgets—cigarette lighters that play songs and flash red, blue, and golden flames, tiny cell phones and beepers edged with green and gold neon that ring to the rhythms of cha-chas and pop tunes. When I admire Danny's lighter, with its engraving of UFOs, he insists on giving it to me. Later he asks me twice, "Are you happy?" A few days later I run into Danny near one of the malls where he works as a security guard. He wears an impressive uniform with several colorful patches, four military-looking stripes, and a large silver badge reading "Supervisor." Silver handcuffs and a ring of important-looking keys dangle from his belt.

The restaurant's Vietnamese American emcee and singer, Juliette, who is outgoing and funny, sits at our front table. Her English is good; she came to the United States as a child in 1975, and grew up attending American public schools. Sara and other patrons take turns singing on the small stage. All the songs are in Vietnamese except two—both the man who joined us earlier and Juliette dedicate a song in English to me, the only non-Vietnamese in the restaurant. (Sara is not yet ready to sing in English.) Juliette talks in English with Tommy a few minutes. When he says something in Vietnamese, she is surprised. "I thought you were American," she tells him. "He is," I say.

Everyone seems happy. Yet I think I pick up some undercurrent of sadness. A Vietnamese friend who joins our group tells me I am imagining it. "This group is not thinking about the past," he says. "They have regular friends, they go to clubs all the time. Danny has become a successful person in the eyes of many people. And Tommy and all these people seem to be doing OK for themselves. To be able to sit and drink and sing this way—they can just enjoy the moment. They are rewarding themselves for being alive. Being alive is a good thing."

As I watched the group at the restaurant, I thought about all the tragedies and suffering they had known in their lifetimes—war, hunger, persecution, loneliness, fear, abandonment, illness and injury, separation from people and things they loved. Their happiness and calm seemed so fragile. Yet these were the lucky ones, at least at that moment. So many others had been lost. Probably half of the Amerasians born during the war must be dead now, some dying as newborn infants, some as toddlers and small children, others as teenagers and young adults. And among those who survived, so many bear scars that can never really be healed.

At this point I am ending my account of the life stories of the Amerasians and the many changes that have taken place in their lives over the years. Each of the main people I have interviewed—Louis, Son, Tiger, Sara, and Miss Dao—is, as of this writing, poised at the edge of major life changes. Louis recently has begun producing musical night club shows, at which he appears to sing as the "star" of these "Vietnamese Motown" productions. Maybe he eventually will become a sort of

Amerasian Berry Gordy. Son, always restless, moved his family near Orange County, where he is buying a house with a small swimming pool. While he works on remodeling his house, hoping to resell it for a profit, his wife, Chi, received her nail license and works in a salon. For a time Son opened a salon nearby, but then sold it. Joe Love, now retired and living in another state, continues to look for Son's father and believes he has narrowed down "candidates" to a small handful of possibilities. Son may yet find his American father. Sara also passed her nail exam and says she soon may go to Vietnam and seek her birth mother. Both Son's and Sara's older children are attending American public schools and are bilingual in English and Vietnamese. Miss Dao, although her health is uncertain, has worked out a balance between a life in Little Saigon and recurring visits to Vietnam, sometimes thinking of involving herself in some kind of activism to help Amerasians. Tiger is due to be released from prison within weeks. Although I do not know where Nan is, I hope and believe she is doing alright.

All of these people, even Tiger in his way, have modest success stories at the point this is written. Yet one cannot know them without knowing there are many wounds still haunting their lives. Moreover, I feel uneasy about drawing conclusions from the stories in this book, because I know such conclusions would be skewed in several ways. For one thing, all the main interviewees, even Nan until recently, led more stable lives, and did not "disappear," or move away, and so I was able to continue to interview them over the passing years. Most important, all the Amerasians whose stories I have concentrated on share one crucial advantage—the devoted love of at least one person at some point in their lives. Sometimes that person was someone they never knew, but a fantasy figure they knew intimately in their own minds.

In writing a book entitled *Surviving Twice*, I have not done justice to the Amerasians who did *not* survive. But using the one-time media estimate at a midpoint in the war of more than 100,000 born, if approximately 30,000 eventually came to America, and perhaps 10,000 remain in Vietnam, then 60,000 are "missing." As I followed the Amerasian population over the years I learned of various categories of their deaths—abandoned and left to die as newborns; killed in battles during the war; dead of epidemics such as measles, malaria, and polio; dead of less serious illnesses and untreated injuries and infections exacerbated by their vulnerability because of malnutrition; deaths during the boat exodus; deaths by suicide. If the figure of 60,000 seems too high, cut it in half—only 30,000 are "missing."

In Vietnam the Amerasians were struggling to survive in desperate times. But after they came to America, they were in a country that was not desperate at all. Thus, their second struggle for survival is much more difficult to justify. The Amerasians, who came with such high dreams, still have never been granted U.S. citizenship, despite the fact that being the child of an American was a requirement of their immigrating. Yet partial amnesties and dispensations leading to citizenship or at least permanent legal residency have been granted to several other immigrant groups in past years. Peter Daniels says he expects massive repercussions for the Amerasians when, under recent laws that affect even legal immigrants, the Amerasians lose such basic benefits as food stamps and medical care. Yet a law, like the one introduced in Congress in October 2003 by Rep. Zoe Lofgren (D-CA) which would give U.S. citizenship to all Vietnamese Amerasians who have come to the U.S. under the Amerasian Homecoming Act, could easily be passed to address their unique situation. At the time this was written, the bill had not been acted upon.

When Does a War End?

Knowing that the life stories of the surviving Amerasians will continue to unfold outside the pages of this book, certain questions arose in my mind: Is the Vietnam War finally really over? And when does a war end? In one way, of course, a war is over when fighting and killing ends. Yet in the case of Vietnam, although the fighting ended long ago, the killing goes on. Every week more Vietnamese—usually children not even born until years after the fighting concluded—die by explosions of ordnance left over from before 1975. Other children, both Vietnamese and American, born with birth defects and a susceptibility to certain cancers, continue to suffer and die from the effects of chemicals sprayed in Vietnam during the war. Many Vietnamese civilians and American and Vietnamese veterans of the war are still paralyzed or crippled by injuries of more than a quarter-century ago. Those injuries burden their victims over their lifetimes, and sometimes bring death, years and years after fighting has ended.

Perhaps a war ends when a new, major war—for example, a "War on Terror"—begins. Such a new war must be big enough and compelling enough to begin a whole new round of not only physical battles but the creation of new beliefs, myths, and fantasies. Or maybe a war ends when people agree on its "meaning," or on the lessons it taught. If so, the Vietnam War is not over, because Americans, at least, are still disagreeing about these things. As one obvious proof of this, witness the vicious battling over the war during the 2004 presidential campaign and the very different responses to it by the two major presidential candidates, George W. Bush and John Kerry. One group feels the lesson learned by the war is never again to fight a "weak" war, holding back America's full military strength, and thereby allowing billions of U.S. dollars to be wasted and thousands of U.S. soldiers to die needlessly. Next time, they argue, we must launch a stronger war, including, if necessary to win, the use of nuclear weapons. But other Americans say the lesson learned is that we must never again engage in a war that has little to do with America's own security, when it has little effect on the United States, and when it would be easy for us to reach peaceful coexistence with whomever is the winner, as we have done many times.

We move into the future, yet, as author William Faulkner said, the past is never past. It is always present, in this case on both a personal and a national level. Whether it is a real past or a past we have made up, it exerts its power. The traumatic memories of the war and its aftermath are often as powerful as those memories of earliest childhood, including those which cannot be remembered consciously but nevertheless influence all our present and future behavior. Memories lie inside us for years like unexploded ordnance that can go off at a touch at any moment, delivering stabbing fragments of pain and reopening emotional wounds that never seem to heal.

A few years ago the *Los Angeles Times*, in an article about U.S. veterans of Vietnam still suffering from post-traumatic stress syndrome more than twenty-five years after the war's end, quoted a 25th Infantry Division vet who had earned both a Purple Heart and a Bronze Star for valor, and who said: "How long is it going to last? When does it go away? Something happened to me [in Vietnam], something was lost. . . . I've stopped the drugs, I've stopped the alcohol—when do you stop paying penance, and move on?"

But perhaps a war can be over when the former enemies reach some kind of reconciliation, as is happening between Vietnam and the United States, when the old warrior leaders on both sides die or fade away and a new generation comes into power. Another question: Did the unresolved presence of the Vietnam War in our memories prevent us, for many years, from getting into a new major war? In the era after the September 11 attacks, Bush administration officials and conservative media seemed to be gliding completely over the Vietnam War as if it had never happened, referring frequently to World War II and celebrating that war's proud victories. So is the effect of Vietnam simply being made moot, or perhaps, instead, "wearing off"? So far, many Americans have not been able to simply shrug, say "mistakes were made," and "move on," to a "closure." We are still trying to make a story or myth about the Vietnam War that enough Americans can both accept and believe.

Maybe at least we can change the treatment of the children of future wars and occupations. Perhaps we can stop believing that such children are just another unfortunate but unavoidable consequence, and find creative ways to address the tragedy of their lives, just as people over the course of history have found solutions to other situations once thought natural and unchangeable.

Maybe one sign a war has ended is the gradual blending of the children of that war, and those children's children. Along with the rusting bombs and tanks America left behind that can still be seen in Vietnam, one can see the half-American faces of now-grown Amerasians, and the part-American faces of their children, who seem to be blending more smoothly into the general population.

In the United States, the Amerasians and their children, along with other Vietnamese immigrants, are becoming part of the ever-changing mixture that is America. In February 2002 in San Jose in northern California, the state's second-largest Vietnamese immigrant settlement, the city's annual Tet Festival kicked off with the "unlikely motto: 'Si, se puede!' [Spanish for 'Yes, we can!']." For the first time in two decades, reported the *San Jose Mercury News*, "the city's large Vietnamese community brought in the new year with Latino entertainers and many of the cultural trappings usually reserved for [the Mexican holiday of] Cinco de Mayo. It's an unprecedented joining of hands between communities that are worlds apart in culture and language, but share neighborhood and business districts throughout San Jose. The weekend . . . will open with the American national anthem sung by a young Mexican singer, and mariachi bands will perform on stage next to Vietnamese pop singers."

Selected Bibliography

Many excellent lists of some of the thousands of books examining the Vietnam War and its aftermath exist elsewhere. The following "Selected Bibliography" is based on materials I found especially helpful in researching and writing this book. It does not include hundreds of news stories on the subject of Vietnamese Amerasians carried in the *Los Angeles Times*, *Orange County Register*, *Nguoi Viet*, and other news publications.

Amerasian Resettlement: Strategies for Success. Conference Proceedings, March 7–10, 1989, Richmond, Va. Sponsored by U.S. Department of Health and Human Services (Office of Refugee Resettlement); Migration and Refugee Services, U.S. Catholic Confererence; Catholic Charities of Richmond.

Ibid., Kelly, Mary Margaret, and Glenn Rogers. *Dynamics of Reunification with American Fathers*. 1989.

Ibid., Mercer, Marie. *American Council for Nationalities Services Guidelines for Assisting Amerasian Clients Requesting Parent Locator Services*. 1989.

Ibid., Podlaski, Ron, et al. *On Fathers of Amerasians*. Vietnam Veterans of America Foundation, Washington, D.C., 1989.

Amerasian Update (every issue, monthly, 1989–94). Issued by InterAction and the Lutheran Immigration and Refugee Service under a cooperative agreement with the Office of Refugee Resettlement. Marta K. Brenden, ed.

Amerasians Special Needs Report. State of California, Health and Welfare Agency, Department of Social Services. 1989.

American Red Cross. *Amerasian Resettlement in the U.S.*, June 1989; *Tracing Procedures for Amerasians Searching for Their Fathers*, Aug. 1990; and *Tracing Services for Vietnamese Amerasians and American Fathers*, Jan. 27, 1992.

Anis, Joyce. "Psychosocial Adjustment of Vietnamese-Americans." Dissertation. University of Minnesota, 1996.

Appy, Christian G. *Patriots: The Vietnam War Remembered from All Sides.* New York: Viking, 2003.

Barnett, Anthony, and John Pilger. *Aftermath: The Struggle of Cambodia and Vietnam.* London: Statesman National Publishing, 1982.

Bass, Thomas A. *Vietnamerica: The War Comes Home.* New York: Soho Press, 1996.

Beschloss, Michael R. *Taking Charge: The Johnson White House Tapes, 1963–1964.* New York: Simon & Schuster, 1997.

Blackstock, Nelson. *COINTELPRO: The FBI's Secret War on Political Freedom.* New York: Anchor Foundation, 1988.

Borton, Lady. *Sensing the Enemy: An American Woman Among the Boat People of Vietnam.* New York: Dial Press, 1984.

Bowen, Kevin, ed., with Nguyen Ba Chung and Bruce Weigl. *Mountain River: Vietnamese Poetry from the Wars, 1948–1993.* Amherst: University of Massachusetts Press, 1998.

Bradshaw, Adrian. "Amerasians Left Behind." *Geographical Magazine,* July 1989.

Branch, Taylor. *Pillar of Fire: America in the King Years, 1963–1965.* New York: Simon & Schuster, 1998.

Chanda, Nayan. *Brother Enemy: The War after the War: A History of Indochina since the Fall of Saigon.* New York: Collier Books, 1986.

Chandler, David P. *The Tragedy of Cambodian History: Politics, War, and Revolution since 1945.* New Haven: Yale University Press, 1991.

Charny, Joel, and John Spragens Jr. Preface by Laurence R. Simon. *Obstacles to Recovery in Vietnam and Kampuchea (Cambodia): U.S. Embargo of Humanitarian Aid.* Boston: Oxfam America, 1984.

CHEER for Vietnam, newsletters, 1997–2004.

Chung Hoang Chuong and Le Van. *The Amerasians from Vietnam: A California Study.* Rancho Cordova, Calif.: Southeast Asia Community Resource Center, 1994.

Coles, Robert. *The Moral Life of Children.* New York: Grove/Atlantic, 1999.

Convery, Anne P. *Amerasians: Relatives Eligible to Follow Per Expanded Amerasian Homecoming Legislation.* Bangkok: International Catholic Migration Commission, March 20, 1991.

Cooper, Nancy. "Go Back to Your Country: Amerasians Head for Their Fathers' Homeland." *Newsweek,* March 14, 1988.

Cummings, Scott, and Daniel J. Monti, eds. *Gangs: The Origins and Impact of Contemporary Youth Gangs in the United States.* Albany: State University of New York Press, 1993.

"Daughter from Danang." Documentary, PBS and selected theaters, 2003.

DeBonis, Steven. *Children of the Enemy: Oral Histories of Vietnamese Amerasians and Their Mothers.* Jefferson, N.C.: McFarland & Co., 1995.

Dellums, Ronald V. *The Dellums Committee Hearings on War Crimes in Vietnam.* The Citizens Commission of Inquiry, ed. New York: Vintage Books, 1972.

DeWilde, Steven R. "Vietnamese Settlement Patterns in Orange County's Little Saigon." Thesis, California State University, Long Beach, August 1996.

Do, Hien Duc. "The New Outsiders: The Vietnamese Refugee Generation in Higher Education." Dissertation. University of California, Santa Barbara, 1994.

Dong-Matsuda, Suzie Xuyen. "A Study of Vietnamese Women's Coping Skills." Thesis. California State University, Long Beach, 1997.

Dorland, Gil. *Legacy of Discord: Voices of the Vietnam War Era.* Washington, D.C.: Brassey's, 2001.

East Meets West, newsletters, 1997–2004.

Elliot, Duong Van Mai. *The Sacred Willow: Four Generations in the Life of a Vietnamese Family.* New York: Oxford University Press, 1999.

Ellis, Claire. *Culture Shock! Vietnam: A Guide to Customs and Etiquette.* Portland, Ore.: Graphic Arts Center, 1997.

Ellsberg, Daniel. *Secrets: A Memoir of Vietnam and the Pentagon Papers.* New York: Viking, 2003.

Emerson, Gloria. *Winners and Losers: Battles, Retreats, Gains, Losses, and Ruins from a Long War.* New York: Random House, 1977.

Engelmann, Larry. *Tears Before the Rain: An Oral History of the Fall of South Vietnam.* New York: Da Capo Press, 1997.

Felsman, J. Kirk, et al. "Estimates of Psychological Distress Among Vietnamese Refugees: Adolescents, Unaccompanied Minors, and Young Adults." *Social Science and Medicine* 31 (1985): 1251–56.

Ibid., *Vietnamese Amerasians: Practical Implications of Current Research.* Washington, D.C.: Office of Refugee Resettlement, Dept. of Health and Human Services, 1989.

FitzGerald, Frances. *Fire in the Lake: The Vietnamese and the Americans in Vietnam.* Boston: Little, Brown, 1972.

Freeman, James M. *Changing Identities: Vietnamese Americans, 1975–1995.* Needham Heights, Mass.: Allyn and Bacon, 1995.

Friedlander, Huyen, and Binh Ha Hong. "Bui Doi: From Children of Dust to Children of Gold." *VIETNOW* magazine, Sept./Oct. 1995.

Guide to Two Cultures: Indochinese. Washington, D.C.: U.S. Department of Health, Education, and Welfare, Social Security Administration, Office of Refugee Affairs, 1980.

Halberstam, David. *The Best and the Brightest.* New York: Random House, 1972.

Hayslip, Le Ly, with James Hayslip. *Child of War, Woman of Peace.* New York: Doubleday, 1993.

Hayslip, Le Ly, with Jay Wurts. *When Heaven and Earth Changed Places: A Vietnamese Woman's Journey from War to Peace.* New York: Plume, 1990.

Hersch, Seymour M. *Cover-Up: The Army's Secret Investigation of the Massacre at My Lai 4.* New York: Random House, 1972.

Hieu Tran Phan. *Coi Nguon Bat An—Roots of Unrest.* Garden Grove, Calif.: Orange County Register, 1999.

Higgins, Marguerite. *Our Vietnam Nightmare.* New York: Harper & Row, 1965.

Ho, Caroline. "Acculturation and Reality-Hypotheticality in Vietnamese Children." Thesis. University of Western Ontario (Canada), 1999.

Huynh Dinh Te. *Introduction to Vietnamese Culture.* Rancho Cordova, Calif., Southeast Asia Community Resource Center, 1996.

Huynh, Thang Mai Tien. "Stress, Current Emotional Status, and Coping Among Amerasian Immigrants." Dissertation. California State University, Long Beach, 1992.

Indochina Interchange. U.S. Indochina Reconciliation Project and Fund for Reconciliation and Development, New York, Sept. 1997 and other issues.

Indochina Issues report. "The Children of the War Start Leaving for America." 1983.

InterAction Amerasian Resettlement Program. Amerasian Families and American Fathers: Considerations for Reponses to Tracing Requests. 1989.

InterAction Amerasian Resettlement Conference, program and notes, 1992.

InterAction Committee on Migration and Refugee Affairs: Analysis of Amerasian/Family Members—Arrivals in U.S. FY '88, '89 and FY '90 First Six Months. 1990.

Isaacs, Arnold R. *Without Honor: Defeat in Vietnam and Cambodia.* Baltimore: Johns Hopkins University Press, 1983.

Karnow, Stanley. *Vietnam: A History.* New York: Viking, 1983.

Kelly, Katie. *A Year in Saigon.* New York: Simon & Schuster, 1992.

Kibria, Nazli. *Family Tightrope: The Changing Lives of Vietnamese Americans.* Princeton, N.J.: Princeton University Press, 1993.

Kiernan, Ben. *The Pol Pot Regime: Race, Power, and Genocide in Cambodia Under the Khmer Rouge, 1975–1979.* New Haven: Yale University Press, 1998.

Kocher, Michael, and Marta Brenden, eds. *Amerasian Resettlement: Building a Network of Welcoming Services.* Conference Proceedings, Los Angeles. InterAction Amerasian Resettlement Program, Office of Refugee Resettlement, Administration for Children and Families. March 15–17, 1991.

Ibid., *Enhancing the Homecoming.*

Kozol, Jonathan. *Ordinary Resurrections.* New York: HarperCollins, 2001.

Ky, Ngugen Cao. *Buddha's Child: My Fight to Save Vietnam.* New York: St. Martin's Press, 2002.

Lacey, Marilyn. *In Our Fathers' Land: Vietnamese Amerasians in the United States.* Washington, D.C.: Migration and Refugee Services, U.S. Catholic Conference. 1985.

Landau, Saul. *The Pre-Emptive Empire: A Guide to Bush's Kingdom.* London: Pluto Press, 2003.

Langguth, A. J. *Our Vietnam: The War, 1954–1975.* New York: Simon & Schuster, 2000.

Lee, Charles F. Report for Congressman Tom Ridge. "Implementing the Amerasian Homecoming Act: A Close Look at the Philippine Refugee Processing Center." Washington, D.C., October 1989.

Leong, Frederick T. L., and Mark C. Johnson. *Vietnamese Amerasian Mothers: Psychological Distress and High-Risk Factors.* Washington, D.C.: Office of Refugee Resettlement., Dept. of Health and Human Services, 1992.

Lifton, Robert Jay. *Home from the War: Vietnam Veterans—Neither Victims nor Executioners.* New York: Basic Books, 1985.

Long, Patrick Du Phuoc, with Laura Ricard. *The Dream Shattered: Vietnamese Gangs in America.* Boston: Northeastern University Press, 1996.

Mabry, Philip James. *"We're bringing them home": Resettling Vietnamese Amerasians in the United States.* Dissertation. University of Pittsburgh, 1996.

Mangold, Tom, and John Penycate. *The Tunnels of Cu Chi: A Remarkable Story of the Vietnam War.* London: Hodder and Stoughton, 1985.

McKelvey, Robert S. *The Dust of Life: America's Children Abandoned in Vietnam.* Seattle: University of Washington Press, 1999.

McKelvey, Robert S., Alice R. Mao, and John A. Webb. "A Risk Profile Predicting Psychological Distress in Vietnamese Amerasian Youth." *Journal of the American Academy of Child and Adolescent Psychiatriy* 31 (1992): 911–15.

McKelvey, Robert S., and John A. Webb. "Long-Term Effects of Maternal Loss on Vietnamese Amerasians." *Journal of the American Academy of Child and Adolescent Psychiatry* 32 (1993): 1013–18.

McPherson, Myra. *Long Time Passing: Vietnam and the Haunted Generation.* New York: Doubleday, 1984.

Merkel, Richard L. *Suicidal Behavior in Vietnamese Refugees: Suicide, Headaches, and the Vietnamese Concept of Self.* Dissertation. University of Pennsylvania, 1996.

Merritt, Nancy-Jo. *Understanding Immigration Law, 2nd Edition: How to Enter, Work, and Live in the United States.* Hawthorne, N.J.: Career Press, 1994.

Mishran, Ahrin. "Vietnamese Gangs: Identity and Discourse in 'Little Saigon.'" Graduate thesis. University of Southern California, August 1993.

Moore, Jonathan. This Way Out: Amerasians Provide an Exit (Vietnam). *"Far Eastern Economic Review,"* July 12, 1990.

Mydans, Seth. "Once Lost in Vietnam, Now Lost in America: Amerasians' 'Homecoming' Is Jarring." *New York Times,* July 7, 1995.

Nam-Hau, Doan Thi. *Traversing Borders: A Cross-Cultural Educational Program (United States, Vietnam).* Dissertation. University of California, Los Angeles, 1999.

Nguoi Viet newspaper, weekly English edition. Westminster, Calif., 1997–2004.

Nguyen, Dung Thi. "Vietnamese Attitudes Toward Mental Illness and the Utilization of Mental Health Services." Thesis. California State University, Long Beach, 1997.

Nguyen, Kien. *The Unwanted: A Memoir.* Boston: Little, Brown, 2001.

Nguyen, Linh Vu Ngoc. "Issues of Pastoral Care Among the Vietnamese Amerasians in San Diego from an Asian Theological Perspective." Thesis. University of California, San Diego, 1996.

Nguyen Ngoc Bich, ed. *War and Exile: A Vietnamese Anthology.* New York: Vietnamese PEN East Coast U.S.A., 1989.

Nguyen, Thanh Son Thi. "Adjustment and Acculturation Problems of

Vietnamese Amerasians in Pittsburgh, PA: A Post-Resettlement Study." Thesis. University of Pittsburgh, 1995.

Nicosia, Gerald. *Home to War: A History of the Vietnam Veterans' Movement.* New York: Three Rivers Press, 2001.

Ninh, Bao. *The Sorrow of War: A Novel of North Vietnam.* Frank Palmos, ed. London: Riverhead, 1995.

Office of Refugee Resettlement. "Amerasian Arrival Data." Oct. 15, 1988.

Pham, Thien Kim. "Coping Methods Used by Vietnamese Refugees and Immigrants." Dissertation. University of Houston, 1993.

Porter, Gareth. *A Peace Denied: The United States, Vietnam, and the Paris Agreement.* Bloomington: Indiana University Press, 1975.

Prochnau, William. *Once Upon a Distant War.* New York: Vintage Books, 1995.

"Psychiatric Problems Among Adolescent Southeast Asian Refugees." *Journal of Nervous and Mental Disorders* 17(2), 1983.

Ranard, Donald A., and Douglas F. Gilzow. *The Amerasians: Perspectives on Refugee Resettlement.* Washington, D.C.: Refugee Service Center, Center for Applied Linguistics, under agreement with the Bureau for Refugee Programs of the U.S. State Dept., June 1989.

Rawlings, Stuart, ed. *The IVS Experience: From Algeria to Viet Nam.* Washington, D.C.: International Voluntary Services, 1992.

Refugee Service Center. Study on Vietnamese Amerasians in America, June 1989

Report to the Congress, Refugee Resettlement Program. Washington, D.C.: U.S. Department of Health and Human Services, Office of Refugee Resettlement, Jan. 31, 1990.

Ibid., Jan. 31, l989.

Ibid., Fiscal Year 1993.

Ibid., Fiscal Year 1995.

Rutledge, Paul James. *The Vietnamese Experience in America.* Indianapolis: Indiana University Press, 1992.

Sager, Mike. "The Dust of Life: Amerasian Children from Vietnam Coming to the U.S." *Rolling Stone* magazine, Nov. 14, 1991.

Sheehan, Neil. *A Bright Shining Lie: John Paul Vann and America in Vietnam.* New York: Vintage Books, 1989.

Snepp, Frank. *Decent Interval: An Insider's Account of Saigon's Indecent End Told by the CIA's Chief Strategy Analyst in Vietnam.* New York: Random House, 1977.

"Southeast Asian-American Communities." *Vietnam Generation* 2:3 (1990).

Southeast Asian Refugee English Proficiency & Education. Austin: Texas Office of Immigration & Refugee Affairs, Texas Dept. of Human Services, April 1994.

Stockwell, John. *In Search of Enemies: A CIA Story.* New York: W. W. Norton & Co., 1978.

Story, Robert. *Vietnam: A Lonely Planet Travel Atlas.* Australia: Lonely Planet Publications, 1996.

Tai Lieu Huong Dan. *A Guide to Resettlement in the United States (Vietnamese).* Washington, D.C.: Center for Applied Linguistics, 1994.

Tal, Kali, ed. *Southeast Asian-American Communities.* Silver Spring, Md.: Vietnam Generation, 1990.

Tien, Liang, and Denny Hunthausen. "The Vietnamese Amerasian Resettlement Experience: From Initial Application to the First Six Months in the United States." *Vietnam Generation* 2:3 199(0).

Tran, Huong Hoai. "The Adaptation of Vietnamese Refugees in American Society." Dissertation. Cornell University, 1994.

Tuong Lam. "Luu Quoc Viet." *Nang Mai* magazine, Oct. 26, 2000.

United States Catholic Conference. In Our Fathers' Land: Vietnamese Amerasians in the United States. Washington, D.C.: U.S. Catholic Conference, 1985.

U.S. Department of State, Bureau of Public Affairs: Amerasians in Vietnam. Washington, D.C., 1988

U.S. General Accounting Office. Vietnamese Amerasian Resettlement: Education, Employment and Family Outcomes in the United States. Washington, D.C.: U.S. General Accounting Office, 1994.

Ibid., 1995.

U.S. NGO Forum on Viet Nam, Cambodia, and Laos, New York, 1991.

Ibid., 1993.

U.S. Senate Committee on the Judiciary, Subcommittee on Immigration and Refugee Policy. Amerasian Immigration Proposals: Hearing before the Subcommittee, Ninety-seventh Congress, 2nd Session. 1982.

Valverde, Kieu-Linh Caroline. "From Dust to Gold: The Vietnamese Amerasian Experience." In *Racially Mixed People in America,* Maria P. Root, ed., 144–61. Newbury Park, Calif.: Sage Publications, 1992.

Vickery, Michael. *Cambodia, 1975–1982.* Boston: South End Press, 1984.

"Vietnam Agrees to Resume Resettling Amerasians." *New York Times*, Sept. 12, 1987.

Vietnam Studies Bulletin, Assn. for Asian Studies, Vietnam Studies Group. Boston, Dec. 1991.

Vietnam Veterans of America Foundation: "Report on the Amerasian Issue." August 1989.

Vietnamese Amerasian Resettlement: Education, Employment and Family Outcomes in the United States. Report to Congressional Requesters, Government Accounting Office. Washington, D.C., March 1994.

Vo, Daniel Van. "Clinical Profile of Vietnamese Refugees with Diagnosis of Major Depression." Thesis. California State University, Long Beach, 1988.

Wain, Barry. *Refused: The Agony of the Indochina Refugees.* Hong Kong: Dow Jones Publishing Co. (Asia), 1981.

William Joiner Center for the Study of War and Social Consequences, newsletters, 1998–2004.

Wolters, O.W., and Huynh Sanh Thong, eds. *The Vietnam Forum #5: A Review of Vietnamese Culture.* Yale University, Winter–Spring 1985.

"The XY Factor: Sex in the Vietnam War." Documentary, History Channel, 2003.

Young, Marilyn B. *The Vietnam Wars, 1945–1990.* New York: Harper Collins, 1991.

Index

About the Author

Trin Yarborough is a journalist whose articles have appeared in such publications as the *Los Angeles Times*, *LA Weekly*, *BAM* music magazine and Amsterdam's *NRC*. In 2001 she was awarded a Rockefeller Fellowship through the William Joiner Center for the Study of War and Social Consequences, based at the University of Massachusetts, Boston, to help complete work on *Surviving Twice*. Born in Oklahoma City, Oklahoma, Yarborough moved to Washington, D.C. as a teenager. She graduated with a B.A. in journalism from the University of Oklahoma, Norman, and for several years covered crime, the courts, religion, and general assignments for the *Houston Press* when it was the *Scripps-Howard* daily. During the 1960s she was active in state politics as the political wife of her former husband's campaigns for governor of Texas. In 1970 Yarborough moved to Cambridge, Mass. for five years, where she studied documentary filmmaking. She then spent five years in Washington, D.C. as an editor and public information officer for The Institute for Policy Studies and its sister think tank, the Amsterdam-based Transnational Institute. Returning to Cambridge, she worked as public information director for the international aid agency Oxfam America, traveling to twenty-three countries in Asia, Africa, and Central America. Yarborough now lives in Santa Monica, California. She has four children and five grandchildren.